THE TOMBS OF MESARA

KEITH BRANIGAN

THE TOMBS OF MESARA

*A Study of Funerary Architecture and
Ritual in Southern Crete, 2800-1700 B.C.*

GERALD DUCKWORTH

First published in 1970 by
Gerald Duckworth & Company Limited
3, Henrietta Street, London W.C.2

ISBN 0 7156 0522 4

Printed and bound in Great Britain by
The Garden City Press Limited, Letchworth, Hertfordshire

To OUR PARENTS
Chesham, Bucks
Bangkok, Thailand

Contents

List of plates

ix

List of figures in the text

Preface

It was less than a year ago that through the kindness of my friend
Peter Warren I acquired a copy of Stephanos Xanthoudides' *The
Vaulted Tombs of Mesara*. I had used the book for many years, and
knew every page and plate intimately. Its importance as the only
major corpus of Early Bronze Age material from Crete, and the
only collective excavation report and discussion of a sizeable
group of Mesara tholoi had long been recognised; so too had its
scarcity. These considerations alone were sufficient to suggest
that the book should be reprinted, but as I worked in the reserve
collections at Iraklion Museum and through the archaeological
journals published since 1924 (when *VTM* was published) it
became clear to me that something more than a reprint was needed.
The superb array of objects illustrated in Xanthoudides' plates
proved to be but samples of a far larger collection of artifacts
never published by him. A study of the journals revealed that
Xanthoudides' fifteen or sixteen tholoi were but a fraction of the
known and excavated total of Mesara tombs; the remainder, with
one or two notable exceptions, were either unknown to, or
ignored by, most Aegean archaeologists. These considerations
prompted me to write to Peter Warren early in 1968, suggesting
that we might consider producing a comprehensive study and
report on *all* of the Mesara tholoi. This project never got under
way for several reasons. Both Warren and myself were busy
writing books on the Cretan Early Bronze Age, as well as various
articles, so that the size of the undertaking was quite beyond our
capabilities, even allowing for the contributions which I hoped
several other scholars would make to the work. There were
complications concerning the large number of tombs dug since
1954 by various members of the Greek Archaeological Service,
the reports on which they naturally were intending to publish
themselves. Finally, steps were already being taken by a number of
young scholars to study and publish the contents of the tombs

xiii

excavated by Xanthoudides. Thus Peter Warren was preparing for publication a definitive study of the stone vases, I had just published my complete catalogue and discussion of Early Minoan bronzes, and Zoes had begun to publish his detailed studies of the pottery of Early Minoan Crete.

Late in 1968, I was invited to address the Prehistoric Society on the subject of "Early Minoan Society and Its Attitudes to Death", the lecture to be given in the following March. I decided to restrict the scope of my lecture to the Mesara tholoi, and during the five months between November 1968 and March 1969 I did much of the research on which this book is based. At the time, I did not envisage writing a book but the subject appeared to arouse so much interest that I felt that there was the need for a more extensive treatment.

The book is not intended to be an all-embracing study of the Mesara tholoi. My aim has been simply to write a book which examined all of the major problems concerning the tombs—their date, their original appearance, their relationship to a cult of the dead, the ceremonies performed in and around them, their origins, and their relationship to the tholos tombs of the Late Bronze Age. I was anxious to present *all* of the evidence on which my arguments were based, but at the same time determined to make the book readable; I did not want it to become a catalogue of measurements and artifacts. For this reason I have tried to pack as much information as possible into the two tables at the end of the book, which present in condensed form virtually everything that is known about the individual Mesara tholoi.

In the interests of economy only a small selection of artifacts from the tombs have been illustrated but I have tried to ensure that the items selected are as representative as possible, in terms of both date and type. Similarly, though the number of plates is restricted, I have found it possible to illustrate all of the structural features which need to be seen in half-tone reproductions. On the other hand the plans of the various tombs have been introduced wherever it was possible to obtain them, and these should be considered as complementary to the constructional details contained in table 1. The difficulties of illustrating the volume have been greatly eased by the kindness of several good friends. Pressure on the available half-tone space was considerably relieved by Mrs M. Maslin's superb line-drawings of the artifacts. The difficulty and expense of obtaining the necessary half-tone illustrations was completely negated by the kindness of the following colleagues and friends who freely allowed the reproduction of their own photographs: Dr St. Alexiou (pl. 2), Professor P. Faure (pl. 3.), M. S. F. Hood (pl. 11), Professor D. Levi (pls 5, 6, 7, 10, 13, 14, 15), Dr I. Sakellarakis (pl. 9), Professor C. Zervos (pl. 1). In addition I was graciously allowed to reproduce plates previously published by the University of Liverpool Press (pls. 4, 8), and by the Italian School of Archaeology in Athens (pl. 12).

I have also received considerable help from various friends during the preparation of the catalogue of sites and the collection of information. Amongst these I am particularly indebted to Dr C. Davaras, Professor P. Faure, M. S. F. Hood, and Dr P. Warren. I must especially thank Douglas Waite for invaluable assistance in the collection of information about recent excavations by the Greek Archaeological Service, and for constantly providing both encouragement and constructive criticism. Similarly, I am grateful to Dr Peter Ucko for reading the text and making a number of helpful suggestions. Finally I must thank my wife for again ensuring that I always began work well-fed and free from the pressing demands of our two children; such was her invaluable contribution to this book.

K.B.

Bristol, November, 1969.

NOTE

Greek place names have been transliterated into English and, in the text, are not given their accents. The accents are however given in the catalogue of sites.

The term *tholos* is used to denote a circular chamber tomb, fully vaulted in stone. We cannot be sure that the Mesara tombs were roofed in this way, and where we are speaking of these tombs, I have therefore used the word "tomb" if possible. In some contexts however it was found desirable to have an alternative word which meant a circular, built, chamber tomb but not necessarily a completely vaulted one. In these places I have used the word "tholos" but without resorting to italics. Thus *tholos* refers to the typical Mycenaean beehive tomb, and tholos to the circular tombs of Mesara.

Chapter One

THE TOMBS DISCOVERED

On his first visit to Crete, in 1894, Arthur Evans visited the museum at Candia (modern Iraklion) and amongst the other material there noted a collection of stone, clay, bronze and gold objects found near Phaistos in the south of the island. There were several marble figurines in the Cycladic style, some small stone vases, a variety of diminutive sealstones in various shapes and carved with elaborate designs, two scarabs, some clay jugs and suspension vessels, a bronze dagger and a harpoon, and several gold, rock crystal and bronze pendants and beads. Although it was to be another five years before Evans discovered Minoan civilisation in his excavations at Knossos, he at once recognised this group of material in Candia as belonging to a pre-Mycenaean era, contemporary with the Egyptian Fourth Dynasty, *c.* 2500 B.C. What he did not, and could not, know at the time, was that he was probably the first archaeologist to see Early Bronze Age artifacts recovered from one of the "vaulted" tombs of the Mesara. The site at which they were found, Agios Onouphrios, is a small white hill a stone's throw north of the palace of Phaistos, and it is now generally accepted that the "Agios Onouphrios deposit" was recovered from a circular Early Bronze Age tomb discovered, looted and destroyed there in the late nineteenth century. Indeed the first of these tombs to be excavated by an archaeological expedition was found less than a kilometre away at Agia Triadha. Here, in 1904, the great tomb "A" was discovered and excavated by the Italians under the direction of Professor Halbherr.

For the first time it was possible to see what one of these communal chamber tombs looked like. Here was a circular wall, two

17

metres wide, enclosing a burial area eight metres in diameter. On the east was a single narrow doorway beyond which, in this particular case, was a complex of small rectangular rooms. Other tombs found later often proved to have just a single room set before the doorway. Inside both the tomb proper and the ante-chambers was a mass of human bones, clay vessels, jewellery, weapons, stone vases and sealstones. The burials represented here numbered not dozens but hundreds, and covered a time span not of decades but of many centuries—as much as a millen-nium in fact. Before long the Italians had found a second tholos, smaller and with a single antechamber, only a few metres from the first.

About the same time as Halbherr began work on the tholoi at Agia Triadha, a peasant from Koumasa, a small village set in the foothills of the Asterousia mountains, about twenty kilometres east of Agia Triadha, took a group of artifacts to the Ephor General of Cretan Antiquities, Stephanos Xanthoudides. It was a small and unimpressive collection of material—three sealstones, a few stone beads, and fragments of a bronze dagger. Xanthoudides however at once recognised their significance and began the first of what proved to be a long series of excavations on the Mesara tholoi. By the time Xanthoudides had completed the excavation of the three tombs which eventually appeared at Koumasa, he had discovered two more cemeteries nearby at Porti and Agia Eirene. These he excavated in the summer of 1906, whilst the Italians under Parabeni were themselves revealing two more circular tombs at Siva, south of Agia Triadha.

By this time, Xanthoudides had acquired a "nose" for these tombs. In 1907, still within a few kilometres of Koumasa, he noticed part of a circular wall protruding above ground at Salame and soon revealed two tholoi here, the second a hundred metres away at a spot called Koutsokera. Then he saw a huge horizontal slab of stone half buried by earth near the church at Christos; another tomb was excavated. Two more tombs were dug at Drakones, after a stream had washed away part of the circuit wall of one of them. In the space of a single year, Xanthoudides had found and excavated five tholoi.

So far, all of the tombs found had been situated south of the Yeropotamos, the river which divides the Mesara east-west. The first tomb to be found north of it was discovered in 1908, when tales of a rich treasure found at Kalathiana in 1854 reached Xan-

thoudides' ears. From the tholos found at Kalathiana, Xanthoudides was able to recover a few tantalising fragments of the wealth
of gold jewellery which had once been buried there. The incredible
pace of discovery now slackened, and no new tombs were found
until Greece and the rest of Europe had already been dragged into
the Great War. Then, in the autumn of 1914, preparations to
build a new church at the village of Platanos led to the discovery
of a new cemetery. Xanthoudides' excavations in 1914–15
revealed a mass of burials, focused on three circular tombs and
produced enough gold jewellery to emphasise what had been lost
at Kalathiana. Two years later Xanthoudides undertook the last
of his tholos excavations, recovering a typical assemblage of
artifacts from an uncertain context at Aspripetra and excavating
what remained of two tombs at Marathokephalon.

Xanthoudides' work over the passage of fourteen years (1904–
18) still provides the backbone of our studies of the Mesara
tholoi. He had excavated fifteen tombs, in addition to a fragment
of another at Christos and the deposit from Aspripetra. The
assemblage of artifacts from these excavations was vast, hundreds
perhaps thousands of clay and stone vessels, sealstones, dagger
blades, figurines, and pieces of jewellery. An account of the
material from Aspripetra and Marathokephalon had been published
in a Greek journal in 1918, but the mass of material and information was still unpublished at this time. To the all important task
of publication Xanthoudides now devoted himself and produced
his definitive account of his excavations in 1924. *The Vaulted
Tombs of Mesara* remains the most important single publication for
our study of pre-palatial Crete. Unsatisfactory by modern standards of excavation and publication, its production was nevertheless a superb achievement on the part of Xanthoudides. Here
we find, described in quite considerable detail, excavations which
had been conducted as much as twenty years previously. Many
items are given a remarkably precise provenance, disturbed
areas are noted, details of stratification recorded, and the text is
abundantly illustrated with a series of fine drawings and photo-
graphic plates. Not a definitive account by current standards perhaps, but a miracle for its time and an object lesson to some of
Xanthoudides' successors.

After Xanthoudides' last excavations in 1918, the discovery and
excavation of the circular tombs ceased almost completely until
the mid-1950s. Marinatos excavated two small but important

tombs at Vorou, not far from Marathokephalon, in 1930 and about the same time discovered and cleared the small circular tomb at Krasi, just south of Mallia on the north coast of the island. This was the first circular tomb of the Early Bronze Age to be discovered outside the Mesara region, but its small size suggested at the time that it might not be strictly comparable to the Mesara tholoi in any case. During his travels in the island however, John Pendlebury noted what he considered to be the remains of two more circular tombs of the Early Bronze Age, one of which was situated at Kalergi, not far distant from Krasi. The other was found at Pedhino in the centre of the great limestone mass of eastern Crete. The question of whether or not the circular tombs were confined to the Mesara was therefore posed but not answered. Pendlebury also noted, during the 1930s, traces of other circular tombs in the Mesara, chiefly in the vicinity of the village of Vasiliki. Pendlebury however did not excavate any Early Bronze Age tholoi, and after Marinatos's excavations, no such tombs were dug until in 1941 the Germans found and excavated a small tomb at Apesokari, east of Platanos. With admirable German efficiency, the report on this excavation was prepared within a year! This, however, was the only tholos excavation in more than twenty years of Cretan archaeological activity following the excavations at Vorou.

In 1954 a new period of discovery and excavation of the tombs was opened with the reports of new tombs at Rizikas and Gorgolaini (the latter just falling within the region of northern Crete) and with the excavation of two further tombs at Rotasi and Viannos. The latter lay some distance east of the Mesara but was of undoubted Mesara type. This was followed in the late fifties by the excavation of a similar tomb at Myrsini, in Sitia, which finally revealed that though the tholoi were most numerous in the region of the Mesara they were also to be found in other parts of the island. A Middle Minoan tomb discovered and excavated on Gypsades at Knossos about the same time emphasised the point. In the Mesara region itself, the late fifties saw the first discoveries and excavations at Lebena and the report of circular tombs at Megali Vrysi. In all, five tombs were eventually excavated in three localities at Lebena. Most of the circular tombs discovered up until 1960 were found in a relatively small area centred on Koumasa, though it was always assumed that similar concentrations existed throughout most of the Mesara and its environs. In the mid-sixties this assumption was shown to be correct as far as the area south of Phaistos was concerned. Where no tombs had previously been known in this area, ten cemetery sites totalling thirteen individual tholoi were found and excavated in the space of four or five years. In addition three more probable or certain sites were discovered but not excavated. Further east, a second tomb was discovered and dug at Apesokari. These excavations were all undertaken by the Greek archaeological service, principally by Dr Alexiou, Dr Sakellarakis, and Dr Davaras. Indeed it is true of the Mesara tholoi as a whole that, unlike the palaces, they have almost all been excavated by the Greeks themselves. The only exceptions are the tombs at Agia Triadha, Siva and Kamilari (dug by the Italians), the small tholos at Apesokari (dug by the Germans), and the late tomb on Gypsades (dug by the British).

The discovery and excavation of the Mesara tombs has been made mainly in two fifteen-year periods of intense activity, between 1904–18, and 1954–69. The result of this activity can be summed up as follows. If we include the late, the atypical, and the unexcavated and uncertain examples of Early Bronze Age tholoi in our total, then we have some sort of information about nearly eighty of these tombs. Of these, about fifty have been excavated, and the identification of the remainder as tombs of this sort and of this period must be examined closely before any of them can be accepted as probable, though unconfirmed, examples. There are several pieces of evidence which one might reasonably expect to find before confirming the discovery and identification of an unexcavated tomb. Obviously one requires traces of a circular structure, normally with walls a metre or more thick and an external diameter between four and fourteen metres. Traces of an antechamber are to be looked for but not expected, since it is clear from many excavated tombs that the relatively flimsy structure of the chambers has led to their complete destruction in the passage of time. Thirdly we should expect to find Early Bronze Age sherds, and perhaps a few fragments of stone vases, obsidian, and human bones strewn in the vicinity of the structure. Finally we must bear in mind the geographical distribution of these tombs. Of the excavated (and therefore confirmed) tombs, only four have been found outside the Mesara and its environs. Three of these, Knossos, Viannos and Myrsini, are late examples of the type (MM.II, MM.I, and MM.I. respectively), and the fourth, Krasi, is unusual for its method of construction, and to some extent its size. Early Bronze Age tholoi, we may conclude, are more likely to be discovered in the Mesara than in other parts of the island.

With these various considerations in mind, we can examine the records, for what they are worth, of the reported but unexcavated circular chamber tombs of the Early Bronze Age. I can personally vouch for three examples which I have seen and examined myself. Two small tombs at Chrysostomos, south-west of Andiskari, were exposed and robbed by a shepherd. Their shape, eastern entrances, and the scatter of Early Minoan I and II sherds, some human bones, and two fragments of Early Minoan III/Middle Minoan I stone vases, make their identification as circular tombs of Mesara type absolutely certain. The third tomb was one situated within a hundred metres of the large Middle Minoan tomb at Kamilari. It lay to the south-east of the excavated tholos, and was almost completely destroyed and looted. Enough of its structure and a few Middle Minoan I sherds survived however to confirm its original purpose, date and appearance.

The remaining tomb reports I classify into five groups— probables, possibles, improbables, rejects, and doubtfuls. There are three probable tombs, including one excavated example where the dating evidence is difficult to evaluate. This is the tomb excavated by Marinatos at Arkhaiokhorapho, south of Siva. A quantity of Late Minoan sherds were recovered from this tholos, the only other dateable find being the top half of a jug, said to be Early Minoan but possibly (from its description) of Middle Minoan I. Marinatos was convinced that this was a looted Early Bronze Age tomb, and I think he was right. The absence of a *dromos* and the situation of the tomb above ground mean it cannot be a Late Bronze Age *tholos*, and the sherd material precludes an Iron Age date for the tomb. The same considerations lead me to identify the remains discovered by Faure at Siderokamino (south of Mallia), as an Early Bronze Age chamber tomb. Here, the surface sherds were mainly of Middle Minoan I (nothing recognisably earlier) and presumably these are indicative of the date of foundation. The circular wall found at Gorgolaini enclosing hundreds of human bones and potsherds, including an Early Minoan askos, is almost certainly a tomb of Mesara type.

Most of the reported tholoi can only be regarded as possible examples owing to a lack of information about their date, their structure, and their purpose. Pendlebury reported possible chamber tombs of Mesara type at five different sites, two of which were outside southern Crete. At Pedhino in Sitia he saw the remains of two circular tombs, associated with handmade sherds of uncertain date, whilst a third tomb was tentatively identified by him at Kalergi, south of Krasi. He records no associated material from here, and all three tombs are therefore of uncertain date. In the Mesara, in the vicinity of the village of Vasiliki, Pendlebury discovered the remains of three circular structures. One of these, at Kokkiniano, produced no sherds, whilst the remaining examples at Plakoura and Merthies were unusual in that they both had a straight wall dividing their interior into two equal parts.[1] From Merthies came sherds of Early Minoan pottery. No excavated tholos has yet produced traces of an interior dividing wall like these at Plakoura and Merthies, and if only for this reason, the identification of these structures as Mesara type tombs cannot confidently be claimed.

Paradoxically, Pendlebury raised doubts as to the nature of the circular wall seen by Evans at Komo, and identified by him as the remains of a circular chamber tomb. According to Pendlebury, the remains appeared to belong to an apsidal building rather than a tholos, but one wonders if Pendlebury had seen the traces of a rectangular suite of outer chambers such as were discovered a few years later at Apesokari, and since then at other tomb sites. The situation of the circular structure at Komo, just to one side of an Early Minoan I-Middle Minoan I settlement is certainly reminiscent of several Mesara cemetery sites. Other possible tombs about which we do not have enough information include examples at Rizikas (circular wall of five metres diameter, built of great stones) Megali Vrysi (great circular structures), and Tsilastra ("a possible tholos"). In addition there are the two deposits of material with no associated structures which are usually thought to have come from destroyed chamber tombs of Mesara type. Of these, the Agios Onouphrios deposit is the better known. There can be little doubt that this assemblage, with its many figurines and its gold jewellery, came from an Early Bronze Age tomb, and that being so it is almost certain that it would have been a tholos. The date and character of the Aspripetra deposit are clearly established by the Early Minoan pottery and human bones found in it, and suggest that it must have come from a destroyed circular tomb.

Two reports which are unlikely to refer to Early Bronze Age tholoi are Faure's report of a circular structure at Elleniko (west of Prina) and Pendlebury's of a small chamber with partially corbelled roof at Paranisi in the Mesara. Elleniko produced no Early Bronze Age material at all and has a Late Minoan III settlement within fifty metres of the "tomb", whilst Paranisi is unlikely to be Early Bronze Age, since Pendlebury does not include it in his list of Early Bronze Age sites. We may, I think, firmly reject Xanthoudides' suggestion that the *tholos* at Praisos was originally constructed in the Early Bronze Age and completely cleared out and re-used in the Geometric period. The design of the Praisos *tholos* is certainly not identical with that of the Mesara tombs, and the quality of the masonry is far better than that found in any Early Bronze Age tomb. On the other hand, the appearance of an antechamber and the absence of any proper entrance passage do bring the tomb into a typological relationship with the Mesara tombs. It would be very satisfying if we could fit the *tholos* at Praisos into the Middle Minoan period, between the latest Mesara tombs and the earliest Late Bronze Age *tholoi*. But it seems impossible to do this, simply because there is no evidence at all for such an early construction date apart from the tomb's typology. The earliest item found in the tholos at Praisos is a Mycenaean gem, and this of course could well have found its way into the hands of the Geometric people who seem to have used the tomb for burials. The excavators were emphatic that there was no Mycenaean or Kamares pottery found in the tomb at all. It is difficult to envisage a cleaning operation in the Geometric period which would not have left at least a few sherds of Minoan pottery on the floor. Tempting as it is to attribute Praisos to the Middle Minoan era, the archaeological evidence will not support such an early date.

There remain a few reports which we can merely query. For example, it is reported that Early Minoan II vessels from a looted grave (almost certainly a circular tomb) at Kaloi Limenes were taken to the Heraklion Museum in 1963. Could this tomb be that briefly reported at Kaloi Limenes a few years later? Similarly, could the two gold diadems from a tomb near Siva, reported *c.* 1954, have come from one of the looted tholoi in this area excavated or noted a few years later—Kamilari II and III for example? Has anything been recovered from, or is anything known about, the large Early Bronze Age tholos which has been verbally reported in the immediate vicinity of Pompia, south of Phaistos? Finally, is there a tomb of this sort at Lukia? On his map showing the proposed route of a Minoan road between Knossos and Phaistos, Evans marked the Mesara tholoi known to him, and included one at Lukia, just north-east of Koumasa. Since all of the other known tombs in this area are also marked on the map, it appears that Evans knew of an additional tholos here. But there are no other reports of this tomb, and Evans nowhere mentions it in his text.

Even allowing for the excavated tombs at Knossos, Viannos, and Myrsini, and the uncertain examples at Kalergi, Gorgolaini, Siderokamino and Pedhino, the distribution of the Early Bronze Age circular tombs of Crete can be seen (fig. 1) to concentrate *Fig. 1* overwhelmingly in southern central Crete, in and around the plain of Mesara. The majority of tombs known at present in fact, are situated in the foothills of the Asterousia mountains or on the edge of the plain, south of the Yeropotamos. We would seem to be justified therefore in thinking of these tombs as characteristic of the Early Bronze Age civilisation of the Mesara and the mountains which surround it. This might help us to understand the remarkable uniformity of the tholos tradition in Early Minoan Crete, several manifestations of which we shall discuss in detail later. The topographical uniformity of the tombs may conveniently be mentioned however at this point.

Virtually all of the tholoi are on elevated ground of some sort. Christos stands on a low mound, Marathokephalon, Vorou and several others on the peak of a small hill, Porti on an upper hill terrace, Chrysostomos on a high promontory, and so on. Very often, in order to maintain an elevated position, the tombs have been built on a slight slope and have necessitated the cutting of a terrace to take them. The most persistent feature of the tombs' location however is their proximity to a contemporary settlement. In every case where extensive excavation or exploration has been conducted, a Minoan village dating at least as early as Middle Minoan I has been found within a short distance of the tholos or tholoi. Again, this is something we shall need to look at in detail later, but for the moment we might mention the tholos tomb at Salame for example, where a distance of only ten metres separated the tholos from the settlement, and Viannos, where an MM.1 house was built right next to a small circular tomb. Clearly, for some reason it was considered important to juxtapose tombs and settlement.

Initially this meant that a village would have one or two

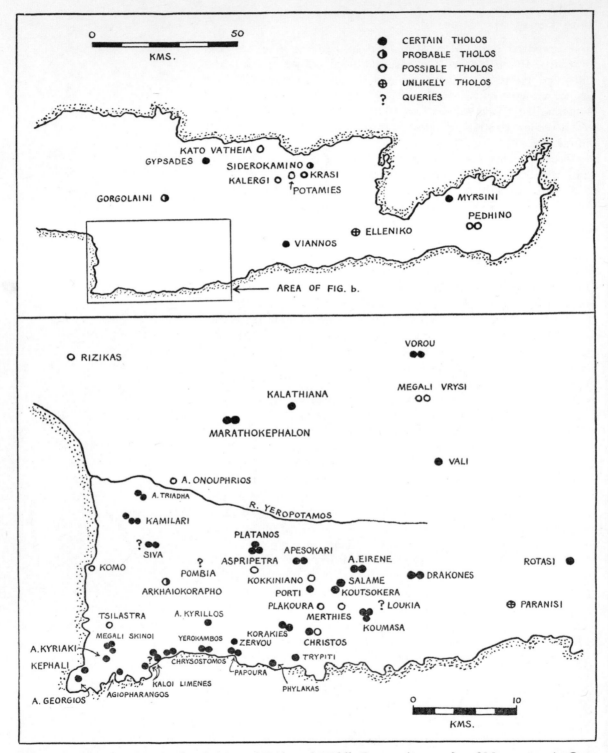

Fig. 1 A map showing the distribution of Early and Middle Bronze Age tombs of Mesara type in Crete

circular stone chamber tombs built to one side of it. These would have an antechamber or antechambers and perhaps stand in an area marked out by a wall, by paving or by stones. In the centuries following the construction of the tombs, however, the cemetery complex would begin to grow. It is clear from the extensive excavations at Koumasa, Porti, and Platanos that periodic clearing of the tholoi was necessary to make enough room for new burials. The remains removed from the tombs were put into the antechambers or into specially constructed store-chambers or walled trenches. As individual burial in a pithos became more common in Middle Minoan I, cemeteries of pithoi began to appear around the tholoi, often concentrated inside flimsy stone-walled huts. By now the cemeteries must have begun to take on an untidy and straggling appearance. At Porti for example Xanthoudides found that "the whole plateau had been a cemetery," with a tholos, a rectangular ossuary, two walled trenches and a mass of pithos burials. The situation at Platanos must have been even more chaotic, but unfortunately Xanthoudides never published a full plan of what he excavated there. From the plan he did publish, and the detailed notes he made about the unplanned features, it is, I think, possible to get some idea of what the cemetery must have looked like by the end of the Middle Bronze Age[2] (fig. 2). Closely grouped together stood three tholoi, each with a group of antechambers before its eastern doorway. Between the tholoi ran a pavement, bounded by a small stone wall. Before tholoi A and Γ, and probably close to B too, were a series of walled trenches filled with material cleared from the tholoi, while just north of tholos Γ were three small groups of rectangular stone huts roofed with clay laid on brushwood. In these were pithos burials and more material from the tholoi. Other pithos burials were scattered in the area, without the protection of these flimsy walled buildings.

Fig. 2

Like most ancient tombs, the Mesara tholoi have been subjected to widespread plunder and destruction. In antiquity itself the temptation must have been great, for the tombs and their contents were easily accessible—one had simply to move the door slab and walk in. Furthermore the periodic clearing and, as we shall see, fumigation of the tombs, gave both the opportunity and the excuse for looting. In several tholos tombs, excavators have been able to point to evidence for plundering being practised whilst the tombs were in use, but nowhere was the evidence

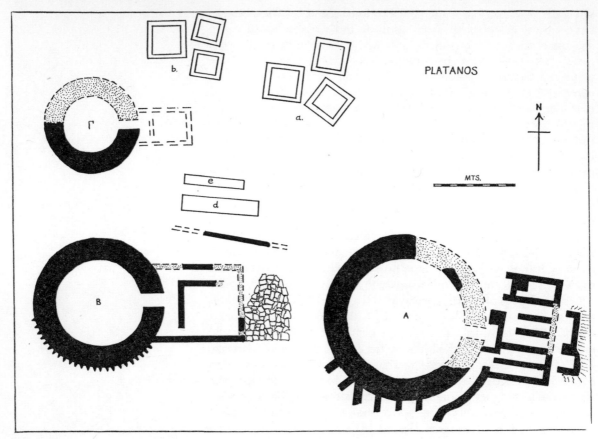

PLATANOS

clearer than at Platanos. Here, Xanthoudides found two distinct strata, the lower of which produced very clear signs of a heavy fire, almost certainly associated with the fumigation of the tomb. This lower level contained, apart from bones, fourteen broken and twisted dagger blades and a few small gold beads. The upper level, representing burials made after the fumigation, was altogether richer and in particular produced a large number of bronzes and a good quantity of gold jewellery. There can be no doubt at all that the fumigation undertaken towards the end of Early Minoan II was used as an opportunity to plunder the old burials of their possessions.

Something of the sort continued at one tholos or another throughout the Bronze Age. Levi noted a very similar situation in

Fig. 2 A reconstruction of the plan of the cemetery area at Platanos, based on the description and incomplete plan published by Xanthoudides

the big tholos at Kamilari, where the earlier deposits had been
systematically looted during Middle Minoan II. Late Minoan looting was detected at Drakones and Agia Eirene, and must be sus-
pected in a number of other tholoi where the remaining material
dates to MM.II but is clearly only a remnant of the original
wealth of the tombs. By the end of the Bronze Age, the looting of
the tholoi must have become much more difficult, for by now the
tombs had collapsed and were rapidly disappearing. Thus, at Agia
Eirene, two Late Minoan sealstones and a bronze ring probably
of similar date were found in the earth covering the burial
stratum. Certainly after the end of the Bronze Age, there is little
evidence for looting and disturbance until relatively modern
times. At Koumasa, a Roman grave was placed on top of the
mound covering tholos B, and another with glass tear bottle and
terracotta lamp was placed in the space between tombs A and B.
A Christian grave was found by the entrance to the tholos at
Christos. But these disturbances are notable for their scarcity; the
Bronze Age cemetery areas seem, for the most part, to have been
deliberately avoided by the people of later antiquity.

Regrettably the same is not true of the modern inhabitants of
the Mesara. Initially perhaps their interest was in procuring an
abundant and accessible supply of building stone. Half of tholos
A at Platanos, for example, was completely destroyed by the
Turkish inhabitants of the village for just that reason. But once
gold showed itself, then the possibilities offered by these stony
mounds of earth were rapidly realised. The sort of frenzied
activity which the discovery of gold set off is very clearly revealed
at Kalathiana. Here, in 1854, some scraps of gold were brought to
the surface and immediately sparked off a wholesale "excavation"
of the mound by the local inhabitants. In their quest for gold they
completely pulled down about half of the circuit wall—which was
well over two metres thick—and became so obsessed by their task
that they began to dig through the soft natural bedrock beneath
the tomb! The holes in the rock were still there to see when
Xanthoudides excavated the tholos more than fifty years later.
The tholoi perhaps escaped lightly, for in the north of the island,
at Arkhalokhori, peasants in search of gold used gunpowder to
blast their way into a sacred cave!

The process continues, perhaps in less dramatic fashion, even
today. In 1966 I was conducted by a shepherd to two small tholos
tombs which he had discovered and looted at Chrysostomos,

overlooking the Libyan sea. He had looted the tombs, he said, using his bare hands and the walking stick which he carried with him. From answers to my questions, and from the fragments of pottery, stone vessels, and human skulls which I was able to pick up, it was possible to estimate that the tombs had been in use from Early Minoan I to Middle Minoan I, and that they had contained a typical sort of tholos assemblage. Rough plans made on the spot enabled me to compile a short report which, together with the finds, was placed in the hands of Dr Alexiou at Iraklion Museum. Unfortunately even this sort of information cannot be obtained in many cases where looting has been thorough and the culprits cannot be found.

Looting however is only half of the particular problem which faces the excavator of a tholos tomb. The other is the length of time over which these tombs were used and the enormous number of burials and funerary ceremonies which must have taken place in them. The results of these factors are that thousands of feet have trampled over the burial deposits in a tholos, many of the deposits have been shovelled out into outside chambers, and others have been swept against the wall to make more space in the centre and near the doorway for new burials. In some tholoi too there is evidence for repairs to the structure or its roof. Tholos Z at Drakones, and tholos ε at Agia Eirene, for example, were both propped up late in their history by the addition of interior buttress walls. For the archaeologist all of this activity, and that of the plunderer, results in disturbance. The tremendous disturbances to which the burial deposits have been subjected explains both the difficulties facing the excavator of a tholos tomb in the Mesara, and the paucity of information which we have about the burials in spite of three dozen excavations. Xanthoudides, Halbherr, and Parabeni were excavating in the days when the science of excavation was still in its infancy; they produced useful and well illustrated reports, but understandably left out much that the modern archaeologist would include as essential. On the other hand the discoveries and excavations made in the last fifteen years have for the most part been disappointingly unlucky. Of the excavated tholoi at Viannos, Apesokari II, Agios Kyrillos, Kephali and Gypsades, none have produced more than a handful of finds, and for this looting must be largely responsible. Only Kamilari and Lebena have yielded material in anything like the quantity and quality which the earlier excavations have led us to expect.

But this is to look on the black side of the picture. The fact remains that today we have *some* sort of information about more than seventy tholoi, and excavation reports, however brief in some cases, for three-quarters of these. The amount of material produced from these tombs runs into many thousands of objects, a good proportion of which have been described and/or illustrated in reports, and certain of which have been subjected to detailed study by students of the Cretan Early Bronze Age. We have the plans of more than twenty tholoi, and a good, if by no means complete, corpus of information about the skeletal remains found in them and the circumstances of their discovery. Furthermore several of the tombs are still exposed and may therefore be visited and studied *in situ* by the more adventurous traveller. All in all, we have enough information to build up a picture of these tombs as they once were, to understand how they were used and for how long, to see what their users believed about death and burial, and to gain some insight into the society of their users and the importance of these tombs in the life of that society.

Chapter Two

THE MONUMENTS OF
A MILLENNIUM

I am aware that the title of this chapter carries a certain ambiguity, and it is my intention that it should. Indeed the purpose of this chapter might be said to be the justification of its title, for here we shall be concerned with the chronological span of the Mesara tholoi and with the main characteristics of Minoan civilisation during that period. The chronological framework for the Minoan Bronze Age was set out by Sir Arthur Evans in the early years of the twentieth century, initially on the basis of changing styles of pottery decoration and shapes. His Minoan Bronze Age was divided into three major periods, Early, Middle and Late Minoan, each of which was subdivided into three sub-periods, I, II, and III. Apart from the changing pottery styles which distinguished the three major periods, one could also point to certain broad architectural distinctions, so that it is possible to use the terms pre-Palatial, proto-Palatial, and neo-Palatial instead of Early, Middle and Late Minoan. These alternatives to Evans's terminology, suggested by the Italian archaeologists, have gained a wide measure of acceptance, particularly as they leave Evans's terms free to be applied as labels to certain pottery styles. There are however inconsistencies in the use of the two terminologies and certainly considerable differences in the way they are interpreted. Thus Middle Minoan cannot be freely used as a synonym for proto-Palatial, since the first palaces are built in the middle of Middle Minoan I, and they are destroyed and rebuilt as the new palaces (i.e. neo-Palatial) at the end of Middle Minoan II. In other words, to say proto-Palatial is to say mid Middle Minoan I–

PLATE I   A view of the plain of Mesara and the Asterousia
mountains looking south from Phaistos

PLATE 2   A view of Lebena II (Yerokambos) showing trilithon door
and huge foundation stones

PLATE 3   The unexcavated tholos at Siderokamino

PLATE 4   Projecting slabs on the outside face of tholos B, Platanos

Middle Minoan II. Middle Minoan III falls in the period of the second palaces, or in the neo-Palatial era. In addition to these inconsistencies there are also the very serious differences in the interpretation of what some of these terms mean, and these are of immediate concern to us, for the differences are greatest in the pre-Palatial or Early Minoan period.

Professor Doro Levi believes the pre-Palatial period to be little more than a sub-neolithic, a sort of transitional phase of perhaps two centuries, between the Stone Age Cretans and the builders of the palaces.[1] His opinion is largely based on his excavations and discoveries at Phaistos, where he has persistently found deposits of the pre-Palatial era containing a mixture of various types of pottery which British, French and American archaeologists believe to represent different sub-periods within the pre-Palatial period. Because they all appear in the same level together, says Levi, they must surely represent a single period during which they were all in usage. In fact Levi was not the first to suggest that the Minoan Early Bronze Age was a fiction. Twenty years before Levi first called Evans's scheme into question, Nils Aaberg had suggested that the Early Minoan and Middle Minoan Ia pottery styles were variations of neolithic pottery, and that Crete was populated by neolithic farmers until the first palaces were erected by immigrants at the end of MM.I.[2] If Aaberg and Levi are right, then clearly we can no longer speak of the Mesara tholoi as the monuments of a millennium!

The views of Aaberg and Levi have found no acceptance amongst other scholars however.[3] Not only do their arguments ignore the mass of distinctive Early Bronze Age artifacts of all sorts found in the Mesara tholoi and elsewhere but they ignore the stratified evidence from many other sites. Dr Warren published a detailed list of Early Minoan stratified and/or homogenous deposits a few years ago, and it is hardly necessary to repeat the information here.[4] It will suffice to mention a few sites where the various sub-divisions of the Early Minoan period are completely vindicated by stratified deposits. Two of our tholoi in fact have produced very clear evidence indeed of the distinctions between Early Minoan I and Early Minoan II, and between Early Minoan II and Middle Minoan Ia. These were the tombs, excavated in 1959–60, at Lebena.[5] In tomb II, Alexiou found an upper level containing pottery of the styles we normally ascribe to Early Minoan II and Middle Minoan I, and sealed

17

beneath this level a second with pottery of the Early Minoan I
styles. The adjacent tomb IIa also produced two levels, here
clearly separated by sand, the upper of which contained Middle
Minoan Ia pottery and the lower Early Minoan II. In other words
the discoveries at Lebena alone demonstrate a stratified sequence
of Early Minoan I, II and Middle Minoan Ia deposits. The Early
Minoan III period is not represented here according to Alexiou,
and although we may have reason to question this view later, for
the moment we will assume that he is right. Certainly Early
Minoan III is best represented in the east of the island, and it is
here that it has been found in a stratified context, between deposits
of Early Minoan II and Middle Minoan I pottery, at Palaikastro.[6]
In addition, its distinctive character is amply illustrated by the
huge deposit of sherds of Early Minoan III style found in the
north trench at Gournia.[7] These sherds are nowhere matched in
the Middle Minoan I deposits in the settlement. Many other
homogenous deposits, and a smaller number of stratified ones,
could be quoted to support those described, but we may simply
refer the reader to Warren's list. Enough has been said to show
that the four periods, Early Minoan I, II, III, Middle Minoan Ia,
exist as distinctive periods in their own right and are represented
by stratified deposits containing characteristic pottery. Before we
attempt to define the chronological limits of the tholoi, we must
briefly describe the various pottery styles which typify these
periods.

Early Minoan I is characterised in the ceramics by four distinctive types of pottery. First there is a pattern-burnished ware,
used mainly for goblets and tall chalices, which we call Pyrgos
ware. Secondly there is red monochrome ware, sometimes burnished, and used particularly for large suspension pyxides. In the
absence of a suitable type-name for this, I would suggest it might
be called Salame ware. The remaining two pottery styles are
distinguished by painted rectilinear decoration. A red or brown
paint on white, buff or pale brown ground is usually called Agios
Onouphrios ware, and is most commonly used for the production
of superb round-bottomed jugs, two-handled bowls, one-handled
cups, and a variety of zoomorphic or related shapes. The other,
rather scarcer style, is a reversal of Agios Onouphrios ware, being
decorated in white paint on a red or brown ground. A fine array
of vases in this style was found at Lebena and I have already
advocated elsewhere that this style should be known as Lebena

ware. The shapes are open pyxides, bowls, two-handled and one-handled tankards, and small jars.

Warren has previously pointed out some of the difficulties of drawing a clear distinction between Early Minoan I and Early Minoan II.[8] The difficulty really is to ascertain whether or not Pyrgos, Salame, Lebena, and Agios Onouphrios wares continued in use in Early Minoan II, and if so to what extent and with what changes in the type of decoration and the range of shapes in which they appear. Sherds of all these wares certainly occur in deposits which are predominantly Early Minoan II, but this need not mean that they represent vases which were being made and used then. They are more likely to represent residual material, and perhaps a few old vases which have remained in use rather longer than the majority of their contemporaries. The mixed deposits encountered by Levi at Phaistos clearly illustrate the dangers involved in accepting that all the sherds found in a deposit are contemporary. It may be that a few vessels of Pyrgos and Lebena wares were manufactured during the early part of Early Minoan II, but if so they were very much in a minority and cannot be picked out in the archaeological record. Salame ware, a rather basic sort of fabric, may well have been made in small quantities over a long period of time, as was its equivalent on the Greek mainland. Agios Onouphrios ware is an altogether more difficult problem. There is no doubt at all that the basic style continued in use during Early Minoan II, but it is equally certain that the style evolved in the passage of time into something different from its original form. One very clear development is the appearance of heavy cross-hatching, usually in large triangular areas, which tends to obscure the shape of the vessel rather than emphasise and enhance it as did the earlier Agios Onouphrios style. This secondary style is particularly clearly represented at Koumasa, and Zoes has proposed that we call this the Koumasa style, but I prefer to stick to the label I gave to it in the *Foundations of Palatial Crete,* namely Agios Onouphrios II ware. This label has the attraction of indicating that the style is a development from the Agios Onouphrios ware of Early Minoan I, and that it belongs itself in Early Minoan II. Another late development of Agios Onouphrios ware would seem to be represented by the great jugs with groups of converging brown lines painted on them found by Warren at Fournou Korifi, near Myrtos.[9] These were present in large numbers in an Early Minoan II settlement. A lot of the pottery here was the mottled ware which we name after the site at Vasiliki in eastern Crete. This is undoubtedly the characteristic ware of the Early Minoan II period, and is used for a very wide variety of vessels—jugs, bowls, "egg-cups", tumblers, plates, and teapots.

Both Warren and myself, however, are convinced that Early Minoan II can be divided into two recognisable phases which we call IIa and IIb. The earlier of these, IIa, is characterised in the pottery record by the short-lived and relatively scarce appearance of fine grey ware, used for small bowls and some finely decorated suspension pyxides. In addition Vasiliki ware at this time is not the dominating fabric which it becomes later in Early Minoan II, nor do we find the elaborate and patently deliberate patterns in the mottled decoration which appear on some of the developed teapots with very long spouts. The later, IIb phase sees the dominance of Vasiliki ware, the disappearance of the fine grey ware, and the production of a small quantity of Vasiliki vessels with white painted decoration on them. In the metallurgical record too, Early Minoan IIb would seem to be a distinctive, and quite important period. The earliest double-axes, spearheads, knives and leaf-shaped razors, all appear in Early Minoan IIb, apart from a small group of elaborated triangular daggers.[10]

Early Minoan III, as a distinct period, has been attacked by several scholars who defend the other sub-divisions of the Early Bronze Age ferociously. For varying reasons Alexiou, Hood, Platon, and Schachermeyr have all agreed that Early Minoan III is not a period of time but a regional style of pottery, confined almost entirely to eastern Crete, where it is contemporary with Middle Minoan I in central Crete.[11] Dr Zoes has demonstrated that this is not the case![12] Early Minoan III, whilst a particularly prosperous and lengthy period in the east of the island, also exists as a distinct period elsewhere. For the subsequent history of Minoan ceramics it is in fact a vitally important period, and the same is true for the history of Minoan metallurgy.[13] Much of the confusion has arisen because the predominant pottery styles in both Early Minoan III and Middle Minoan Ia are all varieties of white painted and dark washed pottery. The Early Minoan III varieties must surely be called Gournia ware after the splendid deposit of sherd material found there. The wealth of decorative motifs cannot possibly be described in a summary such as this, but we may note the emergence of curvilinear designs, including

the spiral. Distinctively Early Minoan III shapes include pedes-
talled teapots, straight-sided cups with *round* handles, and spherical,
rather heavy-looking jugs. Much of the painted decoration has an
exuberance, even an extravagance, not found amongst the pottery
in Middle Minoan Ia deposits. This is altogether more sophisticated and sober, and begins to include polychrome decoration.
In southern Crete plastic ornamentation, by cordons, barbotine,
combing or grooving, comes into vogue. Middle Minoan Ia is a
long period at Knossos, and by no means short even in the east of
the island where Early Minoan III pottery remained in use much
longer. The pottery styles which we call Middle Minoan Ib and II
are virtually confined to a few palatial centres, so that in most
areas Middle Minoan Ia pottery remained in use until the end of
the first palaces, destroyed by an earthquake near the end of the
eighteenth century BC.

These then are the pottery styles on which rests the basis of our
chronological framework for the Minoan Early Bronze Age. Even
those scholars who have rejected Levi's "collapsed" chronology,
however, are at variance with one another as to how long the
Early Bronze Age lasted. Most agree that Early Minoan I does
not begin before *c.* 2600 BC, but in each case this judgement is
based on a misreading of Evans's original excavation report, as
Warren has pointed out.[14] It has been widely assumed that
the Syenite bowl of IIIrd Dynasty date found in the area of the
South Propylaeum at Knossos came from a subneolithic deposit.
In fact there is no reason whatever to assume that this was so;
the vase is regrettably without context. Three fragments of stone
vases thought to be Egyptian, of the late predynastic-Dynasty II
period, were found in the Late Neolithic house in the central
court at Knossos, which contained some Early Minoan I
material.[15] These suggest that the Early Bronze Age may have
begun a century either side of *c.* 2800 BC, and this is implied too
by the C.14 dates for Early Helladic I at Eutresis, *c.* 2700–
2600 BC, since Early Minoan I appears to begin earlier than Early
Helladic I. Egyptian synchronisms, represented mainly by scarabs,
and the C.14 dates for Early Helladic III and Middle Helladic I
at Lerna (where we have Middle Minoan Ia sherds in a Middle
Helladic I deposit), suggest that Early Minoan III ended at
Knossos shortly after *c.* 2000 BC. The end of Middle Minoan II
in the palaces and Middle Minoan I elsewhere must be related to
the seismic disturbances which destroyed the first palaces, *c.*

1700 BC. This then is the millennium of which I write—the period
c. 2800 BC to c. 1700 BC, the period of the Minoan Early and Middle
Bronze Ages.[16]

It was also the millennium of the Mesara tholoi. To write a
detailed discussion of the contents of each and every tholos tomb
with a view to establishing its chronological limits would be a
valuable piece of work, but one which cannot economically be
envisaged here. I have made a careful study of all the published,
and much of the unpublished, material from the tombs listed in
Appendix 3. The dating range suggested by the table for
any tomb appearing in the list, is supported by the appearance
in the burial deposits of that tomb, of the various pottery styles,
gems, bronzework, figurines and other items which are tabulated.

Several points emerge very clearly from the table. Most of the
tombs seem to have been built in either Early Minoan I or Middle
Minoan I. Of the twenty-nine tombs listed, fifteen fall into the first
category and six into the second. It seems certain that there were
many other tholoi built in Early Minoan I, for we have to
remember that sherd material was very rarely published by
Xanthoudides, Marinatos, Halbherr, and other excavators of the
Mesara tombs. For this reason, the earliest pottery from many
tombs, which would have been subjected to the most prolonged
disturbance and the greatest destruction, has probably never been
published. Amongst the tombs not listed in the table there are
several which we know were first used in Early Minoan I (Agia
Eirene e, Chrysostomos I and II, Kephali, Koutsokera, Salame,
Trypiti). Similarly there are several tombs, other than those
listed, which were built in Middle Minoan I (Drakones △ and
Z—possibly built in EM.III— Kamilari III, Myrsini, Vali, Viannos,
Vorou B, and Siderokamino). In contrast to these many tombs of
Early Minoan I and Middle Minoan I, we can point to only seven
tombs which were probably built in Early Minoan II and none
which we can confidently claim to be Early Minoan III foundations. There are in addition two very late tholoi, at Gypsades
(Middle Minoan II) and Kamilari II (Middle Minoan II?). The
forty-five tombs for which a foundation date can be established
with reasonable certainty break down therefore into four groups:

Early Minoan I	Early Minoan II	Middle Minoan I	Middle Minoan II
22	7	14	2

We can conveniently reduce these into two major groups, an early and a late one. The earlier group is the larger, and is concentrated exclusively in the Mesara and its environs, whilst the later group includes several notably small tholoi (Vorou A and B, Gypsades, Kamilari II and III, Apesokari I, Vali, Myrsini, Siderokamino) and a number which are outside of the Mesara region (Gypsades, Myrsini, Viannos, Siderokamino). These tombs in the north and east are perhaps suggestive of a Middle Minoan I date for the reported tholoi at Pedhino(2) and Kalergi.

Already we can see that the tholoi are indeed the monuments of a millennium, for their period of construction spans something like a thousand years, albeit that the activity was concentrated, it appears, at either end of this era. But as the table shows, the tholoi were not simply built over a period of a thousand years, but they were regularly used for burials for that amount of time. At least a dozen tholoi have produced material covering the whole of the Early Bronze Age—Early Minoan I to Middle Minoan I. Furthermore it is clear from tholoi like Agia Triadha B, Platanos A and B, and Porti *II*, that burials in the tholoi did not suddenly stop at some fixed point during the Middle Minoan I period.[17] The tholoi went out of use gradually, odd burials being made in them as late as the beginning of the new palace period in the seventeenth century BC. In some cases they were re-opened and re-used even later. Thus tholos E at Agia Eirene, tholos Z at Drakones, and Kamilari I all contained pottery and traces of burials of the Late Minoan period. In the case of Agia Eirene, this means that the time which elapsed between the deposition of the first and last burials could be as much as fourteen or fifteen hundred years! This is an incredible span of time, and even the prehistorian, who is accustomed to thinking in terms of centuries and millennia rather than weeks and months, must hesitate before glibly committing himself and his readers to such a concept. Yet the truth is that throughout the Mediterranean and western Europe, the third millennium BC is characterised by the erection of great stone chamber tombs of one sort or another, which were used very often for periods up to a thousand years long. The tombs and burials of Spain, southern France, Brittany and Britain, are not perhaps entirely analogous with those of the Mesara, since they appear to have been made for a select few rather than for hundreds, perhaps thousands, as were the Mesara tholoi. But we cannot dispute that the tombs of all of these regions shared the single outstanding characteristic that they were built for a millennium!

In Crete, we may justifiably use the term in its symbolical as well as its chronological sense. The cultural and historical background to the Mesara tholoi is the story of a thousand years of peace, prosperity and progress.[18] At the end of the fourth millennium BC, Crete was still relatively thinly populated, by people who lived either in small village communities like that at Knossos, or in isolated farmsteads like those at Magasa or, a little earlier, at Katsamba. A good many people still lived in caves, such as those excavated at Koumaro, Miamou, and Trapeza. None of these people used weapons, tools or jewellery made of metal, although these things had been manufactured on the mainland of Turkey for more than a millennium already. Crete in fact had little contact with the outside world; its only recognisable import at this time was obsidian from Melos. Commerce indeed had hardly begun in Crete itself at this time. There is no evidence for the emergence of specialist craftsmen or merchants, and none for communal exploitation of natural resources, be they of stone, minerals, fauna, or simply good agricultural land. Communal activities of any kind are difficult to discern, except perhaps in the regular layout of the houses at Knossos. For the most part however, the Cretan of c. 3000 BC lived in a small family group and when he died was buried in a cave used for a small number of other burials, possibly those of members of the same family.

It is still not certain whether Crete received an influx of immigrants shortly after the beginning of the third millennium BC (our tholos tombs may provide us with crucial evidence on this matter in a later chapter), but there was certainly a rapid social and economic development. With the beginning of the Early Bronze Age (i.e. Early Minoan I), we find the Cretan devoted to a communal existence. Villages and small towns are now the norm, and isolated farmsteads are no longer found. Equally the communal tomb is widely adopted, whether it take the form of a circular tholos, a rectangular built tomb, or a burial cave. The new tombs are used for hundreds rather than dozens of burials, and are clearly erected for the use of the whole community or at least a substantial part of it. Economically we see the emergence of specialised craftsmen, initially perhaps only in metalworking, but soon in pottery manufacture as well. Architecturally, as we shall see in the next chapter, the circular tombs, whether vaulted or not were far in advance of any neolithic structures yet found in Crete.

Architectural advance was carried further during Early Minoan II, for now we find the first mansions appearing. Those at Vasiliki and Fournou Korifi contain many dozens of rooms, and feature several architectural forms not previously encountered in Crete. But they represent social and economic advance and change as well as architectural development. Here we find our first evidence for the emergence of a wealthier class in Cretan society, able to build and maintain a mansion the size of many contemporary villages. At Fournou Korifi at least, there was clear evidence too that this wealth was the product of commercial activity, there being ample evidence of an extensive woollen industry as well as a potter's workshop and several magazine rooms containing large storage pithoi. Parallel with this development, further specialised crafts appear, notably the production of stone vases and the manufacture of sealstones. Increased commercial activity however is best demonstrated by the contacts which were now established with the other parts of the Aegean. Whilst it is true that at this time Crete never became as much involved in Aegean commerce as did the Cyclades, the Troad, and the Greek mainland, it is clear that she did not maintain her previous isolation. Some Cycladic influence can be detected in northern Crete during Early Minoan I, but in Early Minoan II it is very much stronger both here and in the rest of the island. Cycladic-style cist graves appear at Mochlos and Sphoungaras, silver and lead artifacts (rare in Crete but common in the Cyclades) are found at half a dozen sites along the north coast, and Cycladic-style figurines appear frequently. The latter are common too in the Mesara, and in addition we find imported Cycladic stone pyxides amongst the Agios Onouphrios material, and a jug which I believe to be Cycladic amongst the pottery from Marathokephalon. Minoan influence in the rest of the Aegean is more difficult to trace, but the foot amulets from Zygouries, Despotikon and Agios Kosmas, and the bottle seal from the last, are typical Minoan types and might even have been made in Crete. Furthermore the earliest Minoan pottery from the island of Kythera would seem to belong to Early Minoan II, and is suggestive of the foundation of the trading colony which we know to have been situated on the island by Middle Minoan I.

These overseas contacts with the rest of the Aegean during Early Minoan II probably resulted in some indirect contact with areas beyond the Aegean. During Early Minoan III the Minoans seem to have established more direct relationships with these regions. The evidence is principally metallurgical, with clear signs of Syrian influence exerting itself on Minoan metalwork, and with some evidence for an exchange of ideas and perhaps even metal artifacts between Crete and the Italian peninsula. It seems likely that these wider contacts resulted very largely from Minoan attempts to find new sources of copper and tin, but the results were of more than metallurgical importance. Both the stone vase and the sealstone industries received a new impetus, the one finding new shapes amongst the Egyptian repertoire and the other new forms amongst Syrian sealstones. Some Cretan industries must have been producing goods for overseas trade— perhaps olive oil and woollens—and other industries must have been created by and for this commerce. Woodworking in particular must have expanded rapidly, for now we see on contemporary sealstones sea-going sailing ships, such as must have carried the Minoan produce abroad. The effects on Minoan society were equally widespread. Harbour towns found a new prosperity, attracting new settlers to them and demanding the creation of specialised trades and offices. The men who controlled the production of the exportable goods, and those who owned and sailed the ships which carried them, must have prospered too. In other words society was being broken down into a greater diversity of classes—distinguished by wealth, by job, and already, one suspects, by status. It was also becoming more mobile, and more flexible; old loyalties were being broken down and new ones taking their place.

Seen in this context, the emergence of palatial society during Middle Minoan Ia is not altogether surprising. As the centres of commerce grew into large towns, it became apparent that communal laws must be made and administered, communal works needed to be efficiently organised, and communal affairs in general had to be overseen. Thus, we suppose, arose the first palace dwellers. Yet even with the emergence of this central authority, Minoan society remained remarkably egalitarian. Houses clustered around the palace, which had no outer enclosure to keep it remote from the mass of the population. There were as yet no rich and isolated burials to denote the rise of a proud monarchy. Prosperity was widespread, and so too was peace. Throughout the thousand years from the start of the

Early Bronze Age to the rise of the palaces, there is no evidence in Crete for major destructions or outbreaks of warfare.[19] Neither the earlier nor the palatial towns erected defensive walls— yet we find them on several Cycladic islands, at Troy, Poliochni, Manika, Raphina, Asketario, Aegina, and Lerna during the Aegean Early Bronze Age. Similarly, the other islands of the Aegean and the Greek mainland did not indulge in the widespread trade that the Minoans pursued, and consequently did not reap its benefits in terms of technical and cultural advance. Whilst the mainland of Greece passed through a somewhat troubled and unrewarding Early Bronze Age, and the Cycladic islands never fulfilled their early promise of cultural excellence, Crete moved forward at an increasing tempo towards the brilliant civilisation of the palatial age. Five hundred years of palatial splendour were preceded by a thousand of prosperous and peaceful development; this is the "millennium" with which we are concerned.

Chapter Three

THE VAULTED TOMBS OF
MESARA?

When the Mesara tholoi were first discovered and excavated, it was widely agreed that originally they had been fully vaulted structures. Xanthoudides repeatedly expressed this opinion throughout his book, and brought forward evidence to support it.[1] Subsequently however, the view came under attack, first from Pendlebury and then from several other British and Greek archaeologists.[2] More recently, Levi, Alexiou and Platon have expressed support for Xanthoudides' view, claiming that evidence from their excavations at Kamilari, Lebena, and Myrsini respectively clearly points to the existence of a full stone vault.[3] This controversy, which continues and with which we shall be much concerned in this chapter, is of considerably wider importance than may at first appear. Clearly the solution to the problem will carry implications for any assessment of Early Minoan building techniques, and in particular for our understanding of the Minoans' ability to create palatial architecture during Middle Minoan I. Equally it will make a vital contribution to the solution of another difficult problem, the origin of the Mesara tholoi themselves, and ultimately, of the population of the Mesara in the Early Bronze Age. Thirdly, the question of vaulting in the Mesara tholoi is closely bound up with yet another controversy— the origins and development of the Late Bronze Age *tholos* tombs of the Aegean.

The evidence at our disposal includes of course examples of an inward curvature on the tholoi walls, of corbelled courses of stonework, and of masses of masonry found collapsed inside the tholoi walls. These things have been discussed at length by others, but we must begin by considering the more fundamental evidence. From the surviving, rather than the hypothetical architecture of the tombs, we must try to assess the technical competence of their builders and the basic strengths and weaknesses of the structures.

The size of the tombs varies considerably, from the tiny tholos at Apesokari, with an internal diameter of a little under two and a half metres, to the great tholos A at Platanos, with a diameter of just over thirteen metres. More than half of the tholoi for which we have details however, have internal diameters of between four and six metres, and three-quarters of them fall within the range four to nine metres. One point of significance in terms of a correlation between size and date of construction, is that eight of the fourteen Early Minoan III/Middle Minoan Ia tholoi are under five metres in diameter. It is likely that the late tholos at Viannos also falls in this group. The best known of this late group is probably the tholos at Apesokari, which has a wall 0.8 metres thick, and which has been quoted as an example of a small, strongly built tholos which was probably entirely vaulted in stone. This should not be allowed to mislead us into thinking that all of the late tholoi are small and thick walled. It is true of Vorou B, but the remaining tholoi for which details are available are more thinly walled than many of their earlier counterparts (fig. 3). It is not of course, simply a matter of comparing the *Fig. 3* actual width of the walls in the various tholoi, but of comparing their width in relation to their diameter. Thus, the great tholos A at Platanos, with its wall two and a half metres thick, is *in effect* more thinly walled than tholos B at Agia Triadha and tholos A at Koumasa, for example, the walls of which are only half the width of Platanos A. This is an important consideration to be borne in mind when we come to decide which, if any of the tombs, could have been fully vaulted in stone. If we were to judge on this criterion alone, then the tombs most likely to have been built in this way would be those at the top of the table in fig. 3A.

But of course there are other factors to be taken into account. A wide wall, whether it be relatively or absolutely so, could not have been built up into a fully vaulted structure unless it was constructed in a suitable manner. Some, at least, of the Mesara tholoi were not. The materials used in the construction of the tholoi were local stone and clay. Whether or not wood was used

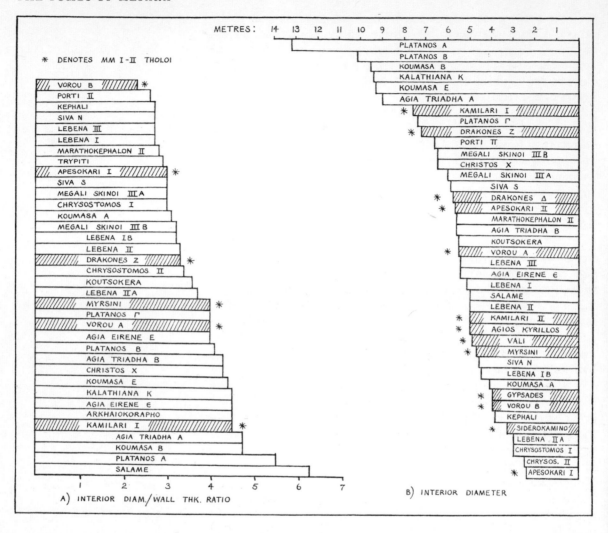

METRES: 14 13 12 11 10 9 8 7 6 5 4 3 2 1

* DENOTES MM I-II THOLOI

A) INTERIOR DIAM./WALL THK. RATIO

B) INTERIOR DIAMETER

to provide a light-weight roof is of course a controversial question to which we must return later. The only possible evidence for wood being used elsewhere in the structure, comes from tholos B at Koumasa. The great central door slab here had two large holes in its northern side and one in its southern which Xanthoudides suggests may have been utilised to take wooden bars, placed across the stone doors.[4] The stone used for construction is

Fig. 3 Diagrammatic representation of (A) the wall thickness/diameter ratios and (B) the interior diameters of the Mesara tholoi

mainly limestone, in pieces ranging in size from a few centimetres diameter, to more than a metre square.

It is significant that some of the largest blocks appear in the
foundation course of the wall. In Koumasa A for example, the
lowest course of stones is comprised of notably larger rocks than
any above it. At Lebena II, great boulders are placed at frequent
intervals around the lowest course of the inside face (pl. 2).   *Pl. 2*
The same is true, to a lesser degree, of the other Mesara tholoi,
and it looks very much as if this was a recognised technique
amongst the tholoi builders. No doubt these huge stones were
intended to anchor the structure as firmly as possible, and to
spread the tremendous weight of the superstructure a little to
prevent its collapse at the base. Normally the builders allowed no
possibility of the tomb "sinking", clearing the earth down to
solid rock before they began to erect the wall. This well-advised
practice might well explain the slightly sunken appearance of the
tholoi, which has previously been attributed to the supposed
origin of the tholos tomb in (a hypothetical) ancestral domestic
architecture. Above the foundations, the construction of the
circuit wall followed one of two practices. By far the most
common method adopted was to build the wall with relatively
large facing stones, on both the inside and the outside faces, and
to pack the centre or core of the wall with stones which were
mainly much smaller and were bonded with clay. The smaller
the stones, the more clay was used, and this is particularly true of
Porti and Apesokari. It is surely significant that these two tombs
have walls which are relatively thick, such as are needed to carry
this sort of construction to any notable height. Within the group
of tombs built in this way, there are many degrees of competence
and skill represented. At the bottom of the scale must come tombs
like those at Chrysostomos, Vorou, and Koumasa, built with
totally unworked stones of medium size, and with little or no
regard to coursing. In some cases, like Chrysostomos and
Koumasa B, there was not even an attempt to produce a smooth
inside face to the wall. Superior to these tombs in the quality of
workmanship are those which reveal the use of worked stones,
but are still built without regard to coursing. This is the case for
example with the tombs at Lebena, where many of the facing
stones were found to have been worked, and a good number even
had one face worked to the form of an arc. Furthermore, a
majority of the facing stones had apparently been carefully

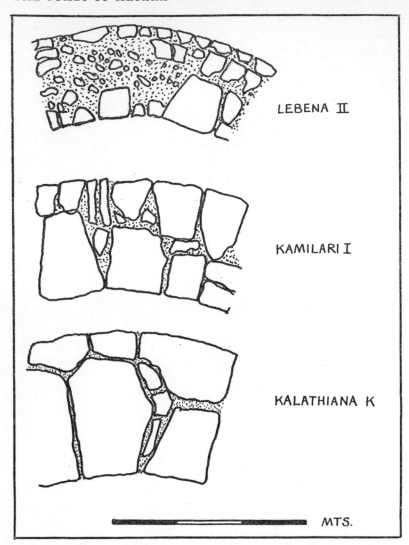

LEBENA II

KAMILARI I

KALATHIANA K

MTS.

Fig. 4 Details of the wall construction in Lebena II, Kamilari I, and Kalathiana

selected for their shape, being either roughly rectangular or wedge-shaped (fig. 4a). When these more regularly-shaped blocks were laid, they were separated from one another by one or two smaller stones and clay bonding. It is surprising that the considerable care exercised in the selection, working, and utilisation of the facing stones here did not extend to the laying of proper courses. In this

Fig. 4

PLATE 5   A general view of the interior of Kamilari 1 showing
the built doorway and regular masonry

PLATE 6   The fallen masonry, as discovered in Kamilari 1

PLATE 7   The antechambers and the huge door slab outside Kamilari I

PLATE 8   A stone vaulted cheese dairy on Mount Ida; early twentieth century

respect, the tholoi at Agia Triadha, Siderokamino, and Agios Kyrillos might be considered more sophisticated structures (pls. 3, 9). At these sites we have tombs built with roughly worked facing stones laid in something approximating to courses. In each case this was probably facilitated by the careful selection of the facing stones, the majority of which seem to conform to some sort of standard, so that the overall appearance of these walls at a distance is not altogether unlike that of a brick wall. This is particularly true of tholos A at Agia Triadha.   *Pls. 3, 9*

Only two of the tombs which have been published and/or seen by the author do not conform to these types of construction, and even these I would hesitate to classify separately. These are the tombs of Kalathiana and Kamilari. Xanthoudides drew attention to the fact that the stone used at the former site was never worked but naturally broke into regular slabs and blocks which gave the appearance of worked stone. At Kamilari however there can be no doubt at all that the stones used to face the wall were very carefully worked. Most of the facing stones have a properly cut face and are cut to the shape of either a rectangle or a wedge. It is not the working or shaping of the stones at either Kamilari or Kalathiana which pick them out as an improved form of structure in comparison to the other tholoi. The important difference is that in both cases, the majority (but not all) of the facing stones are large enough to span half the width of the wall. Thus, by skilful use of stones of different shape and varying size, it was possible virtually to interlock the inside and outside faces of the wall (fig. 4b, c). At both sites added strength was achieved *Fig. 4* by coursing, which in the big tholos at Kamilari was extremely regular (pl. 5). A final mark of sophistication at Kamilari is the *Pl. 5* bonding of the upper courses.

It would be satisfying if we could relate these typological differences in construction to chronological ones, but this is not possible. Amongst the most primitive type of tombs we find the tholoi at Vorou, built in Middle Minoan Ia very probably, whilst amongst the more sophisticated tholoi we find Agia Triadha A (dating from Early Minoan I) and Kalathiana (founded no later than Early Minoan II, and probably before). Though the quality of architecture represented by Kamilari may reflect a genuine advance in building techniques in Middle Minoan I, it must be admitted that the varying standards of construction seen in the other tholoi do not represent varying dates of construction. The stonemason's craft already included in Early Minoan I the ability to work and face building stone, to lay stones in courses, and to lay sturdy and effective foundations. This fact is underlined by the excellence of the doorway constructions in many of the early tholoi.

The methods of doorway construction fall into two very clear categories. Most of the tombs have doorways built on what we might call the trilithon principle, with two huge upright slabs supporting a massive lintel (pl. 2). The tombs at Porti, Koumasa, Agia Eirene, and many other sites are examples of this technique. There are a smaller group of tombs however which have what we may best call "built" doors, where the lintels rest on built jambs (pl. 5). The stones used to build the jambs are usually much larger examples than utilised elsewhere in the structure. Of the excavated and published tombs, only those at Kamilari, Chrysostomos, Agios Kyrillos, Apesokari, Gypsades and Vorou B can certainly be identified as belonging to this group, but it seems likely that Vorou A and the two tombs at Drakones also belonged to this category. There is perhaps a genuine chronological distinction to be made here, for apart from Chrysostomos, all of the tombs with "built" doorways date to Early Minoan III/ Middle Minoan Ia or later. It cannot be claimed that all tombs with "built" doorways are late constructions (Chrysostomos proves otherwise), nor that all tombs with "trilithon" doorways are early examples (the late tomb at Myrsini seems to have had a trilithon door), but it does seem quite clear that the majority of "built" doorways are to be found in the latest of the Mesara type tombs.

So too are the highest of the doorways, a point to which Sinclair Hood has previously drawn attention. The only tombs with doors over a metre and a half in height are those at Gypsades (*at least* 1.5 metres), Agios Kyrillos (1.7 metres) and Drakones Z (2 metres). All three tombs were built in the early second millennium BC. In contrast to these doorways, those in Lebena II and III, and Koumasa E are tiny, Lebena III being only half a metre high! Equally the majority of tombs have a very narrow doorway. The narrowest is certainly that at Apesokari, less than half a metre wide, and only Gypsades and Megali Skinoi A have doors more than a metre in width. Clearly there would have been considerable difficulty in moving corpses, and their bearers and mourners, through doorways of such diminutive proportions, and this is a question to which we must return later. The im-

Pl. 2

Pl. 5

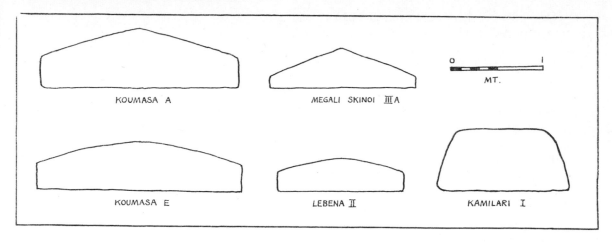

KOUMASA A

MEGALI SKINOI III A

O   I
MT.

KOUMASA E

LEBENA II

KAMILARI I

mediate question which poses itself is why the builders chose to construct such small doors in the first place. One explanation which can be dismissed at once is that they did not have technical competence to build larger ones. We have already mentioned some of the skills of the Early Minoan stonemasons, and to these we can add the evidence from the doorways themselves. The solidity and strength of the constructions is demonstrated by their survival in so many cases until the present day. Furthermore, whichever method of construction was adopted, the stones comprising the door-jambs were always carefully selected and worked. This is even more true of the lintels. Sir Arthur Evans long ago pointed out that at least some of the lintels had been deliberately worked so that their upper sides took the form of a shallow arc or low triangle. Examples of the former type can be seen at Christos and Koumasa E, and examples of the latter at Koumasa A and Megali Skinoi A (fig. 5). There can be little doubt that Evans was right in believing that this was a conscious attempt to disperse the central pressure on the lintel, just as it appears to be in the Lion Gate at Mycenae. Lintels of this sort and size (Koumasa A and E for example have lintel stones 2.2 and 2.3 metres in length respectively) surely imply a certain degree of architectural competence on the part of the people who made and used them. It is hard to believe that such people could not have made their doorways just half a metre or so higher.

One difficulty in erecting high doorways of the "trilithon"

Fig. 5   Lintels with relieving arcs or triangles

Fig. 5

type would be to find sufficiently large slabs to use as jambs, and one might point to the taller, "built" doorways at Gypsades, Agios Kyrillos and Drakones and claim that this was indeed the reason for the low "trilithon" doors of the earlier tombs. But this argument does not stand up to examination either. Two of the earliest tombs, at Chrysostomos, had "built" doors and certainly the great majority of doorways in contemporary domestic dwellings were constructed with built jambs. The "built" doorway was therefore well known to the early tomb builders and even on occasion used by them. Equally, it seems they had little difficulty in finding slabs of sufficient size to make taller jambs, for it seems that all of the tombs were originally closed with huge stone slabs, which in many cases have been found *in situ*. At Kamilari for example, the door slab was a third as tall again as the door, and a second flat slab found lying outside the tomb was a similar height. Had these two slabs been utilised as jambs, the entrance to this tholos would have been raised in height by a third of a metre. The same is true of other tombs. There is no reason to think therefore that the trilithon method of construction is responsible for the low doorways built into the tombs.

As far as we are able to judge, the increased height of the tomb doors built at the start of the second millennium BC was the result of a change of fashion rather than any sudden technological advances. What brought about the change in fashion, and what dictated that the earlier tomb doorways should be small, are questions which again we must defer for later consideration. Similarly we need not concern ourselves here with the details of the various ante-chambers which stood before the entrances to many, if not all, of the circular Mesara tombs. Our concern in this chapter is with the problem of whether or not the tombs were vaulted, and with the evidence relevant to this problem. So far we have seen that the tombs vary in size between two and a half and thirteen metres diameter, and that the diameter of the tomb may be between three and six times as great as the thickness of the enclosing wall. Building techniques varied considerably in quality between one tomb and another, but apparently with no regard to chronological differences between the tombs. Some of the earliest tombs display an architectural competence—to be seen in the working and coursing of the masonry, the shaping of the lintel, and the construction of the doorway—that is never bettered in the later ones. In other words, in terms of engineering ability, there is no reason to suppose that the builders of the latest tombs of Mesara type were notably more advanced than those who constructed the tombs built in Early Minoan I. As far as we can judge, the tomb builders of Middle Minoan I would have been no more, or less, competent to build a vaulted structure than their Early Minoan I predecessors.

No one has yet been able to produce evidence either to confirm or to reject Xanthoudides' original hypothesis that the Mesara tombs were fully vaulted in stone. Sir Arthur Evans enthusiastically endorsed the suggestion in his preface to Xanthoudides' book, although Seager had already expressed the opinion that the tombs were unroofed.[5] During the 1930s opinion swung away from the vault hypothesis, with first Marinatos and Wace rejecting it and then Pendlebury. Marinatos argued principally on the evidence he had derived from his excavation of the two tombs at Vorou, Wace on the general grounds that the methods of construction would not have been able to support stone vaulting, and Pendlebury both on these grounds and on the persistent absence of any clear evidence of a fallen vault within the tombs. More recently Hutchinson has followed Pendlebury, though with reservations about tomb B at Agia Triadha and tomb K at Kalathiana, and Mylonas too has rejected the vault hypothesis, without discussing the evidence at all.[6] The excavations at Lebena, Kamilari and Myrsini however have produced new evidence in support of Xanthoudides' hypothesis, with the result that Alexiou, Levi and Platon (the respective excavators) have all declared the opinion that the tombs were fully vaulted in stone. Matz has followed them.[7] Apart from Levi's quite full treatment of the problem in his report on Kamilari, Hood has discussed the problem at some length.[8] His conclusions were that many of the smaller tombs were completely vaulted in stone, but others were probably built with mud or mud-brick domes on substantial stone foundations. Some form of light superstructure— whether of mud-brick or timber—has been postulated for most, if not all, of the tombs by both Pendlebury and Hutchinson.

The foregoing is but a brief review of the controversy surrounding the "vaulted" tombs of the Mesara, but it will serve to demonstrate the variety of both the solutions and the approaches to the problem. The vault hypothesis has been supported or rejected on a wide variety of grounds, but never on a comprehensive survey of all the evidence available. Nor has anyone approached the problem from the point of view of the engineer, trying to establish what is and is not structurally possible. This we shall attempt to do shortly, but first we may discuss the excavated evidence for and against the vault hypothesis.

The evidence in support of the vault hypothesis falls into four major groups. These are, the evidence for a collapsed vault, the evidence for a corbelled superstructure, the thickness and height of the stone walls, and the evidence for various external supports for the walls. The most widespread evidence is undoubtedly that for a corbelled superstructure, which has been encountered in *at least* half of the excavated tombs. In many other cases it probably existed but has either not received mention in the (often brief) excavation report or else can no longer be identified due to the destruction of the wall down to its last two or three courses. Only once has an excavated tomb been preserved to a reasonable height and yet shown no evidence of a corbelled superstructure. This was tomb A at Vorou, with a wall preserved to a height of 1.8 metres. In addition tomb Z at Drakones, where the wall still stood to 2.2 metres, showed only a slight overhang of the upper courses.[9] Elsewhere the evidence is persistent, even in tombs with walls standing to less than a metre in height. Although he gives no details, Xanthoudides mentions the overhang in describing most of the tombs he excavated, and notes that at Kalathiana, Christos, and Porti, the evidence was particularly plain. Amongst those tombs for which details of the overhang are available, the most pronounced inward lean is to be found in Agia Triadha "A", where the wall is preserved to 1.55 metres high and overhangs its foundations by as much as 0.4 metres. Other notable examples of walls with a marked inward lean are the tombs excavated near Lebena (deviation from upright varying between 1 in 5.5 and 1 in 8.0) and the larger tomb at Chrysostomos (deviation 1 in 6). In every case for which details are available, these inward leans or overhangs have been achieved by the adoption of corbelling. It seems certain therefore that the builders of the Mesara tholoi knew and used the technique of corbelling, and that it was the standard technique employed in the construction of these tombs. What is not certain is the height to which the corbelled walls were taken.

At least nine of the known Mesara tombs survive to a height in excess of two metres. The greatest preserved height yet recorded is 3.4 metres in Megali Skinoi IIIa. Other early tombs which are relatively well preserved include Kalathiana (2.7 metres), Kaloi Limenes II and Agia Triadha B (2.3 metres) and Megali Skinoi IIIb (2.0 metres). Of the late group of tombs, the best preserved is Drakones Z, surviving to a height of 2.2 metres. Three other late tombs, Agios Kyrillos, Kamilari I, and Apesokari II, stand to just over two metres in height (pl. 5). It is clear from these nine tombs, and many others with walls standing well over a metre high, that the circular walls were not intended merely as low stone foundations to carry superstructures of lighter material, nor as low enclosure walls. Both the preserved height and inward lean of many of the walls clearly implies that they were intended to be carried up to a considerable height and at least partially to cover the interior.   *Pl. 5*

This is confirmed by the mass of stone found inside several of the tombs. At Christos, for example, Xanthoudides found what he considered to be "nearly all" of the limestone slabs used for a complete corbelled vault, lying inside the tomb.[10] Alexiou found a great mass of fallen stones in a tomb at Lebena, and Levi has provided us with an excellent photograph which shows a similar situation in the large tomb at Kamilari (pl. 6). Platon considered   *Pl. 6* the quantity of stone found inside the tomb at Myrsini to be sufficient to confirm that there had once been a full stone vault. But in none of these cases do we know precisely how much stone was found collapsed inside the tomb. The only excavator to publish this information was Xanthoudides, who carefully stacked up the stones from inside Platanos B and found them to total twenty-five cubic metres of masonry.[11] The volume of original wall which this stone represented would have been greater than this of course, since one has to make allowance for the considerable amount of clay bonding and packing used in the construction of the wall of Platanos B. Even so, this hardly seems sufficient to have carried the wall up to any substantial height, let alone into the complete vault which Xanthoudides thought it to represent. We shall return to this particular problem a little later.

In the case of Kamilari and Lebena the excavators rightly drew attention not only to the fallen stones but to the nature of the stones and to the way in which they had fallen. A notable number of stones at Lebena seem to have been wedge-shaped and were found to have fallen like "rows of books". Both of these features are strongly suggestive of a collapsed corbelled structure. So too at Kamilari, a large number of wedge-shaped stones were found, often with their thin end pointing in towards the centre of the tomb (pl. 6). Such stones were much more prolific in the fallen *Pl. 6* masonry than they were in the surviving wall, suggesting that the upper part of the structure may have been built in a different way from that which survives intact. This is an important point, since one of the main arguments against full stone vaults in the Mesara tombs is that the wall construction is usually too random and flimsy to allow a corbelled vault to be constructed. The evidence from Kamilari, and perhaps Lebena, suggests that the upper stone-work on the tombs may have been of a rather different character to that employed on the foundations. There is a very clear suggestion of this in Xanthoudides' report on the tomb at Christos.[12] He draws an absolutely clear distinction between the "large and small undressed stones" employed on the surviving lower part of the wall, and the "slabs of limestone" found collapsed into the interior of the tomb. Unfortunately he gives no dimensions of these slabs. In addition to these stones of different shape, size, or rock noted at Kamilari, Lebena, and Christos, Kamilari and Platanos B each produced a very large flat slab which in each case was identified by the excavator as the capstone of a full stone vault. That from Platanos B, an elliptical slab 0.58 × 0.50 metres, was found in the centre of the tomb—a suggestive enough situation, whilst that from Kamilari was found just outside the tomb but is the more impressive "capstone", measuring 1.3 × 1.2 metres.

So far we have looked at what we might call the direct or primary evidence of a vault—that is, at the actual remains of a corbelled roof of some kind. In addition to this evidence there is evidence which is of a more secondary nature; this includes certain features of the tombs which may best be explained as being related to the construction of a corbelled and vaulted roof. One such feature which Hood considers to be significant in this respect is the relative thickness of the walls. About two thirds of the tombs for which we have the relevant information have walls which are a quarter or more as wide as the diameter of the tomb, and in about one third of the tombs the ratio between wall thickness and tomb diameter is 1 to 3 or lower (fig. 3). If the walls were simply *Fig. 3* meant to form enclosures, then it is certainly strange that they needed to be built so thick; the width of the walls is altogether more suggestive of a structure carried up to a height of several metres, if not into a full stone vault.

Additional strength was given to some walls by other means. Some tombs had a notably thickened wall added (either as part of the original construction or subsequently) to one part of their circumference. At Apesokari and Lebena Ib it was on the south side (fig. 28), whilst both tombs at Vorou had a thickened structure on the north and east sides (fig. 6). There may have been something similar on the west side of tholos X at Christos, but Xanthoudides' description ("a kind of supporting buttress") could refer to a wall running outwards from the wall, such as he noticed at Platanos A and Marathokephalon II. At Platanos A six such walls were found within a short distance of each other on the south side of the tomb (fig. 2), whilst at Marathokephalon an unspecified number were found on the north side of tomb II. In both cases Xanthoudides suggests that these walls are buttresses, although those at Platanos look too flimsy to have been used in this way.[13]

Fig. 28
Fig. 6

Fig. 2

In addition to these built thickenings and "buttresses", there are several examples of tombs which have been built against rock faces, possibly with the intention of using these as a sort of natural buttress or counter-force. About a third of the larger tomb at Chrysostomos is built against a rock face on its western side (fig. 33) whilst Lebena I was built against a rock abutment on its north side and a series of large boulders on the south. Less extensive use of natural outcrops of rock was made elsewhere. Finally, we should briefly mention the tomb at Agios Kyrillos. The preliminary report on this tomb does not comment on the fact, but the published photograph of the tomb (pl. 9) suggests that unlike any other Mesara circular tomb yet excavated, this one was sunk into the ground to a depth of almost two metres, being let into the slope of a hillside. If this is correct, then this tomb would have been firmly supported around almost its entire circumference.

Fig. 33

Pl. 9

There is one other piece of evidence provided by the tombs which may possibly be indicative of a full stone vault, but it is ambiguous and extremely difficult to interpret. This is the evidence of the slabs which project from parts of the circumference of several of the tombs. At least ten tombs have produced slabs of this sort, though in widely varying numbers and situations. The most slabs yet recorded on a single tomb were a row of twenty-four on Platanos B (pl. 4) and a row of twelve, six on either side of the door, at Koumasa E. The smallest number yet found on a

Pl. 4

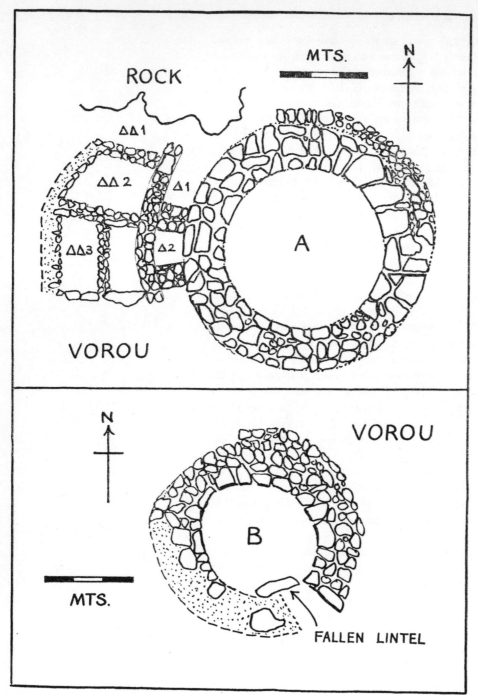

Fig. 6 The two tholoi at Vorou

single tomb were the three discovered at Marathokephalon II. At Kamilari and Koumasa E the slabs were on the east side of the tomb, at Koumasa B and Apesokari I they were on the north, and at Platanos B, Agia Triadha B, and Agia Eirene E the slabs were on the south. No tombs have yet produced slabs on their west side, although at Porti six slabs on the north-east of the tomb were balanced by three slabs on the south-west. Porti and Kamilari are the only tombs yet to produce two separate groups of slabs on opposite sides of the tomb, but multiple rows of slabs (three) were found at Kamilari and Agia Triadha B. The slabs are usually placed between 0.3 and 1.0 metre above ground level and between 0.2 and 1.0 metre apart. In at least some cases, the slabs are carefully shaped, though they may vary between the thick wedge-shaped blocks built into the large tomb at Kamilari and the thin, triangular slabs utilised in Platanos B. In addition to the variety of quantity and situation already demonstrated, it must be emphasised that a good many other tombs with walls surviving more than a metre high have produced no evidence at all to suggest that they ever featured external slabs of this sort. To some extent the variations may have been exaggerated by the destruction of portions of the relevant courses in a tomb, but it can be said with certainty that this is not true of Koumasa B, Koumasa E, or Agia Eirene E, in all of which the greatest preserved height does not coincide with the position of the slabs. This is probably true of several other tombs for which details are not available.

No one has yet offered a convincing explanation of these slabs. There is little reason to follow Parabeni and Xanthoudides who suggested that they were intended to "key" a covering mound of earth, not only because no trace of such a mound has yet been discovered but also because the keying effect of these slabs, which are rarely more than 0.4 metres in length, would be negligible.[14] Xanthoudides' alternative suggestion that the slabs were used as scaffolding by the builders has recently been supported by Levi, and is altogether a more likely solution to the problem.[15] One unsatisfactory feature of it however is that it is difficult to see why such "scaffolding" should only have stretched around a small part of a tomb's circumference. Nor does this solution explain why the builders needed scaffolding which raised them only 0.3 metres off the ground (as at Koumasa E) or why they should take the trouble to so carefully shape their stones (as at Platanos B). As evidence for the construction of a fully vaulted tomb, the slabs are therefore of dubious value, though if one accepts the "scaffold-ing" hypothesis then the implication of the two rows at Kamilari and three at Agia Triadha B is that these tombs were built in stone to at least another metre above their surviving height.

Apart from the evidence derived from the tombs themselves, those who believe that the Mesara tombs were fully vaulted in stone bring two other arguments to support their case. First they emphasise how unsatisfactory are the alternative solutions to the problem of the tombs' roofing. It is highly unlikely that the tombs were completely unroofed, for if so why did their builders give them such thick walls and begin to corbel the superstruc-ture? Equally, the surviving height of tombs like Megali Skinoi (3.4 metres) and Kalathiana (2.7 metres) argues against simple enclosure walls with no roof over the interior. In the case of Kamilari the amount of fallen masonry inside the tomb surely puts the matter beyond doubt. The most commonly proposed alternative is not quite so easily dismissed. Pendlebury and Hutchinson have argued that the tombs were completed by a flat roof of timber.[16] Hood has refuted this suggestion,[17] arguing that such roofs would need internal supports, for which there is no evidence, and that they would be incompatible with the practice of fumigation which appears to have been part of the Mesara tradi-tion. One might also ask again why the trouble was taken to build thick corbelled walls if lightweight flat roofs were to be placed on the tombs. Nor is there evidence from the Mesara tombs for the use of mud plaster on reeds or wands such as was used on con-temporary domestic roofs and the roofs of some of the rectangular ossuaries.[18]

Lack of evidence must also weigh heavily against Hood's own hypothesis that some of the tombs were given a mud-brick vault on a stone base. Mud-brick does of course dissolve, but one would expect some to survive in some of the tombs, particularly as it would probably have been covered by stones tumbled from the lower parts of the wall and therefore protected from the worst effects of weathering. One is therefore left, it appears, with the hypothesis of a stone built vault.

Those who favour this hypothesis produce as their last argu-ment contemporary examples of corbelled vaults from elsewhere in the Mediterranean and later examples from Crete and the Mesara. The two groups of examples together may be taken as evidence for the knowledge of the corbelled vault throughout the

Mediterranean at the time when the Mesara tombs were being built, and for the continuity of the tradition in Crete itself.[19] Particularly significant among the first group of examples are the corbelled tombs of minor officials of the Second Dynasty of Egypt, since although these are built of brick they are roughly contemporary with the beginning of Early Minoan I (and the first Mesara circular tombs) and there is of course a strong school of thought, founded by Evans, who believe that the Cretan Early Bronze Age owes much to Egyptian inspiration. The stone corbelled vaults of the Los Milares culture of Iberia are closer parallels in terms of materials but not techniques, and are more difficult to relate chronologically to the Minoan tombs. Among the second group of examples, there are the small number of Late Bronze Age corbel vaulted *tholoi* from Crete, and perhaps of greater interest the modern cheese dairies of Mount Ida (pl. 8). Xanthoudides drew attention to these in an appendix to his book, and certainly they present some remarkable similarities to the Mesara tombs. The walls are built of medium and small sized stones, only roughly dressed, and the doorways are normally built on the trilithon principle. The dairies vary in diameter between five and eight metres, the range in which about sixty per cent of the Mesara tombs fall. The major difference between the construction of the Ida dairies and that of the Mesara circular tombs is that the corbelled vault of the former is built of very large limestone slabs which enable a relatively low vault to be erected with complete safety.

Pl. 8

The case in favour of the vaulted tomb hypothesis may be summarised as follows. Most, if not all, of the Mesara tombs featured corbelling, and the evidence of fallen masonry and the surviving height of the wall in some of the less disturbed tombs suggests that this corbelling was carried up into a full stone vault. The thickness of the walls, the various methods used to buttress parts of the tombs' circumferences, and the possible evidence for "scaffolding" extending up the side of some of the tombs for about two metres, are all best explained as features necessitated or suggested by the construction of a stone vault. The historical and cultural context of the tombs is quite in keeping with the vault hypothesis.

The case against stone vaulting is to some extent a negative one, since it disputes the validity of some of the evidence *for* vaulting but does not provide a great deal of positive evidence against it.

Of the primary evidence for vaulting—that is the supposed remains of collapsed vaults—the evidence for some sort of corbelling cannot be disputed, but that for both the amount and nature of fallen stonework can, and is. As I mentioned earlier, the only excavator actually to measure the volume of fallen masonry in one of the tombs was Xanthoudides, who found twenty-five cubic metres of stone in Platanos B. If the inward lean of the walls was to be carried up to any considerable height (let alone continued to form a full stone vault) then the amount of clay originally used to bond and pack between these stones could hardly have exceeded two-fifths of the volume of the stone. In other words, the masonry which Xanthoudides discovered is unlikely to have represented a total volume of wall material in excess of thirty-five cubic metres. In the case of Platanos B (internal diameter 10.23 metres, external 15.13 metres) this would have increased the height of the tomb from its surviving one metre to about one and a half metres. Xanthoudides' evidence for a full stone vault at Platanos B is therefore non-existent.

Even the evidence from Kamilari is not as impressive as at first appears. Although Levi has not quoted any figure for the volume of stone found collapsed within the tomb, we can arrive at quite an accurate one, since we know the internal diameter and height of the tomb, and the published photographs and description reveal that the stone completely filled the interior of the tomb. The amount of stone must therefore have been in the region of ninety cubic metres. This would have added a little under two metres to the height of the wall, which, on average, survived to about the same height. The total height of the Kamilari wall therefore, taking into account its present height and the collapsed masonry, was between three and a half and four metres. It would be foolish to assert that the wall was never higher than this, but there is no evidence to suggest that it was. Similarly, the so-called capstone could have been taken to Kamilari for use as an altar slab in the tomb enclosure. There is no evidence to show that it once surmounted a stone vault, and its position when discovered argues, if anything, against that supposition. The "capstone" from Platanos was found in a more significant position, but is very small for the capstone of a vault which, if it existed, must have stood ten metres high. The perforation in this stone, mentioned by Xanthoudides, suggests that it is perhaps better compared to other perforated stones found at

Agia Triadha and Vorou which appear to have served a non-architectural function (see p. 93). As to the wedge-shaped stones, particularly numerous at Kamilari, there is no evidence to suggest that these were carried up into a full stone vault, and more to the point, such stones are by no means commonplace in the Mesara tombs. The appearance of such stones at Kamilari and Lebena is the exception rather than the rule. Buttresses, thickened walls, and rock abutments are more common, but still in a minority, and are too irregular to have supported a stone vault. Usually they give added support to only a small part of the circumference, and never to the whole of it. The alternative method of support, a surrounding mound or bed of earth, is nowhere in evidence in the Mesara tombs, with the possible exception of Agios Kyrillos.

This brings us to one of the more crucial and positive arguments against the stone vault hypothesis, namely that in the great majority of tombs the wall is constructed of stones which are both the wrong shape and the wrong size to enable a corbelled vault to be built. Most of the tombs are built of stones which are block-like rather than slab-like, and which for the most part do not exceed half a metre along their longest side. These stones are laid, apparently in a random manner, with a generous allowance of clay bonding and packing between them. It seems unlikely that such stones could ever have been built into a full stone vault, but we must remember that the supporters of the vault hypothesis are in fact asking us to believe more than that. We are expected to accept that such vaults were not only built but were sufficiently strong to stand for many centuries, often as much as a millennium, in an island which possesses a long and persistent history of seismic disturbances.

If we cannot accept that these vaults were built, then we must find an alternative form of roofing which fits the known facts about the tombs. Apart from Hood's suggestion that mud-brick was used to build a lightweight vault over some tombs, for which there is no confirmatory evidence, the most commonly proposed alternative is that of a flat roof of wooden beams over which was laid other organic material—be it planks, wands, brushwood or whatever. The evidence that such existed is extremely slight. Surprisingly perhaps, the clearest evidence for such a roof is to be found on one of the photos of Kamilari (pl. 10). Here one can see, in the centre of the tomb, the remains of burnt pieces of

Pl. 10

47

wood which, at least as they were found, form a reasonably
coherent pattern. Could these be the remains of a collapsed timber
roof of the type envisaged by Pendlebury and Hutchinson?
Something similar might have existed in Koumasa B where
Xanthoudides mentions "a large hearth" in the centre of the
tomb, denoted by burnt marks on the floor. Hood's objection
that timber roofs would be incompatible with fumigation is not
an altogether valid one, since such roofs could be removed very
easily and quickly, and would enable not only the smoke to clear
but also the fire to burn very much better. Indeed the combina-
tion of a timber roof and the tradition of fumigation might
together provide one of the few acceptable explanations of the
projecting slabs. If a light timber or wickerwork roof capped the
tomb, then the slabs could have been built into the wall to facili-
tate access to it when it needed to be removed. A function of this
kind would allow complete freedom of choice as to the orientation, situation, and quantity of the slabs employed, such as seems
in fact to have operated amongst the builders of the tombs.
Equally it would explain why some tombs apparently never
possessed any such slabs, since there would be other ways of
climbing to the top of the superstructure and the use of projecting slabs would be a matter of choice rather than necessity.

There is however the serious objection raised by Hood, that
roofs of this kind would need some kind of internal supports to
span the relatively large diameters of some of the tombs. No
evidence for such supports has yet been recorded, although one
could argue that timber posts would normally leave no trace unless they were burnt down or placed into post-holes rather
than on large slabs of stone. But the validity of the objection rests
on one's interpretation or reconstruction of two features, namely
the original height and internal diameter of the tombs and the
type and weight of the hypothetical timber roof. For the former
figures it is possible to make some approximate calculations based
on the information provided mainly by the tomb at Kamilari but
also on that provided by the tombs at Lebena, Agia Triadha and
Chrysostomos. We know from these tombs that the lower courses
of the wall were built with an overhang of about 1 in 6, although
at Agia Triadha the overhang was as great as 1 in 4. As with the
later tholoi, we should expect the overhang to increase somewhat
above the first few courses, and the evidence from Kamilari,
Lebena and Christos where considerable amounts of stone from

PLATE 9   A view of the tholos at Agios Kyrillos

PLATE 10   Part of the interior of Kamilari 1, with the funerary deposit
swept to the wall and traces of burnt timbers showing
in the centre of the tholos

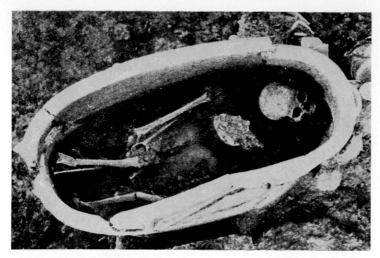

PLATE 11   One of the larnax
burials in the tholos on Gypsades,
Knossos

PLATE 12   Room L, outside
tholos A at Agia Triadha, with its
thick deposit of clay cups

the higher levels were preserved, suggests that this was achieved by the use of wedge-shaped slabs or slabs larger than those used in the lower courses. The original height of the tombs is unknown, but we have seen that at Kamilari the evidence suggested a minimum height of about three and a half to four metres. If, for the moment, we assume that four metres *was* the original height of the wall, then we can calculate that the internal diameter at the top of this wall would have been in the region of five metres. If the wall had stood to about five metres originally, then the internal diameter at the top would have probably been about four metres. It would be no problem to find beams of Cypress wood to span this sort of distance, nor even, for that matter, the seven metres internal diameter we can estimate for the largest of the tombs, Platanos A. The thickness of the tomb walls might suggest that the timber roof was in fact comprised of a series of such beams, laid next to one another across the space at the top of the tomb, although a much lighter structure could have been constructed of wickerwork on a cross-frame of timbers. If one is not prepared to accept the hypothesis of a full stone vault, then a timber or timber-framed roof of this sort is apparently a viable alternative.

It is still, however, an hypothesis and like the case in support of the vault hypothesis, the arguments in support of it are inconclusive owing to the scarcity and ambiguity of the evidence. Ambiguity is perhaps the crux of the problem. There are some tombs, like Kamilari and Lebena, where the evidence for a stone vault looks convincing (though not conclusive) and others, like Platanos A and Koumasa B, where the possibility of the walls being carried up into a full stone vault seems remote in the extreme. The ambiguity extends beyond individual tombs to various features of the tombs' architecture. Various forms of buttressing are used on some tombs but not on others, and where they are used it is in an irregular and unsystematic way. Several of the tombs are well built of quite regular, large, blocks of stone, but many others are constructed of small and completely irregular stones. In a few tombs there are considerable quantities of fallen masonry, but in most there is relatively little stone debris. Some tombs have projecting slabs on the exterior, in varying numbers and situations, while many tombs have no such slabs. There are other relevant features—the "capstones" and evidence of burnt timbers for example—which occur all too rarely to be held as

reliable evidence for the form of the tombs as a whole. All too
often we find ourselves arguing from a small part of the evidence
and ignoring the lack of evidence, or even contrary evidence,
from the majority of the tombs. One way round this problem
would be simply to assume that some tombs were completely
vaulted in stone and others not. This is what Hood and Hutchinson have suggested, their alternative forms of roofing being mud-
brick and timber respectively. But this solution runs contrary to
the very strong impression one gets from the Mesara circular
tombs of an established uniformity. This may seem a strange
statement to make after writing the preceding paragraph; yet as
we progress with our study of the tombs, their contents, and the
rituals and beliefs associated with them, this impression will
become stronger. Though details in the methods of construction,
the design of the ante-chambers, and the situation and surround-
ings of the tombs may vary, the type of burial, the type of ritual,
and the type of tomb remain constant. The difference between a
fully vaulted tomb and one partially open to the sky is not one of
detail, but a fundamental one of concept. Thus, if one believes
that Lebena II was fully vaulted, then one can hardly postulate an
open-centred roof for other tombs built in Early Minoan I. This is
not necessarily to say that *all* of the Mesara tombs must have had
either a fully vaulted or a flat roof; there *could* be differences of
roof type amongst tombs erected at different times. If the concept
of the tomb changed over the course of centuries then so too
might the architectural form in which the concept was embodied.
In other words, our late group of tombs (Early Minoan III–
Middle Minoan I) *could* have been roofed, perhaps, in a different
way to the earlier tombs. Furthermore, taking into account the
conservatism implied by the very construction of these late tombs,
we need not expect all of the late tombs to follow the new style (if
such a change took place at all). Some tombs might well be built
according to the old pattern. Again, of course, we have entered
the field of conjecture, but it is an interesting hypothesis and for
the moment we might briefly follow it to see if there is any
evidence which might support it.

We noted earlier that both the size and style of doorway may
have been changed by the tomb builders of Early Minoan III and
Middle Minoan I. The only tombs with doorways more than a
metre and a half high are three of late date (Gypsades, Drakones
Z, Agios Kyrillos), while all of the late group of tombs for which

we have the relevant details prove to have built doorways rather than trilithon ones.[20] Other changes in construction techniques are less uniform, but the most carefully built tombs, using worked stones of regular size and shape, laid in courses, are all late tombs —Kamilari (pl. 4), Siderokamino (pl. 3), and Agios Kyrillos (pl. 9). Some of the late tombs of course, are very poorly built. There is one other trend which may be detected amongst the late tombs, namely that towards a smaller diameter. Over half of the Early Minoan III/Middle Minoan I tombs are less than five metres in diameter, while less than one in three of the earlier tombs fall below this figure. We might justifiably claim therefore that changes in the construction of the circular tombs were introduced during Early Minoan III/Middle Minoan I. Most of these changes were straightforward structural ones, but the decision to build higher doorways was a change of fashion for which there appears to be no technical motivation whatever. This feature at least, might therefore represent the evolution of a new concept of the tombs. New concepts in burial customs were certainly manifesting themselves in Early Minoan III with the appearance of the larnax and pithos burials, and as we shall see, some of these burials are found inside the circular tombs. Nevertheless, interesting as these changes in the construction of the tombs and perhaps in the concepts associated with them may be, they are hardly distinctive enough for us to assert that the form of the tombs must have been changed radically at this time. The only changes which might perhaps have been associated with the change from an open-centred roof to a full stone vault are the generally smaller diameters and the appearance of at least some tombs with walls built of regular, coursed masonry.

It seems that we have now exhausted all of the evidence from which we might hope to find a solution to our problem, but there remains one approach to this problem which neither we, nor others previously, have attempted—the approach of the civil engineer. It must be said at once that the civil engineer cannot provide us with a calculated and mathematically proven answer to our most basic question—could the Mesara tholoi have been successfully constructed with a full stone vault? Both of the engineers that I consulted were certain that the construction of the tholoi walls was, in every case, too random to allow a theoretical analysis of their strengths and weaknesses; it was simply not possible to say whether or not they would have collapsed had they

Pls. 4, 3
Pl. 9

been fully vaulted in stone.[21] There were, however, a number of points which could be made about strains and stresses and the technological problems involved in the construction of a corbelled vault. Taken together, these points perhaps provide us with some indication of the direction in which a solution to the problem may lie. The basic pressures which would be exerted in a corbelled vault would be in three directions, inwards, outwards, and downwards. The inward and downward pressures combined would be at their greatest in the uppermost parts of the vault, but there would also be great vertical pressure on the inside of the wall base. Similarly the greatest outward pressure would be met at the base of the wall on the outside of the structure, although there would be lesser outward pressures higher in the wall. There is some evidence to suggest that the Minoans may have tried to counteract the inward and downward pressures. Maslin drew attention to the frequent insertion of small stones between the larger blocks of masonry (fig. 7). This feature is to be found not   *Fig. 7* only on many of the Early Bronze Age tholoi but on several of the Late Bronze Age tombs as well. Small stones used in this way might represent nothing more than packing, but Maslin suggests that they may have a greater structural significance than this. The insertion of such stones between the relatively even edges of two larger blocks would result in greater friction and thus help to counter the inward and downward pressure of the two blocks. In other words, this may have been a measure deliberately adopted to increase the stability of the structure. The downward pressure at the base could not have been relieved in any practical way, but its effects may have been countered by the use of particularly large rocks, often of triangular or sub-triangular shape, in the foundation course of the wall. Smith, incidentally, reports that the limestones used in the construction of the tholoi are certainly strong enough to have taken the pressures which a full stone vault would have imposed on them.

There are no indications, however, that the Minoans took effective steps to counteract the outward pressures which would have been exerted in a structure with a corbelled vault. The erection of tombs against rock abutments (Chrysostomos, Lebena I, for example), with thickened sections of wall (Apesokari I, Vorou A), and possible "buttresses" (Platanos A, Marathokephalon II), would be totally inadequate to counter such pressure, for the

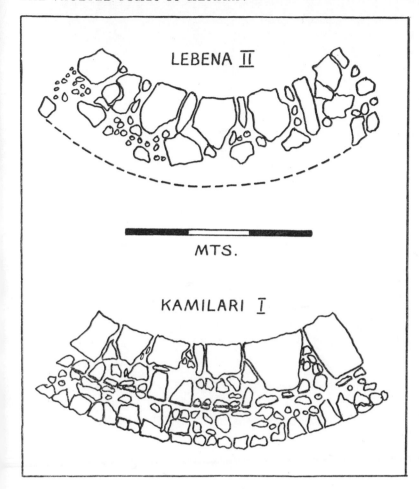

LEBENA II

MTS.

KAMILARI I

Fig. 7 Detail of the walls of Lebena II and Kamilari I showing the alternation of large and small stones in the construction of the inner face

simple reason that a counter-force would be needed round the entire circumference of the tombs. There can be little doubt that other reasons apart, this was why the Late Bronze Age *tholoi* were dug into hillsides or covered by a mound. It also probably explains the high "beehive" vault of these tombs, since apart from the use of some form of buttressing round the outside of the tholos wall, the other way to reduce the outward pressure would be to build a high vault. The Early Minoan tholoi *could* have been built with high "beehive" vaults; but not only do the small amounts of debris found in and around the tombs suggest otherwise, but it is doubtful whether this measure alone would have been successful.

Both Maslin and Smith, therefore, are dubious as to the ability of the Mesara tholoi to have supported full stone vaults, particularly over the course of a millennium in an earthquake prone island. Yet tombs like Megali Skinoi IIIa, Kalathiana K, Agia Triadha B, and Kamilari I survive to sufficient height to show that they must have originally been built to a substantially greater height. Their corbelled superstructure, furthermore, reveals that their inner diameter decreased as their height increased. If the tholoi were not fully vaulted in stone, and we have no evidence of mud-brick superstructures, then I suggest that they were roofed with timber which covered a relatively small aperture created by the use of the corbelled superstructure. At Kamilari I for example, we estimated that if the tomb was originally five metres high, then the central aperture would have been no more than four metres in diameter. A light timber roof, capable of removal by three or four men, could easily have been constructed to cover such an aperture. I asked both Maslin and Smith if an incomplete vault of this sort was likely to have been stable. They agreed that theoretically at least, each course in the wall should be stable and that a third, half, three-quarter or full vault would all, in this case, be stable. Smith was uncertain whether or not in practice the Mesara tholoi would have been unstable if left with a half or three-quarter vault. Maslin felt there was no reason to think that they would not be stable in this condition, and emphasised that it was the upper-most parts of the corbelled vault which present the greatest technological and constructional problems. In other words, in terms of stability the three-quarter vault was as good as the full vault, and in terms of ease of construction it was far better.

There remains the possibility that some of the late tombs of Mesara type were in fact fully vaulted in stone. Of the excavated tombs of this group, only one—that at Agios Kyrillos—was apparently supported round its circumference by the shallow hill-slope into which it was built. But we simply do not know enough about Myrsini, Viannos, Vali, and Siderokamino to be certain that these tombs did not have a retaining bank of earth round their circumference. The smaller diameters of the Middle Minoan I tombs would certainly have facilitated the construction of full stone vaults, and both Maslin and Smith agree that the use of regularly shaped blocks laid in courses, such as appear in several of the Middle Minoan 1 tombs, would also have enabled a more controlled structure to be erected with consequent improvements to stability. There are therefore, some structural grounds for supposing that some at least of the Middle Minoan 1 tombs may have been fully vaulted in stone. The excavations at Arkhanes have added historical grounds for the same supposition and we shall discuss these in the closing chapter of the book. Nevertheless, on the evidence of the monuments themselves and the engineers' assessment of them, it looks as if for most of the tombs, Xanthoudides' title—The Vaulted Tombs of Mesara— was a misnomer.

Chapter Four

GRAVE-GOODS

It is clear from the relatively few unplundered tombs which have been excavated, that the circular tombs of the Mesara originally contained a mass of grave-goods of a remarkably varied nature. Some of these have proved more attractive to looters than others, so that the majority of tombs contain only a few fragments of gold jewellery and not many bronze objects either. In recent times looters have been less selective, since complete pots, stone vases, sealstones, figurines and amulets are all in demand in the antiquities market. Apart from looting, the objects have also suffered of course from centuries of disturbance during the time the tombs were in use and from the effects of heavy falls of masonry during the time when they were falling into decay. Pottery has naturally suffered a great deal in this respect, and in several of the tombs he excavated, Xanthoudides records that only sherds were found. Finally, the natural processes of decay have no doubt completely destroyed many organic objects which were placed in the tombs. In particular one thinks of clothing, to which a handful of pins and button-like stones perhaps attest, and small personal objects of wood. In addition to the considerable number of tombs which have been almost entirely cleared out by looters, there are many more for which we have only the briefest of reports. Our idea as to what constitutes a typical assemblage of material from a Mesara tomb is therefore very largely determined on the basis of finds made in about one-third of the excavated tombs.

These finds, usually dominated by vessels of various sorts and materials, tell us a great deal about contemporary life in the Mesara. Indeed, but for the objects recovered from the circular tombs, our knowledge of the civilisation of Early Bronze Age

Crete would be severely limited. Not all of the objects found in the tombs, however, reflect contemporary life. It is clear that some of them were manufactured exclusively for use in the burial chamber, and in this chapter we shall look at the two categories of objects separately.

By far the commonest finds in the tombs are clay vessels of various sorts which were used in contemporary settlements. None of the excavated tombs for which we have any details at all lacked clay vessels, although they were scarce in Platanos A, Agia Eirene E and e, and several other tombs.[1] The most common vessel was the clay cup (fig. 8). The earliest examples were often *Fig. 8 second left* finely painted in the Agios Onouphrios style, and usually possessed a single handle dropped from the rim. Others were produced in "Lebena" ware, and took a form more akin to a tankard, *bottom left* with a straight-sided cylindrical body and a single low-set handle (Lebena). Early Minoan II cups are not common in the tombs, but broad, round-bottomed examples with a single handle occur *third right* sporadically (Koumasa) and since Warren's excavations at Fournou Korifi, some of the straight-sided cups with plain red or brown wash on them must be regarded as possible examples of Early Minoan II tumblers. Cups of Early Minoan III date seem to be more numerous, but some which we ascribe to this period may belong to Middle Minoan I. Straight-sided cups with simple *top left* designs painted in white on a dark wash are recognisable enough (Koumasa), but many dark-washed cups with rounded sides and either one round-sectioned handle or none at all are more difficult to place precisely. There can be no doubt that the great mass of clay cups found in the tombs belong to Middle Minoan I. The variety of form is a wide one. Goblets may have a small pedestal or *top right* a flat base but flaring sides. Handled cups may have straight, curved or carinated walls, and either broad, flat handles or *third left* rounded ones. Many are simply covered in a dark wash, but others are quite elaborately decorated with white and sometimes red or brown paint. Outnumbering all of these varieties however *bottom right* is the ubiquitous conical handle-less cup, or "ash-tray" as it is known in archaeological circles. Some of these have bands of red, *top right* black or brown paint around their rim or just below it, but for the most part they are undecorated and do not carry a wash. They *second right* were clearly mass produced in large numbers, and in Middle Minoan I, though they are quite common in domestic deposits (at Phaistos for example), they appear in vast quantities in the

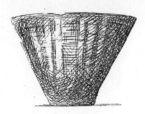

KOUMASA (H.4)

LEBENA (H.7)

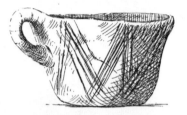

LEBENA (H.9·3)

PORTI (H.7·2)

PLATANOS (H.7)

KOUMASA (H.4·5)

LEBENA (H.6·4)

PLATANOS (H.5·5)

Fig. 8 Grave goods. Clay cups of Early Minoan I– Middle Minoan I (measurements in cms)

tombs. Kamilari for example produced about a thousand cups, the great majority of which were of this sort. Other large groups were found at Apesokari I, Agia Triadha A, Vorou, and at Lebena. Cups therefore appear in relatively small numbers in the Mesara tombs until Middle Minoan I, or perhaps late in Early Minoan III.

Next to the cups, jugs and "teapots" are the most common clay vessels. These vary greatly in type and style (fig. 9). Amongst the earliest are elegant round-based jugs decorated in the Agios Onouphrios I style. Their Early Minoan II successors include a few "Vasiliki" jugs, others of plain fabric, and the first "teapots". A few of these, like one from Porti, are of the well-known "Vasiliki" type, but the Mesara also produces its own characteristic type, well represented at Koumasa, perhaps developed from spouted bowls. Other Early Minoan II jugs from Koumasa are painted in the Agios Onouphrios II style and sometimes stand on tiny feet. In view of the scarcity of Early Minoan III light-on-dark style in the Mesara, it is more difficult to pick out Early Minoan III jugs amongst the various tomb assemblages, though there is no reason to think that jugs were not included amongst the grave-goods of the Early Minoan III phase. Jugs which almost certainly belong to this phase include some with pellets on the neck and white bands painted on the natural buff clay (Koumasa), others of typical "Vasiliki" shape but covered with a dull, dark wash (Platanos), and "teapots" similar to Vasiliki ones but without their pedestal and covered in a dark wash (Drakones). These teapots are a transitional type, perhaps, between the true Vasiliki and Koumasa teapots of Early Minoan II, and the flat-bottomed, straight-sided teapots of Middle Minoan I, which appear in considerable numbers in the tombs at Kamilari, Koumasa, Kalathiana and elsewhere. The ordinary jugs of Middle Minoan I are similar in shape to the Early Minoan II and III ones, but are decorated very often in either polychrome or barbotine. Some are decorated, rather hideously, in both. In addition to these various common forms of jug there are a few jugs with narrow necks and tubular spouts which project from the side wall of the vessel. These have no recognisable Early Minoan ancestors. For the most part however, the jugs found in the Mesara tombs can be seen to belong to a line of descent stretching from the Early Minoan I jugs through into the Middle Minoan II period. After

Fig. 9 third right

bottom left

bottom right
second left

third left

second right

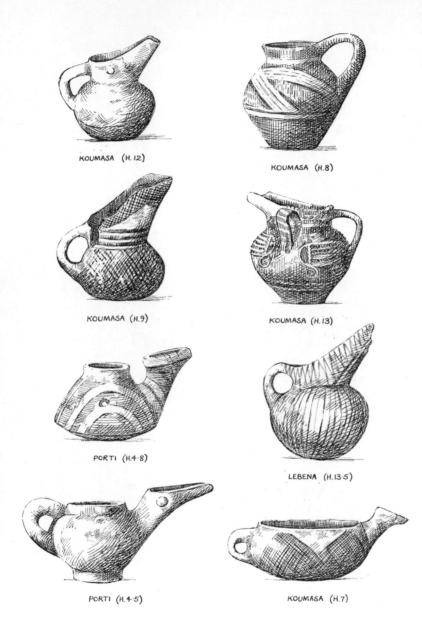

KOUMASA (H.12)

KOUMASA (H.8)

KOUMASA (H.9)

KOUMASA (H.13)

PORTI (H.4·8)

LEBENA (H.13·5)

PORTI (H.4·5)

KOUMASA (H.7)

Fig. 9 Grave goods. Jugs and "teapots" of Early Minoan I–Middle Minoan I (measurements in cms)

PORTI (H.7)

KOUMASA (H.8)

LEBENA (H.9)

KOUMASA (H.7.3)

KOUMASA (H.6)

LEBENA (H.8.3)

PORTI (H.4.5)

PORTI (H.4.5)

Fig. 10 Grave goods. Dishes and bowls of Early Minoan I–Middle Minoan I (measurements in cms)

their introduction in Early Minoan II, the "teapots" too regularly form part of the tomb assemblages.

The other type of domestic pottery vessel which appears in quantity in the tombs is the dish or bowl (fig. 10). From the first, they appear in several varieties, although there is a notable preference for two-handled examples during Early Minoan I (Lebena). Most of these early bowls are decorated in the Agios Onouphrios I style and feature rounded bottoms, but flat-bottomed dishes with deeper sides and straighter walls also appear. Two-handled bowls are scarcer during Early Minoan II but rounded bottoms persist, usually associated with Agios Onouphrios II decoration, and the first spouted bowls appear. Normally the spout projects from the rim, but occasionally it may be pushed through the wall of the vessel (Koumasa). Handles are placed either vertically or horizontally, and either opposite the spout or, less frequently, on one side of the vessel. This latter fashion is developed and becomes popular during Early Minoan III, various deep-sided bowls with short spouts projecting from the rim, featuring side-handles in preference to those opposite the spout (Porti). Some of these vessels become deep enough to be classed amongst the first of the two-handled bridge-spouted jars so typical of the Middle Minoan period (Platanos). In Middle Minoan I dishes appear in greater numbers and varieties than previously. Handle-less examples are notably prolific and vary in shape from low, conical examples to others which resemble pie-dishes and sugar-bowls (Porti). Both open and closed-mouth spouted bowls occur, usually with two handles, and other two-handled vessels of this group resemble fruit-bowls. Decoration may be simple or non-existent, but often is elaborate and polychrome (Platanos). Barbotine decoration is less common than amongst the jugs.

Apart from certain types of vases which seem to have been produced principally for funerary use, there are only two other groups of clay vessels which appear in any quantity in the Mesara tombs, and neither is represented throughout the Early Bronze Age. An early type which is rarely found after Early Minoan IIa, is the pyxis (fig. 11). In Early Minoan I cylindrical pyxides in both plain buff fabrics and in Agios Onouphrios I ware are frequently found in the tombs (Salame, Marathokephalon). In addition spherical pyxides with suspension lugs, in plain red or brown fabrics or sometimes of Salame ware, are also found in Early

Fig. 10 third right

second left

third left

top right

second right

bottom

top left

LEBENA (H.13·5)

KOUMASA (H.7·5)

PLATANOS (H.7)

LEBENA (H.12)

KOUMASA (H.11)

A. ONOUPHRIOS (H.8)

KOUMASA (H.7·5)

Fig. 11 Grave goods. Two-handled jars, pyxides, and "fruit-stands" or lids, of Early Minoan I–Middle Minoan I (measurements in cms)

Minoan I deposits (A. Eirene, Koumasa). In Early Minoan IIa the spherical pyxides are usually made of fine grey ware and carefully decorated with incised herringbone and other patterns. A fine selection of these, including some with three or four feet, were found at Koumasa. Probably contemporary with these are a few unusual cylindrical pyxides including plain examples from Platanos, a footed one with a conical lid from Agia Triadha, and some footed ones rather carelessly decorated with incised patterns of Agios Onouphrios derivation from Koumasa. Pyxides later than these are difficult to find.

Fig. 11 bottom right

top right

The other group of vessels, the two-handled closed-mouth jars, are common only in deposits of Early Minoan I and Middle Minoan I date (fig. 11). Elegant round-bottomed Agios Onouphrios jars with short, straight collars are quite common in Early Minoan I deposits, and at Lebena at least were accompanied by vessels in "Lebena" ware, of similar type but with shallower bodies and taller, cylindrical necks. A few of the Agios Onouphrios jars from Lebena might date to Early Minoan II. Apart from these however, the next major group of two-handled jars with closed-mouths belong to the Middle Minoan I period. For the most part, these are rather heavy-looking vessels with two handles placed horizontally high on the shoulder (Lebena, Platanos, Agios Onouphrios).

second right

top left

second left

In addition to pottery vessels, other functional artifacts placed in the tombs included a wide variety of tools and weapons (fig. 12). A good many of these were made of copper and bronze, and by far the most common in this category were the dagger blades. More than half of the tombs for which we possess any details at all of the finds are known to have yielded dagger blades. We can perhaps get some idea of their abundance from Platanos A, where about eighty daggers were found, and Agia Triadha A which produced about fifty. The daggers fall into two basic classes, the short, triangular ones and the long, narrow daggers. Both probably appeared first in Early Minoan I, and certainly both were in use during Early Minoan II. Thereafter the triangular dagger very rapidly went out of fashion and the long dagger was the only type in use. There were more than a dozen varieties of this weapon, including examples with both prominent and decorative ribbing dating to Early Minoan III and Middle Minoan I. The only other weapon represented in the tomb deposits is the spear, and this is known only from single spearheads found at

Fig. 12 top right bottom left

PLATE 13 The "altar" and inverted clay cups outside the large
tholos at Kamilari

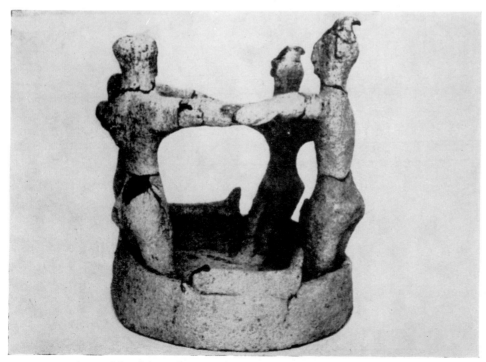

PLATE 14 A model of four dancers from the large tholos at Kamilari

PLATE 15   A model depicting a ceremony of uncertain
significance, from the large tholos at Kamilari

PLATE 16   The Agia Triadha sarcophagus, depicting funerary
or post-funerary ritual in the Late Minoan period

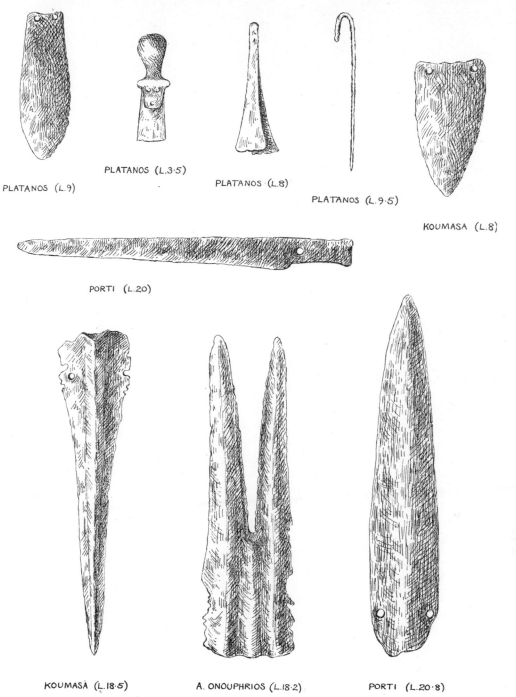

PLATANOS (L.9)

PLATANOS (L.3·5)

PLATANOS (L.8)

PLATANOS (L.9·5)

KOUMASA (L.8)

PORTI (L.20)

KOUMASA (L.18·5)

A. ONOUPHRIOS (L.18·2)

PORTI (L.20·8)

Fig. 12 Grave goods. Bronze tools and weapons of Early Minoan I–Middle Minoan I
(measurements in cms)

Marathokephalon and Porti. In addition a few bronze tools have been recovered from the circular tombs—awls (Agia Triadha, Platanos, Koumasa), knives (Koumasa, Porti), needles (Siva, Platanos) and a chisel and saw from Koumasa. Obsidian blades on the other hand are almost as common as bronze daggers, examples being recorded from about a third of the tombs. For the most part the obsidian found is in the form of long, narrow blades, but it is worth noting that cores were found in tomb B at Platanos and in Marathokephalon II, and both cores and flakes in tomb B at Koumasa. Two tombs, Drakones Z and Agia Triadha B, yielded rare examples of Early Minoan stone axes, and from the latter also came some stone mace-heads. Like the bronze tools however, such finds are the exception rather than the rule.

Fig. 12 bottom right

centre

The other manufactured artifacts which we find in the tombs and which seem to have been manufactured originally for use in life, are those which we might call "personal effects"—sealstones, toilet implements, amulets, figurines, jewellery, and other treasured possessions. The artifacts most commonly found are sealstones, which are recorded from about two-thirds of the tombs for which details are available (fig. 13). Several tombs have produced a dozen or so seals but larger groups were found at Platanos, Lebena I, and Agia Triadha. Tomb A at Agia Triadha for example produced more than a hundred sealstones. None of these can be dated to Early Minoan I, and there is no evidence from Crete for the production of sealstones before Early Minoan II. Most of the Early Minoan II seals which have yet been discovered have been found outside of the Mesara, but there are a few sealstones from the Mesara tombs which belong to this period. They fall into two stylistic groups.[2] The more prolific is the geometric style which features two basic motifs, the cross and the over-all grid pattern. Several examples of the former were found at Agios Onouphrios and Agia Triadha, and the latter site produced examples of the other pattern as well. The second style, which I call the "free style", uses representational designs as well as abstract ones, and shows none of the discipline or the love of the straight line apparent in the other style. Curving lines loosely drawn are the norm, and good examples of this type have been found in the tombs at Koumasa and Platanos, and in the Agios Onouphrios deposit. A few sealstones decorated in this style belong to Early Minoan III, if we are to judge from the designs carved on their second face. Platanos 1092 for example features

Fig. 13 bottom centre

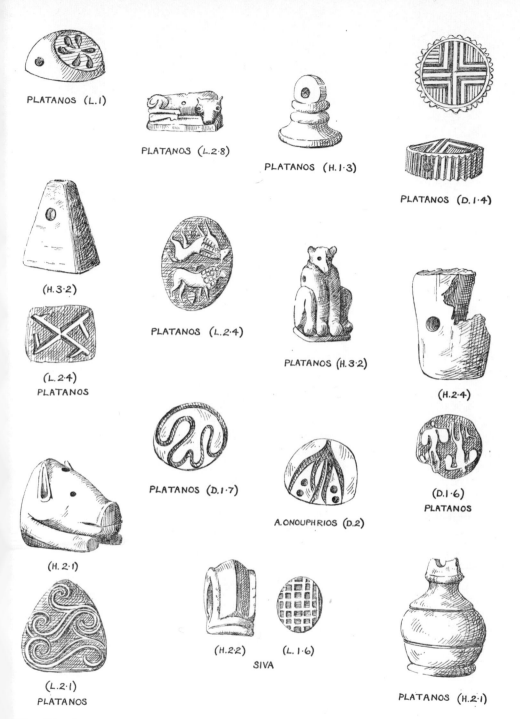

PLATANOS (L.1)

PLATANOS (L.2.8)

PLATANOS (H.1.3)

PLATANOS (D.1.4)

(H.3.2)

PLATANOS (L.2.4)

(L.2.4)
PLATANOS

PLATANOS (H.3.2)

(H.2.4)

PLATANOS (D.1.7)

A.ONOUPHRIOS (D.2)

(D.1.6)
PLATANOS

(H.2.1)

(H.2.2)   (L.1.6)
SIVA

(L.2.1)
PLATANOS

PLATANOS (H.2.1)

Fig. 13.   Grave goods. Sealstone designs and shapes of Early Minoan II–Middle Minoan I
(measurements in cms)

one design of two human figures in "free style" and a second of four lions in the impressionistic style of Early Minoan III and Middle Minoan I. Designs like this last become common in Early Minoan III and Middle Minoan I, probably reflecting new contacts with the eastern Mediterranean. Spiraliform decoration too is a popular Early Minoan III sealstone design, seen on examples from Platanos, Koumasa, Agia Triadha and Kalathiana. It is probably to this period that we may ascribe some of the zoomorphic sealstone shapes too, like the trio from Platanos (pig, cow and monkey) and the doves from Agios Onouphrios and Koumasa. In Middle Minoan I the plain cylindrical, conical and bottle-shapes of the earlier sealstones are joined by a variety of new ones, including flattened cylinders, low button seals, three-sided prisms and varieties thereof, and the first signets. Alongside the continuing animal friezes appear simpler designs of stylised flowers or stars, and there is also a return to the superimposed cross design first used in Early Minoan II. We are not certain of the significance of any of these designs, although the appearance of many of them in the Phaistos inventory of sealings, dating just a little later, suggests that they were in someway intended as a means of identifying a person, place or commodity.[3] It has been usual to think of the sealstone designs as being the equivalent of a man's signature, and despite the similarity between many of the designs—and the confusion which this might have caused—this still seems to be the most valid interpretation of them.

Like the sealstones, we may assume that the amulets were worn by their owners, suspended from a thread (fig. 14). As we might expect, many of the amulets are unique and cannot be classified on either typological or chronological grounds. The remainder fall into four groups, two of which are particularly distinctive. The largest group, but perhaps the least coherent, are the zoomorphic and anthropomorphic amulets. Many of them represent quadrupeds of uncertain identification, although the appearance of bulls-head amulets suggests that some of the quadrupeds may be bulls too (Koumasa, Platanos). Amulets in the form of a fish were found at both Koumasa and Agia Triadha, and there are a few in forms which may represent birds (Platanos). Almost as common as the zoomorphic and anthropomorphic amulets are those which have no distinctive shape whatsoever; that is to say, they are simply "pebbles" which have been perforated for suspension. They are not however natural pebbles,

Fig. 13 centre right

bottom left

top left
top centre

top right

Fig. 14 centre
bottom
second left
top centre

68

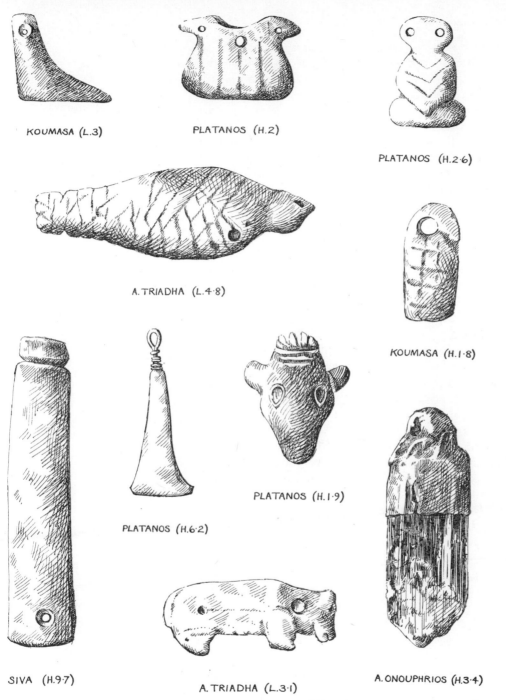

KOUMASA (L.3)

PLATANOS (H.2)

PLATANOS (H.2·6)

A. TRIADHA (L.4·8)

KOUMASA (H.1·8)

PLATANOS (H.6·2)

PLATANOS (H.1·9)

SIVA (H.9·7)

A. TRIADHA (L.3·1)

A. ONOUPHRIOS (H.3·4)

Fig. 14 Grave goods. Amulets of Early Minoan I–Middle Minoan I (measurements in cms)

since they are usually carved from steatite or serpentine. The use of this stone may have a particular significance which we shall mention in a moment. Most of the amulets of this type are completely undecorated, but simple designs have sometimes been incised on one surface, like the grid pattern on one from Koumasa and the flower on another from Siva. The third group of amulets are perhaps the most interesting for several reasons. These are the so-called "foot amulets", a dozen of which have so far been recorded from the Mesara tombs and about as many from the rest of the island.[4] Many of them probably date to Early Minoan II, although the evidence for this comes from two examples found on the mainland of Greece (Agios Kosmas, Zygouries) and a third found on Despotikon, rather than from Crete itself. All of these amulets represent the human foot and ankle (in contrast to the Egyptian "leg amulets" with which they are often compared) and the majority are made of serpentine. It is clear from examples found at Tylissos, Phaistos, and the two mainland sites mentioned above, that these amulets were worn in life as well as in death. Their function however is uncertain. The most attractive hypothesis at present is that they represented protection against snake bites. This view is based on the material used (serpentine—which according to Pliny was thought to possess this very power), on the appearance of votive clay feet in a shrine of the Snake Goddess at Mallia (in the Late Bronze Age), and on the sudden decline in the usage of the foot amulet in Middle Minoan I when the peak sanctuaries (probably dedicated to the Snake Goddess) were becoming established. It may be that from Middle Minoan I onwards, protection from snake bites was sought from the deity rather than from the amulet.

Fig. 14 second right

top left

Finally there is a small group of bronze amulets which take the form of pendants in the shape of a toilet scraper. These are so thin that they could never have fulfilled their normal function, and it is thought that they must have possessed amuletic values.[5] If this was the case, then it must reflect to some extent on the function and meaning of the other toilet scrapers. Only four of these scraper amulets have yet been found in the Mesara tombs, at Kalathiana, Christos and Platanos (2).

centre left

The scrapers themselves are probably the most prolific of the toilet implements found in the tombs. About a dozen tombs have produced a total of nearly thirty examples. There are several varieties of type, but basically all consist of a small bronze blade

which was hafted in a bone, ivory or wooden handle (fig. 12). *Fig. 12 top left*
The signs of wear along the edge of the blade suggest that they
were used in a grinding operation, which in view of their size
could only have been associated with the preparation of cosmetics
of some sort. The amuletic variety, briefly discussed above, is
perhaps suggestive of a ritual context for the use of the scrapers
and the cosmetics which they ground and applied. In this connection, the appearance of several scrapers in the deposits in the
sacred cave at Pyschro is perhaps significant. Other toilet implements found in the tombs are depilatory tweezers and razors
(fig. 12). Tweezers are almost as common as scrapers, about two *top centre*
dozen pairs have so far been recovered from the tombs, dating
(like the scrapers) from Early Minoan II to Middle Minoan I.
Whether or not scrapers and tweezers were first produced during
Early Minoan I we cannot say. The earliest of the razors are also
of Early Minoan II date, but the characteristic leaf-shaped variety
first appear in Early Minoan III. About twenty razors have been *top left*
discovered in the Mesara tombs, although it is as well to remember
that some of the obsidian blades may have been used as razors.

Few of the tombs have failed to produce various items of
jewellery. Beads from necklaces are by far the most common, but
finger and hair rings, pins, and various pendants also appear, as
well as a number of gold diadems and associated pieces. Most of
the beads are spherical or cylindrical in form, but there is a wide
range of materials used, ranging from clay, through various types
of stone (green, blue, black steatite and serpentine, red sard, rock
crystal) and faience to gold. The gold beads are often more
elaborate, with repoussé, appliqué or granulated decoration *Fig. 15 centre*
(Platanos, Koumasa, Kalathiana) and barrel or lentoid shapes *bottom*
(fig. 15). It seems likely that the clay and stone beads were in common use throughout the period, but most of the gold beads
probably date to Early Minoan II and III. The same may be said
of the other gold jewellery, since a diadem was found in an Early
Minoan II level at Lebena and a gold pendant in an Early Minoan
II level in Platanos A. On the other hand gold jewellery is almost
completely absent from the Early Minoan III and Middle Minoan
I tombs. The only tomb of this date known to have produced
gold-work is Kamilari I, and here there were but a few fragments.

Gold rings were found at Koumasa, Porti, Platanos, and
Kalathiana, and heart-shaped or triangular pendants at Platanos *centre left*
and Agia Triadha. More elaborate and unusual pendants include

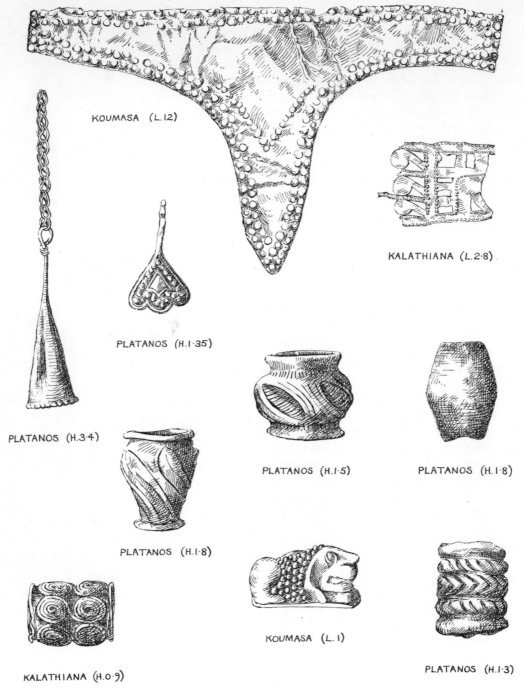

KOUMASA (L.12)

KALATHIANA (L.2·8)

PLATANOS (H.1·35)

PLATANOS (H.3·4)

PLATANOS (H.1·5)

PLATANOS (H.1·8)

PLATANOS (H.1·8)

KALATHIANA (H.0·9)

KOUMASA (L.1)

PLATANOS (H.1·3)

Fig. 15 Grave goods. Gold jewellery of Early Minoan II–Middle Minoan I

a cheeky toad found in Koumasa B, and a variety of shapes (snake, bi-spherical, "pocket-watch") from the Agios Onouphrios deposit. One imagines that many of these gold rings, beads, and pendants belonged to the same people who owned the splendid diadems found in Platanos A, Agia Triadha A, Kalathiana, Porti, Koumasa A and B, and Lebena I (fig. 15). For the most part these are flat bands of gold, narrowing at either end and decorated with a few simple designs in repoussé. Most of them were never long enough to completely encircle an adult head, but strands of gold wire found in the same deposits probably served as ties to knot at the back of the head. More elaborate examples were found at Kalathiana, Lebena and Koumasa, and stray gold leaf pendants at Agia Triadha and Platanos recall the leaf attachments of the elaborate diadems from the Mochlos cemetery in the east of the island. Unfortunately we cannot be sure how many of these diadems are represented by what remains to us, since many are but small fragments and others are so narrow that they might be bangles or armlets rather than diadems. At Platanos, in tomb A, it is clear that there were many diadems, three of which were found intact and "numerous" others in fragments, apart from "dozens" of narrow strips of gold. On the other hand, the sizeable group of gold jewellery in Agia Triadha A included only one fragmentary diadem.

Apart from the gold jewellery the tombs contain, in very small quantities, a number of other objects which we may assume to have been treasured personal possessions. These are objects which would have been difficult to obtain since they came from beyond the island, and mainly from the eastern Mediterranean. Nevertheless at least ten tombs are known to have produced items of this category. Some of these have yielded a single Egyptian or Syrian scarab (Lebena I, IIa and Aspripetra) whilst Lebena II produced a scarab and what appears to be a rare Minoan imitation of an Egyptian claw-foot goblet. An Egyptian stone vase was however found in Agia Triadha A, and this tomb has produced several other imported items including a scarab, cylinder seal, and fragmentary Syrian dagger. In addition a peculiar bird-vase from Agia Triadha has very close parallels in Syria. Other Syrian daggers were found at Platanos, one in tomb A and another in tomb B, which also produced a cylinder seal and three scarabs. A further Syrian dagger was found at Koumasa, but the most significant finds here were three silver daggers of Italian type. A

Fig. 15 bottom centre

top

top right

73

copper example of this type of weapon was found in the Agios Onouphrios deposit, along with four scarabs and two Cycladic marble pyxides. Finally, the tomb at Marathokephalon yielded a small decorated jug of Cycladic type. In addition to these various items, we should of course bear in mind that many of the artifacts we have already discussed were in fact made of imported materials. Many of the sealstones and some of the pendants were made of ivory (from Syria or Egypt), and the gold for jewellery was probably brought from the east Mediterranean. The source of the silver used so rarely for earrings (Vorou, Platanos) and pins (Porti, Platanos) may have been Cycladic but the daggers from Koumasa and Agios Onouphrios allow the possibility that it came from the west Mediterranean,[6] particularly since it occurs so infrequently in Crete. Obsidian of course would have come from Melos, and one other Cycladic import has yet to be discussed, namely marble, mainly in the form of figurines (fig. 16).

In fact, Renfrew's recent study of the "Cycladic" figurines in Crete has revealed that the great majority of them are almost certainly native products.[7] An exception is the fine folded-arm figurine found at Koumasa, which falls into Renfrew's "Spedos" *Fig. 16 left* type. Nearly all the rest belong to a distinctive Minoan variant labelled the "Koumasa" type, since five examples of it were found in or around the tombs at this site. Other Mesara tombs producing figurines of the "Koumasa" variety include Platanos *bottom right* (1) and Lebena (3). Since a Cretan source of "Island marble" has now been found, there is no reason why all of these figurines should not have been manufactured in Crete from local stone.[8] In addition to these folded-arm figurines, there are other limestone and marble figurines from the Mesara tombs which also fall into the broad category of "Cycladic" figurines. These include the featureless and limbless type found in Troy I (Agios Onouphrios, Lebena II), and the curious broad-bodied and short-legged *centre* Agios Onouphrios type (also represented at Lebena).

The second category of figurines, those with only schematic rendering of the torso and with rounded or pointed bases, might be derivatives of the Cycladic figurines.[9] The more numerous type, with arms across the body (indicated only by one or two incisions) and pointed base, would seem to be related to the folded-arm figurines. The relationship is also suggested by the rather spade-like faces typical of this group (fig. 16). The best known groups of these figurines were found at Platanos and Agia *top centre*

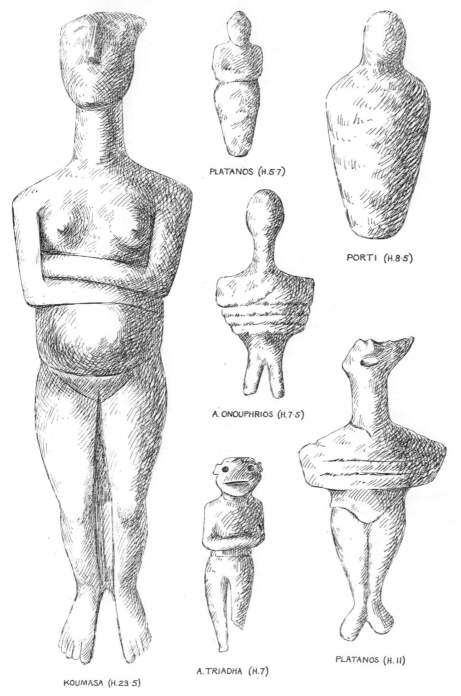

PLATANOS (H.5.7)

PORTI (H.8.5)

A. ONOUPHRIOS (H.7.5)

KOUMASA (H.23.5)

A. TRIADHA (H.7)

PLATANOS (H.11)

Fig. 16 Grave goods. Anthropomorphic figurines of Early Minoan I–Middle Minoan I (measurements in cms)

Triadha, and the type may date as late as Middle Minoan I. The other variety within this broad group have rounded heads, almost cylindrical bodies with no features marked on them, and rounded (as opposed to pointed) bases. These are less common, but examples were found at Koumasa, Agia Triadha and Porti. *Fig. 16 top right* Although they are broadly comparable to the pointed-base figurines, they may be considerably earlier, since they might be considered a Cretan variant of the "Apeiranthos" type of Cycladic figurine. Finally we might include here a cross-like limestone figurine from Platanos which looks very much like a "Phylakopi I" type figurine, which would date it to Early Minoan III or Middle Minoan I.

There is a third group of figurines found in the tombs, which are those which attempt to show the human body in a realistic manner. These are normally of stone or ivory, the latter almost invariably revealing considerably more detail than the former. Men and women are modelled in about equal numbers, but there is a notable correlation between male and ivory figurines, and between female and stone ones. Whether or not this is significant is uncertain. The women invariably stand with arms raised between the breasts and dresses reaching to the ground (Agia Triadha, Koumasa) while the men are normally naked but for a loin-cloth (Porti, Siva, Agia Triadha). The most splendid male *bottom centre* figure yet recovered was that recently found at Agios Kyrillos, very similar to the ivory one from Porti, but made of clay and much larger. Even better was the superb agrimi found near the tomb at Porti, but strangely this is almost the only animal figurine found on the site of a circular tomb in the Mesara. A rather crude bull figurine was found at Platanos, and two small bulls outside the tombs at Koumasa, but that is all.

All of the artifacts which we have discussed so far in this chapter are items which are common to both funerary and domestic deposits, though because of the rarity of excavated Early Bronze Age settlements examples from tombs are far more numerous than those from houses. Some authorities might dispute that the Cycladic figurines were used in life, but there are now sufficient examples from contemporary settlements to be sure that this was the case. The vast numbers found in the cemeteries on the other hand certainly suggest that it was regular practice to bury these figurines with their owners. The use of the figurines in the realistic style in Minoan settlements is now well

established by Warren's discovery of several in the mansion at
Fournou Korifi,[10] apart from isolated finds in other settlements
(Vasiliki, Palaikastro). Only for the pointed and rounded base
figurines does it remain to establish a non-funerary period of use.
None have yet been found in Early Minoan houses, but if one
accepts the suggestion that they are a late Minoan development
of the Cycladic folded-arm figurine, then like that type they would
presumably have been used in life as well as death.

For the most part, the artifacts which appear to have been made
exclusively for use in the tombs are vessels of various types. The
most prolific, undoubtedly, are the small stone vases.[11] Almost
all of the excavated tombs have produced at least a few stone
vases, but the cemetery at Platanos produced many hundreds,
and other large groups were found at Koumasa and Kamilari.
The majority of the vessels found fall into two types, the "birds-
nest" bowl and the flat-bottomed, straight-sided cup (fig. 17). In   *Fig. 17 third right*
addition there are a variety of other shapes found in small
quantities—ladles, goblets, jars, jugs, bowls, handled cups,   *Fig. 17*
boxes, and even the occasional "teapot". With the exception of
the "teapots" and handled cups, all of the shapes share one thing
in common: they are all in miniature and are most unlikely to
have served any useful purpose in everyday life. This impression
is confirmed by the almost complete absence of stone vessels in
contemporary settlements. I understand from Dr Warren that
there are only half a dozen fragments of stone vases from Early
Minoan domestic sites. Unless these vessels had a particular
funerary function this discrepancy is hard to explain, all the more
so since the colourful stones in which they were manufactured
(limestone, marble, brecchia, alabaster, steatite, schist, and
serpentine) made them extremely attractive. The earliest of them
date to Early Minoan II, and include bi-conical and rectangular
pyxides, spouted bowls and ladles, all manufactured in green
chlorite or chlorite schist. Examples of these vessels have been
found in half a dozen Mesara tombs.[12]

Warren is convinced that the mass of the stone vases, showing
signs of the use of the tubular drill, must date to Early Minoan III
and Middle Minoan I.[13] I am not entirely happy about this,
particularly in view of the fine collection of vases from Mochlos,
some of which appear to be in Early Minoan II contexts, but there
is no doubt that *most* of the Mesara vases belong in the later
periods. In fact, I believe that a great many of them belong in

PLATANOS (H.7·7)

PLATANOS (H.5·1)

PLATANOS (H.5)

PLATANOS (H.2·8)

PORTI (H.5)

PLATANOS (H.4)

KOUMASA (H.5)

PLATANOS (H.3·2)

Fig. 17 Grave goods. Stone vases of Early Minoan ii–Middle Minoan i (measurements in cms)

Early Minoan III or early in Middle Minoan I. This is because there is some evidence to suggest that the "birds-nest" vases, the cups, and the bowls, were fulfilling the same sort of functions as the conical clay cups, and these we found suddenly grew numerous in Middle Minoan I tomb deposits. That is to say, the clay cups may have replaced the majority of the stone vases in the funerary tradition. If we look at the proportion of clay cups to stone vases in the Middle Minoan I tombs this situation seems to be clearly revealed. Kamilari I for example produced more than a thousand cups but only seventy stone vases, the two tombs at Vorou yielded over sixty cups in contrast to half a dozen of stone, and Apesokari II contained hundreds of clay cups and little more than a dozen of stone. These figures may be contrasted with those for earlier tombs. Koumasa B for example produced more than seventy stone vases and only a handful of clay cups, while Agia Triadha A yielded about fifty stone vases from within the tomb, and as many clay ones from the latest (Middle Minoan I) deposits in the antechambers. Before Early Minoan III, the need for cups was presumably met by the one- and two-handled cups and tankards which we discussed at the beginning of this chapter.

One group of stone vessels which deserve particular mention are the so-called "kernoi",[14] small vessels, often rectangular in shape, with two, three or four cylindrical holes in them (Platanos, Koumasa). The outside faces of these curious vessels are usually *Fig. 17 bottom left* decorated with incised designs based on hatched triangles, semi-circles, diamonds and panels (fig. 17). It has been customary to date these "kernoi" to Early Minoan I and II, comparing their form to late predynastic examples from Egypt, and their decoration to that of the Early Minoan II green chlorite pyxides and spouted bowls. If Warren is right about the tubular drill however, they cannot be earlier than Early Minoan III, and certainly an analysis of the decorative motifs employed on the "kernoi" and on the Early Minoan III and Middle Minoan I "birds-nest" bowls reveals a close relationship between the two groups of vessels. It therefore seems more likely that the rectangular stone "kernoi" date to Early Minoan III and Middle Minoan I. There were earlier "kernoi" however, though they are rare. Clay examples were found at Koumasa, including the unusual "condiment set" on a stand in fine grey ware of Early Minoan II, and at Lebena. These may have had even earlier prototypes like the dish with three compartments found in a neolithic level at Knossos. In addition there are some small "kernoi" of two circular stone cups joined together which, despite the use of a circular drill on most of them, might be as early as Early Minoan II. One from Drakones was made from the green chlorite so typical of Early Minoan II stone-working.

Sir Arthur Evans believed that the fore-runners of the stone "kernoi" were the so-called lids or fruit-stands found in some of the Mesara tombs and elsewhere in Crete (fig. 11). Xanthoudides was convinced that they were lids, and Seager that they were "fruit-stands". Neither of these solutions is acceptable, for it remains true that there are still no vessels to go with the "lids", and too many of the "fruit-stands" have small and uneven "pedestals" which would never have allowed them to stand. I would agree with Evans that the vessels were probably produced for ritual usage, though I do not see how they can be fitted into the "kernoi" tradition. The characteristic features of these "lids" are a dish-shaped body, a handle mounted in the centre of the base, frequently a burnished fabric, and occasionally a herring-bone pattern of incisions around the rim. If we are to see them as ritual vessels, then I suggest we compare them with the Cycladic frying-pans, which share some of the features mentioned above and are strangely absent from Early Minoan II Crete, although they are common in parts of the Greek mainland, and Cycladic figurines, as we have seen, were by no means scarce in Crete. These "lids" certainly appear in Early Minoan II, and it may be significant that in three of the five tombs where they appear, Cycladic figurines have also been found. At Agia Triadha there were no such figurines, but there were the pointed base variety which we suggested might be a derivative type from the Cycladic folded-arm figurines. Like the figurines however, the "lids" do appear in some domestic contexts and might have been made for use in life as well as death, whatever the function they fulfilled.

Fig. 11 centre

The same can hardly be claimed for the zoomorphic and anthropomorphic jugs and vessels found in the tombs, and absent from the settlements.[15] About a third of the tombs excavated have produced vessels in this category, although the only ones to produce them in quantity were the cemeteries at Koumasa, Platanos and Lebena. Some of the Lebena vessels dated as early as Early Minoan I, and others here and at Koumasa belonged to the following period. Other examples from Koumasa, Platanos, Agia Triadha, and Agios Kyrillos date to Early Minoan III and

Middle Minoan I, so that the use of these vessels appears to cover the whole of the Early Bronze Age. Lebena produced some of the most individual of the zoomorphic vessels, including one delightful example in the shape of a pig. There were also some *Fig. 18 second right* other weird shapes which whilst not falling into the category of either zoomorphic or anthropomorphic vessels, deserve mention. These included barrel-, gourd- and boat-shaped pots. Other unusual zoomorphic designs from elsewhere include a tortoise found in Koumasa B and a shell from Agia Triadha. For the most part however, the vessels fall into three clear categories, bird-vessels, bull-vessels, and vessels in the form of a woman (fig. 18).

The bird-vases are not in fact a very uniform group at all. The earliest of them is probably a vessel from Lebena II which appears to have a bird in flight rising from either end of the body. There *lower centre* are a small group of vessels, ranging from Early Minoan II to Middle Minoan I in date, which portray a bird with no legs and only the most meagre of wings and tails (Koumasa, Platanos). A second group are characterised by four short legs and distinct wings and tails (Koumasa, Platanos). In addition there is a squat *top right* jug from Koumasa which is perhaps intended to represent a bird sitting on its nest (it has a tail and two wing-like handles), and a curious vessel looking rather like a chicken, and finding remarkably close parallels at Byblos, from Agia Triadha.

The bull-vases are more uniform, although two slightly unusual ones without legs and with box-like bodies were found at Koumasa. The remainder are all modelled realistically with horns *bottom right* and legs prominently featured. Two of them, from Porti and Koumasa, are of particular interest since they have human figures hanging from the horns and at once suggest some con- *centre left* nection with the bull-games of the palatial era. No Early Minoan I bull-vessels have yet been discovered, but some, like the one with acrobats from Koumasa, may plausibly be attributed to Early Minoan II. We cannot be certain about the date of these; they could be later, and certainly some bull-vessels, like that from Agios Kyrillos, are of Middle Minoan I date.

All of the woman-vases yet discovered in the Mesara come from a single cemetery, that at Koumasa. One of them was preserved intact, while three other broken examples were found. All of them have box-like bodies of identical shape to those used on the two unusual bull-vases from the same site. The complete example

81

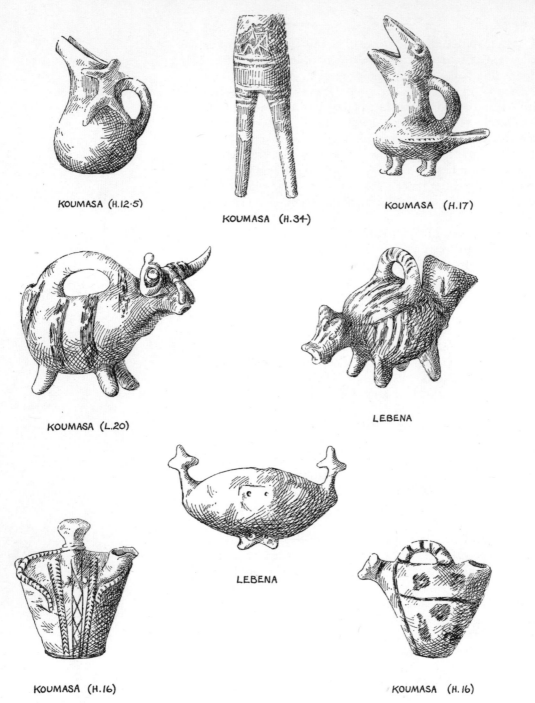

KOUMASA (H.12·5)

KOUMASA (H.34)

KOUMASA (H.17)

KOUMASA (L.20)

LEBENA

LEBENA

KOUMASA (H.16)

KOUMASA (H.16)

Fig. 18 Grave goods. Zoomorphic and anthropomorphic vessels of Early Minoan I–Middle Minoan I (measurements in cms)

has a head which is featureless but for a ridge indicating the nose. Around the neck and shoulders is draped what can only be identified as a snake. The other three vessels all preserve traces of a similar creature round the neck and/or shoulders. The decoration of the complete example in the red-on-buff style, together with the "Cycladic-like" head suggest that it may date to Early Minoan II, although one of the other vases is decorated in the linear white-on-black style of Early Minoan III. *Fig. 18 bottom left*

There are a number of other vases which may be termed anthropomorphic with varying degrees of certainty. A vessel in the form of a woman with a long dress and a girdle round her waist was found at Koumasa, close to one of the woman-vases. From Koumasa too came three plain jugs with human figures modelled clinging to the rim or handle, and a curious pair of votive or ritual "trousers". Two more pairs of these were found at Platanos, and a fourth pair at Marathokephalon. Finally we might mention here the three clay phalli found at Platanos, and the six discovered at Koumasa. They are not hollow vessels, but their ritual purpose is presumably linked in some way with either the bull-vases or the woman-vessels. *top left* *top centre*

The various vessels we have been discussing were probably used in association with the libation stones and palettes found in some of the tombs. In each of the tombs at Vorou Marinatos found a large cylindrical stone with a perforation at its centre. A similar stone was discovered at Arkhaiokorapho, while in tomb A at Agia Triadha two large flat stones with perforations were also found. The so-called cap-stone which Xanthoudides found in Platanos B may well have been a sixth example. Whether or not Marinatos was correct in identifying the Vorou stones as being used for libations is uncertain, but it is at least a reasonable hypothesis. Half a dozen tombs have proved to contain limestone palettes, and Koumasa B produced as many as seven. They are completely standardised, all of them being flat rectangular slabs of limestone with a groove running round the four edges. In addition to four palettes, the tomb at Porti also produced a clay "offering table" of circular shape with three short legs.

There remain three small groups of objects which may not have been manufactured exclusively for use in the tombs, but whose presence there may have a particular significance. At least six tombs have yielded finely made whetstones with one or two perforations (fig. 14). These may have no exceptional significance, *Fig. 14 bottom left* but they immediately recall the distinctive group of Wessex Culture burials from Britain, where whetstones form a common part of the "dagger grave" assemblage.[16] It may be of some interest to mention that commonly associated with the whetstones and daggers in these grave groups are tweezers and pins.

Double-axes have been found on only three cemetery sites in the Mesara, Kamilari, Platanos and Apesokari, but the ritual associations of the double-axe in Crete and the unusual form which some of the axes from the cemeteries take is sufficient justification for mentioning them here. Two sheet bronze axes found outside the tombs at Platanos were clearly intended for ritual usage, and a small, bronze double-axe pendant found inside tomb A was presumably considered to have an amuletic value. In the second tomb excavated at Apesokari, a small black steatite double-axe and others of bronze (size and type unknown) were discovered in the larger of the two rectangular rooms situated before the entrance. Half of a double-axe found inside Kamilari II is suggestive, perhaps, of ritual breakage.

Fig. 25

Finally there are the lamps discovered in seven or eight of the excavated tombs. Most of these are small, saucer-shaped lamps of clay, but a fragmentary one found in Koumasa E had a tall pedestal with barbotine decoration. Lamps of both this and the simpler type have been found in domestic contexts, but their appearance in the tombs probably implies that along with torches they had a part to play in the funerary ceremonies. A unique lamp in the form of a circular hut with doorway and windows was found at Lebena, and is to some extent paralleled by a lamp with cut-out windows and modelled animals found in the east of the island at Sphoungaras.

These then are the grave-goods found in the Mesara tombs, covering a period of more than a millennium, yet showing a certain uniformity throughout the period. Objects originally manufactured for use in life always seem to form the major part of the assemblage, and those artifacts manufactured for funerary use are always relatively few in number, with the exception of the stone vases in Early Minoan III and early Middle Minoan I. Certain items appear to be particularly prevalent as grave-goods— daggers, jugs, dishes, cups, jewellery, and sealstones—and these seem to be items which were common possessions in life. On the other hand none of these items occur in anything like sufficient quantity to go round all the burials that were probably made in the tombs. Their significance therefore has still to be evaluated. So too has that of the distribution of finds in and around the tombs, and that of the various funerary artifacts. I have deliberately refrained from interpreting the usage of zoomorphic vessels, palettes, stone vases and the like, since their interpretation must clearly be closely related to any discussion of burial ritual and attitudes to death and the dead, and these are the subject matter of our next two chapters.

Chapter Five

THE BURIAL OF THE DEAD

In our discussion of funerary rituals and customs, we shall attempt to distinguish between Minoan attitudes to burial and Minoan attitudes to death, since as we shall see, the two are not necessarily complementary to each other. The purpose of this chapter is, in effect, to describe an Early Minoan funeral in the Mesara. As with most cultures which followed a tradition of communal burial, this is not an easy task. Constant disturbance of existing burials by the making of new ones, together with the occasional fumigation or clearing of the tombs and their subsequent looting in the case of the Mesara cemeteries, has completely confused the skeletal and other remains. It is no longer possible to say which artifacts went with which corpses, or even to be sure of the posture in which the bodies were laid to rest. There are only three features of the funerary tradition associated with the Mesara tombs which can be established without discussion and interpretation. The first of these, that burials were made in communal tombs, is self-evident. The second, that inhumation was the rule, might be disputed in view of the charred bones found in many of the tombs which might be interpreted as evidence of cremation. But the discussion of the use of fire in the tombs in the next chapter will show that the bones were charred by fumigatory fires and not crematory ones. Thirdly, it cannot be disputed that a large number of grave-goods were deposited in the tombs, and the personal nature of many of these suggests that they were buried there with their owners. In other words we may say at the outset of our discussion, that corpses were inhumed in a communal tomb together with some of their personal possessions.

86

In view of the mass of unarticulated bones found in these tombs, it is surprising that only one archaeologist, Enrico Stefani, has ever suggested that the corpses were allowed to decompose outside the tombs and that only disarticulated bones were placed in the tomb itself.[1] Though one might expect complete disturbance of the earliest burials, it is certainly strange that none of the latest ones remain articulated—if they were articulated when they were buried. Stefani suggested that the bodies were placed in larnakes until they were decomposed, and these could have been placed in the antechambers to the tombs whilst decomposition took place. But larnakes only appear in Early Minoan III and later contexts, so that the earlier burials could not have been left to decompose in them. This is not in itself a sound reason for rejecting the hypothesis that the circular tombs were in fact ossuaries pure and simple, but there are other reasons for doing so. Even at Agia Triadha, one complete skeleton was found, and Evans, visiting the site at the time of excavation, noted indications of articulated limbs.[2] Other complete skeletons were found at Vorou and Gypsades, and probably at Lebena, where Alexiou describes their posture.[3] Xanthoudides too must have found incomplete skeletons *in situ* since he also describes the posture of the corpses in the tombs.[4] It seems therefore, that scarce as the evidence is, several tombs have yielded complete or fragmentary skeletons *in situ* which on the one hand confirm that at least some bodies rather than bones were placed in the tombs, and on the other tell us something about the posture and orientation of the burials.

The two skeletons found *in situ* at Agia Triadha and Gypsades both had their knees bent so that they were in either a contracted or flexed posture. Evans noted bent knees among the articulated limbs at Agia Triadha, and Xanthoudides presumably noted the same among the bones in the tombs he excavated, since in the conclusion to his report he describes the burials as being laid in the "contracted" position. There can be little doubt therefore that burials were made in this posture, but it is equally clear that extended burials were also made. Alexiou states that the burials in Lebena I were "extended inhumations", and Marinatos describes several skeletons in the extended position found in both the tombs at Vorou. Though we have no details to confirm it, it is likely that the extended bodies were probably laid on their back and the contracted or flexed ones on their side. The only direct evidence of the original orientation of the bodies is from Vorou, where the bodies were mainly aligned east-west, with the head *facing* west (and presumably, therefore, actually placed on the east). I think some confirmation of this may be sought in tomb A at Agia Triadha. Banti published a detailed plan of the finds made in this tomb, and although the skeletal remains drawn on the plan show no clear indications of their original orientation, one group of artifacts do. These are the forty or so bronze daggers found in the tomb, three-quarters of which were found with their point facing west (fig. 19). This is unlikely to be coincidence, and if it is not it presumably represents their original orientation. This is important since we know that in life the Minoan male wore his dagger at his hip, with the point, as one would expect, facing the feet (see the Petsopha figurines).[5] It is likely, though not certain, that in death he would be buried with his dagger in the same position. It may be relevant to mention here the "triangular" flint daggers of the Remedello culture of central Italy, for which I have argued a Minoan derivation, which are found in contemporary graves at the waist of the dead man.[6] If this was the practice in Crete, then the orientation of the Agia Triadha daggers suggests that here at least, the bodies were laid with the feet to the west, and the head to the east. A general east-west orientation for the bodies might be postulated in any case, since the great majority of the circular tombs have their entrance to the east.

The earliest burials in most of the tombs were laid directly on to the cleared rock surface, unless they were laid on matting or some kind of wooden stretcher, either of which would have long since rotted. In a few tombs however, material was deliberately introduced into the tomb and used to make a laid floor on which the earliest burials were placed. At Koutsokera the floor was simply twenty–thirty centimetres of pure earth beaten hard, and a similar floor was found at Gypsades. At Drakones Z and Platanos B on the other hand, the floors were made of sand and gravel from nearby streams and in Platanos "A" of red clay. The most elaborate floor was that found in the almost destroyed tomb at Kamilari (II) where the rock had been covered with a thin layer of beaten earth which formed a bed for a floor of polygonal slabs.[7] In other cases "floors" of white sand or earth were laid over earlier burials, usually at an important time in the tomb's history. In Lebena IIa and Platanos A for example, white floors were laid immediately

Fig. 19

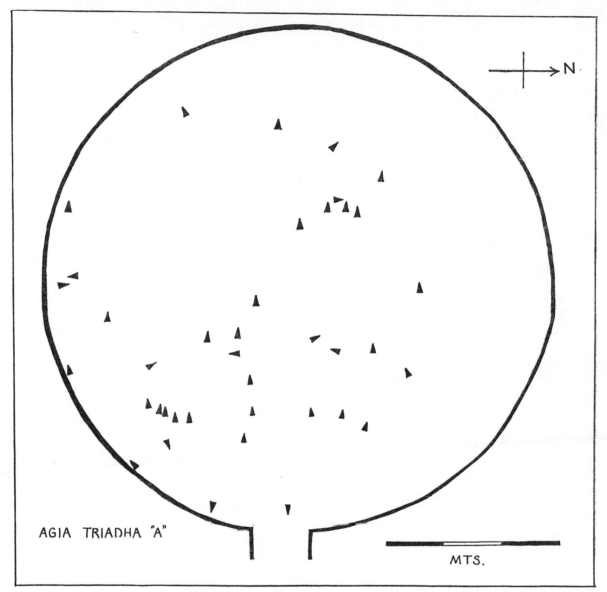

Fig. 19 A diagram showing the orientation of dagger blades, as found in tholos A at Agia Triadha

over the remains of a fumigation fire, while in Vorou A it separated extended inhumations on the ground from burials in pithoi and larnakes. A major clearing out and cleaning up of Koumasa E was also followed by a white clay "floor" being laid over the existing remains, which here had been swept to one side.[8] The use of a white material for floors laid after clearing or fumigation seems persistent and one wonders if it was chosen deliberately to symbolise, perhaps even confirm, the purged state of the tomb. The significance of the original laid floors is more difficult to understand since so few tombs have them; yet where they occur it is clear that the builders of the tomb had gone to considerable trouble to introduce them. The important point however is not, I think, the differing use of rock and laid floors but the apparently universal clearing of the existing soil which for some reason was not considered suitable for use in the tomb.

It seems clear that some, if not all, of the burials were accompanied by a group of artifacts, although nowhere has this yet been clearly demonstrated owing to the confused state of the burial stratum. One hopes that the final publication of the Lebena excavations may provide some examples of burials with firmly associated grave-goods. At present however our ideas of a typical assemblage are really no more than conjecture. The persistent looting, to which we have referred several times already, means that we are not able to judge whether or not all of the burials were originally accompanied by grave-goods. The only artifacts which we might expect to survive in anything like their original quantity are the sealstones, since they are usually small enough to become lost very easily in the mass of debris on the tomb's floor, and were also too personalised to be of much value perhaps to the Minoan looter. On the other hand, there is the very real possibility that many early seals were made of wood, so that we may well have lost a large proportion of the seals originally placed in the tombs. Furthermore, only certain types of people may have worn and owned sealstones so that the number of sealstones need not indicate the number of burials which were accompanied by grave-goods of some kind. Two late tombs, Vorou A and Gypsades, provide us with some evidence as to the situation in Middle Minoan times. At Vorou the finds made with both the extended skeletons and the burials in pithoi and larnakes were very few in number. Most of the skeletons on the floor lay near clay vessels and the odd stone bowl, but several of the larnax and pithos burials contained no finds at all. Others contained a single clay cup. Just outside tomb B at this site, a skeleton was found with some handleless cups and a pair of bronze earrings. At Gypsades the remains of two burials were found inside the circular tomb, on a newly laid and raised floor. The only other artifacts found in the tomb were some clay vessels and figurines, which in the circumstances seem likely to have belonged with the two burials. The impression from these two tombs is that grave-goods were few in the Middle Minoan period, but the mass of material from Kamilari 1 suggests that this was not necessarily so, although the number of burials here was far greater than that at Vorou or Gypsades. For the main period of the circular tombs, we can only say that we do not know if everyone was buried with grave-goods but it seems likely that they were. Certainly the universal rite (and right) of burial in a circular chamber tombs suggests a society where there would be no social or political barriers to burial with one's possessions. The limitation was presumably one of wealth, and there could have been very few indeed who did not possess a few clay vessels, some clay and stone jewellery, and perhaps a dagger if he were a man.

Many of the burials were presumably better equipped than this, and on the basis of the frequency of finds from the various tombs one may envisage a common assemblage for a Minoan male comprising a jug, a bowl, a cup, a necklace or amulet, a dagger, and perhaps a stone vase and a sealstone. Men of wealth or rank may have possessed, and been buried with, a little gold jewellery, a fine ceremonial whetstone, or an imported dagger or scarab. The Minoan woman would have been buried with a similar assemblage except that the dagger may have been replaced by toilet tweezers or scrapers, and that figurines would probably have featured more prominently among the female burials, since we believe many of them were originally made for the use of women in childbirth.

Apart from these typical assemblages, some of the rarer finds in the tombs hint at grave-goods which were placed in the tomb not so much because they were a man's personal possessions but because they were the tools of his trade (fig. 12). For example the *Fig. 12* leather-cutter from Marathokephalon (the only example yet known from the Early Bronze Age) was presumably buried with a leather-worker, and the saw and chisel from Koumasa with a carpenter.[9] Other possibilities include the loomweight from

Platanos, perhaps buried with a wool-worker, the unfinished stone vase from the same site (buried with a lapidary?), and the obsidian cores from Koumasa, Platanos and Marathokephalon, which may have belonged to men who procured and worked this valuable material.[10] One wonders too if the spearheads from Porti and Marathokephalon were the possessions of fishermen, as the harpoon from Agios Onouphrios and the net-needle from Platanos surely were.[11] Finally we might mention one curious omission from the grave assemblages—cooking vessels. Their absence implies perhaps that women were buried as 'mothers' or 'wives' rather than as 'housekeepers'.

Fig. 12 bottom centre

The other clay vessels placed in the tombs, however, have yet to be discussed. While a man or woman might possess his own, personal, cup or goblet, and possibly his own plate or bowl, it is unlikely that he had a personal jug. It seems altogether more probable that these various vessels were placed in the tomb as containers for food and drink rather than as personal possessions. Yet the only food remains found in all of the excavated tombs are a few animal bones from Lebena I and II and Agia Triadha A, the shells of edible marine molluscs in Lebena II and Agia Triadha A, and olive seeds from Lebena II.[12] Some food remains may have been missed in excavations, and liquids of course would have vanished leaving scarcely a trace, but nevertheless the scarcity of food remains from the tombs cannot be denied. There is thus no reason whatever for supposing that the bowls originally held food for the dead, or for that matter, that funerary feasts took place inside the tombs, as Alexiou has suggested. The bones, seeds and shells could have got into the tomb in several ways, not least as expressions of a man's vocation, as hunter, farmer, or fisherman. We may return to the problem of the jugs, cups and bowls in a moment.

The rituals enacted inside the tomb itself at the time of burial appear to have been very simple and very few. The corpse must have been dragged through the low, narrow doorway, by one or two men already inside the tomb. They would probably have already lit small fires in bowls, on small clay tables (as at Porti) or in the broken base of a pithos (as at Vorou),[13] on which they burnt aromatic substances to cover the stench of the tomb. With them they would have brought a small lamp and possibly torches. Alexiou noticed that the lintel of Lebena II was blackened on its underside by the passage of torches in and out of the tomb, and

Levi thought that some of the burnt timber he found in Kamilari I came from torches. The body and its offerings were laid, head to the east it seems, on the floor, or after the tomb had been in use for centuries, simply on top of existing burials (Lebena I). The presence of large stones with holes in them in Vorou A and B, Agia Triadha A, Arkhaiokhorapho, and perhaps Platanos B, are certainly suggestive of libations poured in the tomb during the funeral.[14] This might well explain the common presence of jugs in the tombs, since jugs used for pouring libations of a funerary nature would probably have been deposited with the body rather than brought out of the tomb and returned to normal usage.

There is however one other possible explanation for the appearance of jugs and cups, and perhaps dishes, in the Mesara tombs. This is that they were used in some sort of "toasting" ritual involving the drinking of ? wine poured from a jug into one or several cups, which when they had fulfilled their function were left in the tomb with the newly buried body. Some sort of token feast may have accompanied the "toasting"—pieces of meat, fruit, or bread being taken into the tomb in a bowl or dish which was then deposited with the jug and cups. A "feast" of this sort would have left no trace but for the clay vessels in which it had been contained. Some sort of "toasting" ritual was almost certainly practised outside the tomb, as we shall see shortly, but the evidence for this suggests that such rituals took place in Early Minoan III and Middle Minoan I. Is it possible that before this time the ritual always took place *inside* the tomb?

Many, possibly all, of the tombs had small rectangular ante-chambers in front of their doorways (fig. 20). Their walls were *Fig. 20* built of small stones and clay, were relatively thin, and never stood to more than two metres in height, one imagines. They were probably, though not certainly, roofed over with a flat roof of mud or clay laid on brushwood and beams. Their most remarkable feature is undoubtedly their small size. Even at Platanos A, a tomb with an external diameter of about eighteen metres, the antechamber was only 2.75 × 1.5 metres. The largest antechamber yet recorded is in fact that discovered in front of Apesokari II, measuring 3.5 × 2.3 metres, whilst the smallest is probably Koumasa A, a tiny 1.45 × 0.8 metres. Their purpose is uncertain, but they were clearly regarded as an integral part of the tomb, since like the tomb itself, their floor was always cleared right down to rock, giving the impression of a small sunken

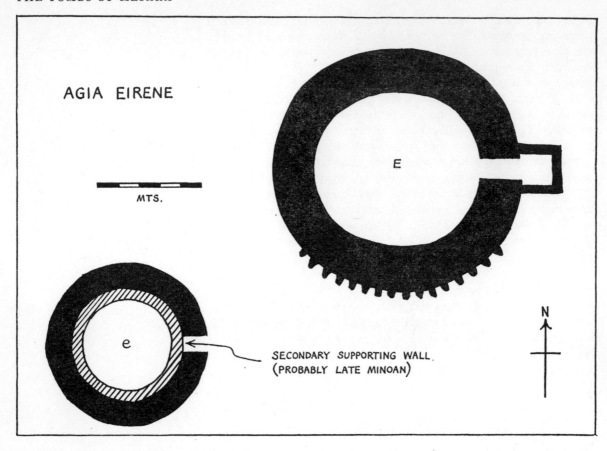

AGIA EIRENE

MTS.

E

e

SECONDARY SUPPORTING WALL
(PROBABLY LATE MINOAN)

N

chamber. Xanthoudides commented that in Koumasa E, the difference in height between ground level and the floor of the antechamber was perhaps sufficient to have necessitated the use of a small ladder. The close relationship between the antechambers and the tombs suggests that the former's function was associated with rituals performed at the time of burial. That is to say, they were a part of the tomb and like the tomb were only entered for the purposes of burial.

It may well be that the term *antechambers* is a particularly apt one and that they were regarded as precisely that by the Minoans. Here the body could have been placed before burial, awaiting entry to the tomb. How long it might have remained there we cannot say, although there are several ethnographic parallels

Fig 20 The cemetery at Agia Eirene (reconstructed from Xanthoudides' description)

where the body remains unburied until putrifaction sets in.[15] At the time of the burial proper, the antechamber may have become the focus of part of the ritual. Certainly those entering the tomb would have to pass through the chamber, and the persistently small size of the chambers suggests that rituals here and in the tomb were probably attended by only a small group of people. Unfortunately we cannot demonstrate that the antechambers were kept clear, as they needed to be, of bones and grave-goods, since once the tombs themselves became full, burials took place first in the doorway, then in the antechambers and finally in the rooms beyond the antechambers, where such existed. Nevertheless, with rooms so small, it is quite certain that they must have been kept completely clear of all debris while burials were still made in the tomb chamber, since otherwise it would have been impossible to open the great stone doors, let alone take the body into the tomb.

In addition to small antechambers commonly found before the doorways of the Mesara tombs, many of the tombs had a series of other chambers which were built on to the antechamber and the east side of the tomb. Some of these, like the narrow chambers outside Platanos A and Porti (figs. 2, 24), are clearly huts or lined pits *Figs. 2, 24* into which material removed from the tomb was thrown, and we shall consider these in the next chapter. But most of the chambers were more nearly square and, originally at least, were not intended as storage space for bones and other material cleared from the tomb. In general these outer chambers do not show the uniformity of the antechambers, but there are a group of seven or eight tombs all of which have outer chambers built to a similar design. The tholoi where one of these suites of chambers have survived intact until the present day—Apesokari I (fig. 28) and II, *Fig. 28* Agios Kyrillos (pl. 9) and Kamilari (fig. 21)—are all late tombs, *Pl. 9, Fig. 21* and a fifth example probably existed at Viannos,[16] another late tomb. It is tempting to think of this as a late feature of the Mesara tomb tradition, but a sixth suite of this type almost certainly existed at Platanos B, a seventh probably outside Platanos Γ14 (fig. 2), and possibly an eighth outside the southern tomb at Siva *Fig. 2* (fig. 32). All of these belong amongst the early group of tombs, *Fig. 32* although the possibility must remain that the suites of outer chambers were added to these tombs at a late date.

These suites comprise a small antechamber, a larger outer chamber, and a narrow corridor-like room running along the side of both rooms. In some cases—Apesokari I and Agios Kyrillos

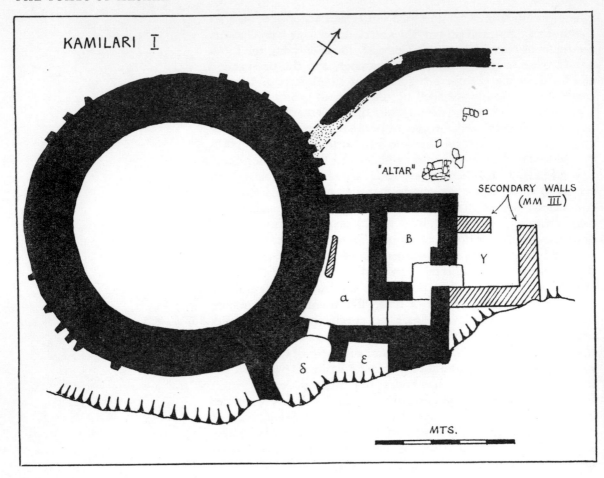

Fig. 21   The large tholos at Kamilari (Kamilari 1)

for example—a fourth, medium-sized room is added to the east of the largest room. At Kamilari, Levi was able to establish that the fourth room was an addition to an original three-roomed suite.[18] In addition to these tombs with a standardised suite of outer chambers, there are several others with outer chambers which were built to no uniform plan. Lebena II for example has four rooms, including an antechamber, built in an L-shaped arrangement (fig. 22), while Agia Triadha A has a curious complex of small chambers and corridors which basically comprises a central corridor with three chambers either side of it and an antechamber at its far end (fig. 23).

Fig. 22

Fig. 23

96

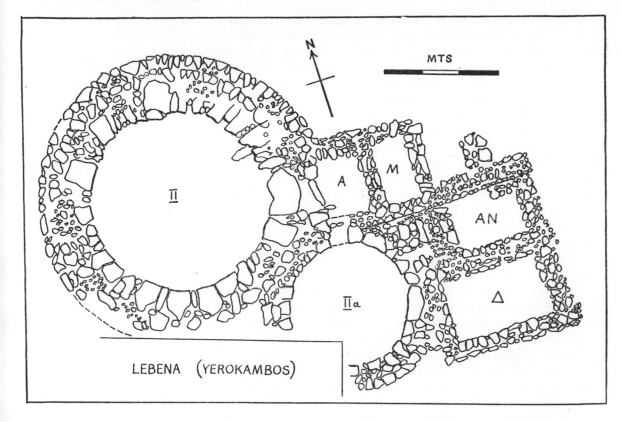

N

MTS

II

A M

AN

IIa

Δ

LEBENA (YEROKAMBOS)

The purpose of the outer chambers, like that of the ante-chambers, is often obscured by their secondary uses as dumping space for material taken from the tomb (perhaps by looters) or as additional burial chambers when the tomb proper became full. The appearance of a group of tombs with a uniform suite of outer chambers however argues strongly in favour of a uniformity of purpose, and probably of ritual. Unlike the ante-chambers, the outer rooms do not seem to have been "sunk", so that they may not have been considered to have so intimate a connection with the tomb chamber itself as did the antechambers. Furthermore there may be some significance in the fact that at least six of the eight tombs in this group were fronted by some sort of pavement, usually of undetermined extent, implying a relationship between the suites of outer chambers and open-air ceremonies of some kind.

Fig. 22 The "twin" tholoi at Lebena, Yerokambos (Lebena II and IIa)

The finds from the outer chambers are in several cases significant and helpful in understanding the purpose of the rooms. At Apesokari ii, the antechamber contained two stone vases but hundreds of clay cups, while the larger, outer room contained a small number of stone and clay vases but also the bronze and steatite double-axes.[19] The outer rooms at Agios Kyrillos produced several stone and clay cups, a bull rhyton and the clay statuette of a Minoan male.[20] In the two chambers immediately outside Vorou A (Δ1 and Δ2) were found only jugs and conical cups, and a single "bell" idol. These rooms had apparently been deliberately kept clear of burials since the three rooms beyond them were all filled with burials and debris from the tomb.[21] This was true of most of the rooms outside Agia Triadha A, but room L contained a mass of conical cups (pl. 12).[22] We do not yet have enough information about the contents of the rooms outside Lebena ii, but we know that one of them, AN, contained many conical cups and a number of jugs.

Pl. 12

Among the finds mentioned above, the conical cups are by far the most prevalent, and there can be little doubt that they played an important part in the ceremonies taking place in these outer chambers. Dozens, sometimes hundreds, were found in the chambers outside Apesokari ii, Agia Triadha A, Kamilari i, Lebena ii, and Vorou A, and always they were concentrated into a single room. The room, and therefore one supposes the situation of the ritual, varied. In Apesokari i and ii it was the antechamber (which in tomb ii, we may recall, was the biggest yet discovered) and the antechamber was presumably the scene of the ritual at Agia Triadha A too, since the cups were found in room L, a magazine-like chamber opening off one side of the antechamber itself (fig. 23). The same appears to be true of Vorou A, where it was the two rooms nearest the tomb which contained the cups. At Lebena it was the third room which held the cups, and at Agios Kyrillos they were found principally in the middle room.

Fig. 23

That the ritual was considered important, probably obligatory, we cannot doubt, since not only was it so prevalent but the rooms in which it was practised were kept free of burials wherever this was possible, even when the rooms around were being pressed into service as burial chambers. I have already mentioned that this was so at Vorou, but it is true also of Agia Triadha A, Lebena ii, Agios Kyrillos and Apesokari ii.[23] At the latter there were in fact three burials in the antechamber, but their relatively un-

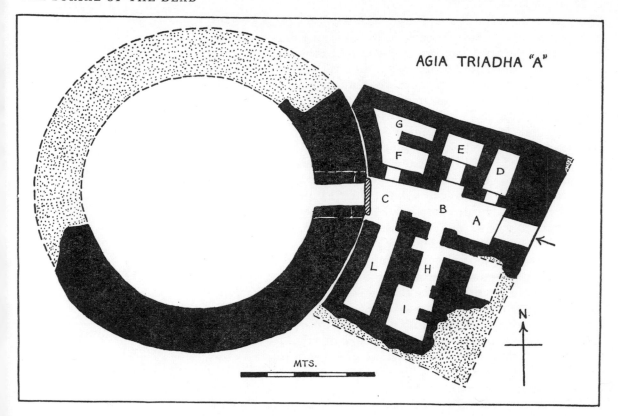

AGIA TRIADHA "A"

MTS.

N

disturbed state suggests that they were put there towards the close of the tomb's life, and they contrast markedly with the heap of bones found in the large room beyond the antechamber. One wonders what happened at those tombs where no large ante-chamber or suite of outer chambers existed. It seems likely that the ritual was sometimes performed in the open air. At Vorou, where the chambers are a late addition (to a late tomb), groups of conical cups and a few jugs were found outside both tombs.[24] But there is one other obvious explanation to be considered, namely that the rituals took place inside the tomb.

I suggest that the nature of the ritual performed in the outer chambers was identical to that which we discussed earlier and which took place inside the tomb—that is, some sort of "toast-ing". The difference between the situation of the ritual is probably to be explained on a chronological basis. We have already noted

Fig. 23 The large tholos (A), and its antechambers at Agia Triadha

that most of the outer suites belong with tombs of the late group, and in the case of Agia Triadha A, which is an earlier tomb, the contents of the antechambers belong almost exclusively to Early Minoan III and Middle Minoan I. In other words, we may reasonably suggest that during Early Minoan III the situation of the "toasting" ritual was gradually removed to the chambers outside the tomb. This hypothesis gains plausibility when we bear in mind the other changes in burial tradition and tomb architecture which took place during Early Minoan III in the Mesara. Indeed one other change in this particular ritual may be noted, and that is the switch from ordinary drinking cups and goblets to small, conical cups with very little capacity, apparently mass-produced for ritual purposes. Most of the conical cups, if not all, appear to date to Middle Minoan I (and later), so that one can suggest that the change in both the situation of the ritual and the vessels used in it took place then, rather than in Early Minoan III. There is an alternative hypothesis however. In the previous chapter I drew attention to the marked correlation on several sites between large numbers of stone vases and small numbers of clay cups, and vice-versa, suggesting that the "birds-nest" bowls and shallow stone cups were fulfilling the same function as the conical clay cups. If that were so, then the use of stone or clay cups may represent variations in local fashion or it might represent a chronological difference. On the whole the latter is more plausible, as long as one allows the possibility of considerable overlap in the use of the two types of "cup", since in several tombs clay and stone cups have been found alongside one another.

We get a slightly clearer impression of the "toasting" ritual from the outer chambers than we do from the tombs proper, simply because there is so much less disturbance of the remains. Two points seem reasonably clear. The number of people participating in the actual drinking of the "toast" was small. Both inside and outside the chambers at Vorou, Marinatos consistently found that conical cups were grouped in twos and threes.[25] Secondly, when the "toasts" had been drunk, the cups were placed on the ground in a uniform position. This varied from cemetery to cemetery, but on any cemetery site seems to have been consistent. Thus at Vorou, Kamilari, and Agios Kyrillos cups were always placed in the inverted position (where they were found undisturbed) and at Agia Triadha, in room L, all the cups were placed mouth upwards (pl. 12).[26]

Pl. 12

We have still not really discovered the purpose of the outer chambers, for the "toasting" ritual could be practised in a reasonably large antechamber, as appears to have been the case at Apesokari II, Agia Triadha and perhaps Vorou. If the antechamber was the scene of "toasting" in Apesokari II for example, why had the tomb's builders bothered to build a suite of rooms here? It seems that there must have been some other ritual performed at the time of burial, which we might guess involved rather more people than did "toasting", to judge by the large room which regularly lay in front of the antechamber in these suites. We might postulate too that among those who attended the rites in the outer, large room were those who were not so intimately involved in the burial as those who moved into the antechamber and finally into the tomb with the body. If we are right in assuming that the antechamber was considered a part of the tomb proper, whereas the other, outer chambers were not, then those who entered the antechamber for a short time entered the domain of the dead. Their involvement in the burial must therefore have been considered to be spiritually as well as physically greater than that of those who remained in the outer chamber.

There are few clues as to the sort of ritual practised in the outer chambers. The best is probably the altar found in the centre of the largest chamber in Apesokari I (fig. 28). If this altar was used during funerary proceedings (and we will discuss in the next chapter the possibility that it was used in post-funerary ritual) then it was presumably used either for the deposition of votives and sacrifices, or else for the pouring of libations. Evidence favouring the former suggestion is the discovery of the votive double-axes in the large chamber at Apesokari II, while the pouring of libations in the middle chamber at Agios Kyrillos is suggested by the discovery of a bull vessel in the corner of the room.[27] Both rites could have been performed of course.

Further evidence that libations, in addition to "toasting", accompanied burials is suggested by discoveries made in and around those tombs which did not possess outer chambers. Early Minoan I and II zoomorphic and anthropomorphic vessels have been found inside the tombs at Lebena, Koumasa and Porti,[28] so that we might add these to the evidence in support of our hypothesis that in the earlier part of the Early Bronze Age rituals were performed inside the tomb. Furthermore, if this were so, then it is most probable that the libations poured were of a funerary

Fig. 28

nature rather than a post-funerary one. That the funerary rituals were later switched to outside the tomb, as we have suggested for the toasting and the pouring of libations, is perhaps confirmed by the situation at Koumasa. I have just mentioned that Early Minoan II libation vessels were found here, three or four of them in tomb B. Immediately outside tomb B were found three more such vessels (fig. 27), but all of these were decorated in the white-on-black style of Early Minoan III and Middle Minoan I.[29] The types of libationary vessel involved—bird vessels, bull jugs, and woman vases—remain identical in Early Minoan III and Middle Minoan I to what they were in Early Minoan II. Thus it seems reasonable to suggest that the libations were poured for the same purpose and in the same ritual; only the situation of the ritual changed. If this was so, then we may reiterate that the libations were probably funerary rather than post-funerary.

Fig. 27

We are now able to summarise what we have learned about the burial of the dead in the Mesara tombs. Burial it seems, was not a particularly elaborate affair. The body was placed in the ante-chamber perhaps weeks or even months before the funeral took place. At the funeral would be, perhaps, only two or three chief mourners and a larger, but still small, group of close relatives. The chief mourners entered the tomb with the body, which had to be dragged through the smaller doorway of the tomb—perhaps by two men specifically appointed to the task. Inside the tomb, by the light of lamps or torches, the body was laid to rest, head to the east, accompanied by the most personal possessions of the dead man or woman. The mourners poured and drank a "toast", and perhaps ate a token meal, leaving the jug, cups and bowl with the body. Before or after the deposition of the body, libations were poured from a ritual vessel in the shape of an animal, a woman, or a bird. These short and simple rituals were originally practised in the tomb itself, but later were more commonly performed outside the tomb chamber, either in the antechamber or in the large outer chamber. Where the ante-chamber was too small and no outer chambers existed, the rituals were practised in the open air immediately before the antechamber. Several of the tombs built towards the end of the Early Bronze Age had a special suite of rooms erected before the entrance to the tomb, presumably to be the situation of these rituals.

This is of course a conjectural picture, based on archaeological evidence, and a relatively small amount of it at that. We can have no knowledge at all of any rituals which were performed entirely without the aid of inorganic artifacts, and only an impression of those that were performed with them. Nevertheless the picture I have painted is not at variance with the overall impression which emerges from the tomb assemblages of the Mesara. The great mass of grave-goods are personal belongings, and it is only a minority that were specially manufactured for use in the tomb. The most prolific of these, the stone "vases", were probably used in a very simple rite, which for want of a better word we may call "toasting". Simplicity of ritual, however, need not imply a simplicity of concept on behalf of the tombs' users. I have not attempted to discuss the meaning of the "toasts" and libations, nor that of the deposition of the deceased's personal belongings. Neither have I examined the question of post-funerary rites. These are all topics which are part of the larger topic with which the next chapter is concerned, namely the attitude to death and the dead.

Chapter Six

DEATH AND THE DEAD

We have seen in the previous chapter that the people of the Mesara buried their dead with ritual which was both simple and traditional; basically it varied little from tomb to tomb and burial to burial, as far as we are able to tell. There may have been changes which evolved over a period of time, but these were apparently in the location, rather than in the nature and form, of the ritual. The strength of both the ritual and other traditions associated with the circular tombs is such as to suggest that these traditions were founded on an established concept of death and on a consistent attitude to the dead.

Most of the evidence which we discussed in the previous chapter suggested that the dead were respected and that efforts were made to ensure their protection and well-being in some sort of existence beyond death. Care was exercised in the orientation of the body, and the dead man or woman was buried with all of his or her personal belongings which might be needed or missed in the next world. The mourners apparently partook of wine and perhaps food, the remaining portions of which may well have been left with the deceased. In addition libations were poured, presumably to seek protection or a blessing from a deity or spirit thought to be responsible for the dead. All of this would seem to imply belief in some sort of physical after-life, and we are justified therefore in considering other evidence which may confirm this.

One point which might be significant in this respect is the orientation of tombs and bodies east-west. We mentioned in the previous chapter the evidence for the bodies being laid with the head to the east, but we have not previously discussed the orientation of the entrance to the tomb. It has been usual for writers discussing the tombs to state simply that the entrance was to the east. This orientation of the entrance, together with that of the bodies, to the east is at once suggestive of a connection with the rising sun.[1] In a funerary context it may clearly be related to a belief in the revival of the body after death. However, if the orientation of the body and the tomb entrance were both considered to be essential for this revival, we should expect the eastern orientation to be universal for bodies and entrances. The evidence for the orientation of the bodies is relatively scant, but at present we know of no undisturbed skeletons which were found differently oriented. On the other hand, contrary to popular supposition, there are several tholoi in the Mesara which do not have their doorways aligned to the east. At least five tombs have their doorway on the south-east, of which Vorou B and Drakones Δ are late tombs, and Lebena 1b, Trypiti, and Marathokephalon 11 are early ones. The tomb at Myrsini has its entrance on the north-east. The greatest deviations from the norm are in Lebena 11a, Korakies N, Kaloi Limenes 11, and Kephali. The doorway to Lebena 11a is on the north, and although this is presumably so that the tomb can use the same antechamber as tomb 11 (to which it is, uniquely, attached) the fact that such a concession to convenience could be made suggests that tradition rather than religious necessity demanded that the entrance be on the east. The south facing entrances of Kephali, Kaloi Limenes 11 and Korakies N, and the other deviating entrances mentioned, point to the same conclusion. Thus, the eastern orientation of *most* of the tomb entrances is significant in respect of the strength of the Mesara funerary tradition, but not, I believe, in relation to any belief in a physical after-life.

One point which must be significant in this respect, however, is the concept which lay behind the structure of the tomb itself. Evans was convinced that the origin of the circular tombs lay in circular dwelling huts, and Xanthoudides followed this thought to its logical conclusion and claimed that the tombs were houses for the dead. Pendlebury's similar claim for the rectangular tombs in the east of the island is more reasonable since plenty of rectangular houses are known in Neolithic and Early Bronze Age Crete.[2] But no circular houses of this period have been discovered in Crete, and only the Lebena hut-lamp suggests that they *might* have existed.[3] On the other hand, the circular tombs might well represent caves, but whether those used for habitation or those

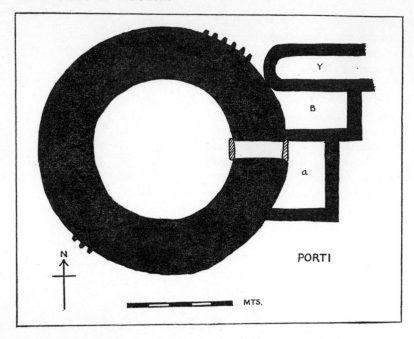

Fig. 24   Porti, tholos II

used for burial is uncertain. We must return to the vexed question
of the origin of the Mesara tombs in the last chapter, but for the
moment we may suggest that there is no sound evidence that they
were imitations of circular houses. That they were regarded as
either artificial burial or artificial habitation caves is quite possible.
The form of the tomb therefore contributes little to our understanding of the concept behind it.

One architectural feature of tombs Platanos A and Porti II
which does perhaps reflect the concept behind their construction
is the group of long, narrow rooms to one side of the antechamber. At Porti there are just two of these "rooms" or walled
trenches (fig. 24), but at Platanos A there were at least nine and   *Fig. 24*
perhaps twice as many originally (fig. 2). These rooms at once   *Fig. 2*
recall the rectangular ossuaries being used elsewhere in Crete
during the Early Bronze Age. Well known examples from
Palaikastro, Mochlos and Arkhanes have their interiors divided
into a series of long, narrow rooms like those seen at Porti and
Platanos. The group as a whole are reminiscent of the magazines
of the palaces, which excavations at Fournou Korifi have now
shown to have Early Bronze Age predecessors.[4] The contents of

the chambers at Porti and Platanos are such as to suggest that they were constructed like magazines because they were intended to fulfil a similar function—in this case the storage of the bones of the dead which had been removed from the tomb proper. Room γ at Porti for example was found to be "filled to the brim" with bones, amongst which were a few clay vessels. Artifacts were more numerous in the rooms outside Platanos A, but apart from room a, which may have served as a depository for stone toasting cups (like the very similar room L at Agia Triadha A), the rooms were all full of skeletal remains.[5] It is significant I think that at Porti no metal artifacts at all were found in the two magazine rooms, and at Platanos only one was found in the storage chambers compared to about seventy inside the tomb.[6] Objects of gold and bronze would have been the most attractive plunder for those engaged in cleaning out the earlier tomb deposits, and their complete absence from these magazine-like rooms is, I think, suggestive that the contents of these rooms were skeletal remains deliberately cleared from inside the adjacent tomb.

There is evidence from several other sites which points very clearly indeed to the conclusion that both the clearing and looting of tombs were a regular and accepted feature of life in the Mesara during the Early Bronze Age. In some tombs, where the total number of burials was not too great, it may have been thought sufficient simply to sweep earlier remains to the side of the chamber, leaving a clear floor space in the centre on which new burials could be laid (pl. 10). Clearing operations of this sort have been noted at Kamilari and Koumasa E.[7] At Kamilari and Koumasa E however, there is reason to think that the clearing operations may have been directly related to looting activities.[8] The large-scale removal of skeletal remains from inside the tombs can be detected at several sites. In Platanos A for example, two distinct levels were found in the burial deposit, the lower of which contained only small fragments of bone and a few broken artifacts.[9] It seems entirely reasonable to suggest that the mass of bones found in the store-rooms outside this tomb came originally from this lower level. Tomb Γ at Platanos also contained very few artifacts and bones, but it was surrounded by several walled trenches and small rectangular buildings in which masses of bones and smaller quantities of artifacts were found.[10] Concentrations of skulls in Platanos B, Koumasa B, and Agia Triadha A seem to represent the systematic retention and collection of

Pl. 10

crania which had become separated from their disturbed, and eventually removed, skeletons.[11] In the previous chapter we mentioned the dumps of skeletal material found in the outer chambers of some of the tombs—Apesokari II, Agios Kyrillos, and Agia Triadha A for example. The evidence from these and other tombs points unequivocally to the deliberate clearance of earlier burials to make way for new ones.

In a number of cases tomb clearance was preceded, followed, or replaced, by fumigation. We have mentioned in previous chapters the evidence which suggests that in some cases the burning found in the tombs resulted from the accidental firing of a timber covering (Kamilari) or from the use of torches or small fires to burn incense (Lebena II). There are several other tombs however where the burning is far too extensive to be explained in terms of torches or incense hearths, and where there is no suggestion from the charred remains that timber roofing was involved. Furthermore, as we shall see, in some cases the evidence of fumigation *inside* the tomb can be related to other evidence for it found outside the tomb. Xanthoudides believed that some of the extensive areas of burning he found in the tombs were evidence for the consumption of funerary feasts, and Alexiou's observations in the funerary cave at Kanli Kastelli pointed to a similar conclusion for a contemporary tomb in the north of the island.[12] We have already seen however that in the Mesara tombs there is no evidence at all for funerary feasts, except perhaps for token ones, and that the burial rituals were on the contrary kept simple. That we are dealing with examples of fumigation rather than traces of funerary ritual is confirmed by the irregularity with which the evidence appears. Several tombs—Marathokephalon II, Christos, Kalathiana—revealed no trace of fire within them, and the same is true of Agia Eirene E and Platanos B, tombs which stand next to others which have produced evidence of internal fire.[13] In other words, it seems clear that the use of fire inside the tombs was adopted when it was considered necessary and not as part of an established funerary ritual.

The clearest examples of fumigation were the deposits found in Platanos A and Lebena IIa. At Platanos, the existing burial stratum was almost entirely removed from the tomb and a fumigatory fire was then lit, charring the few remaining bones and artifacts and heavily marking the floor.[14] New burials, dating from Early Minoan III onwards, were made above the fumigated stratum. In Lebena IIa there appears to have been no clearance of the tomb before fumigation, and after it the charred remains were covered by a clean layer of white sand and the tomb re-used.[15] Platanos Γ may have been subjected to at least two clearing operations, one of which involved fumigation. The oblong trenches and rooms built near this tomb to take displaced funerary remains included two walled trenches (like those at Porti) containing unburnt bones and a few cups.[16] Tomb Γ however had clearly been fumigated at some time in its history, and the clearance which followed this event is probably to be connected with the charred bones and artifacts found in a small group of rectangular huts labelled γ by Xanthoudides.[17] Other tombs where evidence of fumigation was noted include Agia Eirene e, Koumasa B, Drakones $\varDelta$, Porti, Megali Skinoi, and perhaps Siva N.[18]

Already our *interpretation* of the grave-goods and burial rituals as evidence for a belief in a physical after-life are found to be in contradiction to the *facts* about burials in the tombs. Disturbance, clearance and fumigation of skeletal remains such as we have discussed above, all imply that there was no concern for the physical body of the dead, once it had decomposed and become a skeleton. Despite the grave-goods and rituals, this is hardly surprising, since each and every opening of a communal tomb like those of the Mesara must have impressed upon those involved in the funeral the frailty and impermanence of the human body. The practice of fumigation and clearance implies that the people of the Mesara recognised that the body decays, and were prepared to give recent corpses priority of space over the skeletal remains of those long-since decomposed.

Looting, on the other hand, implies not merely lack of concern for the physical remains of the dead, but lack of respect for the dead, their personal belongings, and the sanctity of the tomb. There is no doubt, however, that looting of grave-goods was practised by some of the inhabitants of the Mesara during the Early Bronze Age. Xanthoudides emphasised the notable scarcity of grave-goods in the lower and earlier deposits at Marathokephalon II, Koumasa B, and Platanos A; yet we know from unplundered tombs like Lebena II that the early deposits in the circular tombs were at least as rich as, probably richer than, the late ones.[19] In Platanos A the clearance and fumigation of the existing remains at the end of Early Minoan II was accompanied by a systematic looting of the grave-goods. They did not reach the magazines outside, in which the masses of bones were found, and were presumably stolen by those engaged in the clearance work. In the lower level there remained a single gold pendant and two beads, and fourteen copper daggers—all of which were far too badly twisted, rotted and broken to be of any use. In Koumasa B the earlier burials were swept to one side to make room for new interments, and here too the opportunity had been taken to remove anything of value from the burial deposit. In contrast the later burials were found mixed with numerous grave goods. Levi noticed an identical situation in Kamilari 1, and a similar course of action had been undertaken at Koumasa E, except that having cleared and looted the existing burials, the people using this tomb appear to have abandoned it.[20]

We must thus envisage a situation where people were burying their dead with personal belongings, often including valuable weapons, tools or jewellery, which they knew would be stolen at a later date. Indeed, at the very time that they were burying their dead, they themselves might be taking earlier grave-goods from the tomb. Why then did they bother to deposit grave-goods at all, particularly when it is clear that they did not believe in a physical after-life for the body? There are two likely solutions to this problem, either or both of which may be correct. The personal nature of the grave-goods suggests that they may have been deposited because they were thought to be close to the spirit or personality of the dead. Their retention in the house of the living would be to deprive the deceased's spirit of a visible (and lasting) expression of personality, and it might also invite the return of the deceased's spirit to the house of the living in search of this lost part of its personality.[21] Alternatively the personal belongings of the dead may have been deposited alongside the body in order to placate the dead while the physical body survived. Once the body had decomposed, and certainly once its skeleton had been disturbed and been partially dispersed or broken, it may have been deemed safe to remove grave-goods. Fortunately, metal objects, which were probably the most desirable of the grave-goods, could also be melted down and given a completely new identity. Whichever of the two solutions suggested is considered the more probable, and the solutions could be complementary to one another, we have moved a step forward in our understanding of the Minoan attitude to death and the dead. The first solution implies a belief in a spirit existence, and the second a belief in some sort of temporary after-life for the corpse.

Evidence that something of this sort was envisaged by the people of the Mesara is I think provided not only by the subsequent removal of grave-goods but also by one or two peculiar features of the burials in Vorou A, and by the doors and doorways of the tombs as a whole. Marinatos noted and recorded several examples of larnakes and pithoi stacked on top of each other in Vorou A. This need not be significant in itself, but in some cases the covering pithos or larnax was completely empty and had apparently been placed in position in this condition.[22] Whether these empty covering vessels were completely unused or whether they had been cleaned and emptied and re-used in this way we cannot say, but it does appear that they were intended to act as heavy lids or covers for the burial containers beneath them. Other larnakes and pithoi had heavy clay lids to cover them. It appears that by Middle Minoan I at least, it was considered important to securely cover a coffin or jar containing a burial. This could have been for the protection of the corpse, but one other detail noted by Marinatos suggests that it may rather have been for the protection of the living. In many of the pithoi, he found large stones and in at least one case it was certain that the stone had been placed in the jar at the time of burial, as the jar itself was still covered.[23] I agree with Marinatos that such stones were probably placed on the head of the corpse in order to weigh it down—if only symbolically. That is to say, the dead were regarded with a certain amount of fear and hostility as long as they possessed an articulated body.

There is no evidence for similar measures against the newly dead during Early Minoan I–III, but this need not mean that measures were not taken. For example, if the bodies had been bound with ropes no evidence at all would remain to us in the confused mass of bones in the tomb. However two measures designed to confine the dead within the tomb can, I think, be identified. One of these is the use of a huge stone slab as a door. About a dozen tombs have been found with these slabs *in situ,* the most impressive being that at Kamilari I where a carefully worked slab, 1.3 × 1.1 × 0.14 metres, blocked the entrance (pl. 7). I am convinced that these huge slabs were intended to keep the dead in rather than the living out. We have already seen that looting was a recognised and accepted part of funerary

Pl. 7

tradition in the Mesara, so that there would be no reason to block the entrance to keep out plunderers. Equally if a doorway was needed for the sake of "completeness", then a wooden one could have been used with much greater ease than the cumbersome stone slabs which were utilised. The size and weight of the slabs, and their position at the entrance to the tomb itself rather than the antechamber, suggest that they were intended to keep the newly dead inside the tomb. The use of both inner and outer door slabs in Porti II was presumably considered an extra precaution.

In contrast to the size of the door slabs, the doorways themselves, we may recall, are ridiculously small. Only two tombs have doorways which exceed a metre in width, and several have doors less than 0.75 metres wide.[24] Equally, only four tombs have doorways as much as a metre and a half high,[25] and the majority of doorways are less than a metre in height! These minute entrances are even more difficult to explain than the great door slabs which blocked them. They solved no structural problems, but presented a great many physical ones when it came to make a burial. Their only purpose could have been to discourage and prevent the dead from leaving the tomb. This I think was the main purpose too of placing the personal belongings of the deceased in the tomb with him. The intention was not merely to placate the dead, but to give him no excuse or reason to return to the house from which he had been brought. If we are right in these interpretations of the evidence, then we must assume a belief in a period after death when the spirit still inhabited the body and the body was in some way mobile. The restrictive measures we have discussed would have been of little use against a disembodied spirit.

This brings us to the particularly difficult question of the Minoan attitude to a spirit existence after death. We have already discussed the possibility that the personal possessions deposited in the tombs included some items which were not merely possessions but which in varying ways were regarded as palpable expressions and extensions of the man's personality or identity. Thus his sealstone was an integral part of his identity, and so too were the tools with which he had worked. Objects like these may well have been regarded as essential parts of the tomb assemblage, providing a link between the physical and the spiritual world; while the spirit remained in the body it would feel the need for these things. Once the body had decomposed and the physical home of the spirit was gone, then presumably these physical expressions of the personality would no longer be required or invested by the spirit.

Apart from these manifestations of the spirit or personality, there is a little evidence to suggest that the Minoans may have regarded the skull as intimately connected with personality and identity. This seems to have been a common attitude among prehistoric peoples and an entirely comprehensible one.[26] In the Mesara tombs it may be represented by the heap of skulls found in Koumasa B, the concentrations of skulls in Platanos B and Agia Triadha A, room G, and by at least two otherwise complete skeletons at Vorou which had had their skulls removed.[27] Inside the tomb chamber of Agia Triadha A it was also noted that dozens of skulls were found on the original rock floor of the tomb, often in groups of between three and six crania, with little or no associated skeletal material.[28] Agia Triadha A is one of the tombs where there is clear evidence for the removal of remains to some of the outside chambers, and the most reasonable explanation of these groups of skulls on the original floor of the tomb, is that they were deliberately left as they lay when the skeletal remains that went with them were cleared out. If this were the case, then it would certainly imply that a particular significance was thought to attach to the human skull.

The skulls and the highly personal grave-goods are not, of course, sufficient evidence to claim confidently that the people of the Mesara believed in a spirit existence after death. The sort of evidence we need to make such a claim is that which points as unequivocally as possible to the existence of post-funerary rituals performed in or by the tombs. There would seem to be several pieces of evidence which point to the practice of such rituals. The frequent construction of outer chambers which appear to have been designed and originally used as the location of ritual is suggestive of post-funerary rites. We must bear in mind the evidence we discussed in the previous chapter which indicated that two rites which were probably practised in these outer chambers—toasting and the pouring of libations—were essentially funerary rituals performed at the time of burial. This does not mean that the outer chambers could not also have been used for post-funerary ritual, but it is difficult to point to any evidence which suggests that they were. Some of the finds made in the outer chambers are suggestive of the deposition of votive offerings (to the deity of the dead?). At Vorou for example, room Δ2 produced a "bell idol", an artifact not usually found in a funerary context. In fact a group of about eighteen such idols were found under the wall thickening on the outside of this tomb, so placed as to suggest that they were a "foundation deposit".[29] One other notable find in Vorou A, room Δ2, was a "snake pithos"—a jar with four vertical handles each comprised of three loops. It recalls the snake tubes from the well known Late Minoan shrine at Gournia, and from the peak sanctuary at Koumasa, which was its contemporary and not many kilometres distant from Vorou across the plain of Mesara.[30] Like the "bell idol", the snake vessels are normally associated with household or peak shrines and their appearance in the outer chamber of a circular tomb must thus be regarded as significant.[31] In this particular case this is emphasised by the vessel's association with a very clear example of ritual breakage. Inside the "snake pithos" was a similar but smaller pithos, which had had to be broken to get it into the larger one. Ritual breakage is rare in Early and Middle Minoan Crete, and I know of no examples from this period which are associated with funerary ritual, unless the half double-axe from Kamilari II was ritually broken.[32]

Both the snake vessels and the "bell idols" are found in the Household Shrines of the Neopalatial period, and it may therefore be significant that other artifacts associated with these shrines also occur in the outer chambers of the circular tombs, or immediately outside them. The large chamber at Apesokari II for example, contained a small steatite double-axe and others of bronze. This is a remarkable parallel to the "Shrine of the Double-Axes" at Knossos, where a small double-axe of steatite was found leaning against one of a pair of sacred horns.[33] The hole in the centre of each pair of horns was almost certainly to take the shaft of a bronze or gold double-axe which had been removed from the shrine, one supposes. Sheet-bronze axes of the type used in this way were found outside Platanos A (fig. 25), one of them immedi- *Fig. 25* ately outside the destroyed doorway and antechamber.[34] Another common feature of the Household Shrines, the circular, tripod table, is represented in the Mesara tombs by a single example, found just outside Porti Π, which had an antechamber but no outer rooms. Just two metres beyond the entrance to this tomb, Xanthoudides also found a superb votive clay agrimi.[35] This

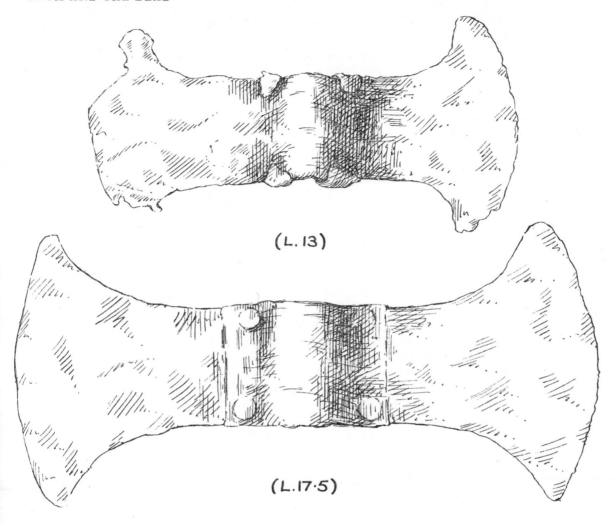

(L. 13)

(L.17·5)

object, the agrimi jug from Kamilari, room γ, and the two votive agrimi horns found inside Platanos A, are again unusual finds in a Minoan cemetery.[36] Models of the agrimi and his horns are normally found in sanctuaries, and more particularly peak sanctuaries. Finally we may mention the horns of consecration, a regular part of the Household Shrine assemblage. No individual examples of the horns of consecration have yet been found in a circular tomb, although several bull vessels have, as we noted in

Fig. 25 Two ceremonial double-axes found outside tholos A at Platanos

the previous chapter. However, in the outer chambers at Kamilari, Levi discovered a group of clay models, at least two of which have a series of sacred horns adorning their perimeter (pl. 14).   *Pl. 14*

These models are central to any discussion of the concept of death as it was held by the builders and users of the Mesara tombs, for Levi has offered an interpretation of them based on the belief that they witness to a cult of the dead.[37] In view of the evidence we have already discussed, which points overwhelmingly to the conclusion that the tomb users did not believe in a physical after-life, Levi's interpretation, if accepted, would presumably imply post-funerary ritual associated with the concept of a spiritual after-life. Apart from a number of fragmentary clay figures and models, there were three in good or fair condition which Levi discussed in detail. The least well preserved of these was on a circular base, around the perimeter of which there remained two crudely modelled horns of consecration. Part of the perimeter was taken up with a modelled doorway in which stood a human figure. The centre of the model featured a low table, at which stood another human figure, back to the door. Across the table from this figure was a third person, in this case seated at the edge of the table. Levi's interpretation of this scene as a domestic one with religious undertones may well be correct. He believes that in the context of the tomb the model represents preparations for funerary ritual, but even if this is correct there is no way of determining whether the ritual was performed during or after burial. As evidence for the preparation of a token funerary feast, the model has interesting possibilities, but as evidence for post-funerary ritual it is of little value. The same may be said of the second model, also sporting sacred horns around its perimeter, which shows four people dancing in a circle (pl. 14). This is a   *Pl. 14* most important model to find in a tomb and we shall discuss it more fully in the next chapter, but it has little to offer as evidence for a cult of the dead and post-funerary ritual.

The third and most complex model cannot be so lightly dismissed from our discussion. The basis of the model is a rectangular structure which has one solid wall (in which there are three "windows") and three open sides. Originally there was a roof of some sort supported at the rear on the top of the solid wall and at the front on a pillar at either corner. Against the solid wall are seated four figures in human form, so arranged as to form two pairs. Their arms are stretched on to their knees and in front of each of them is a cylindrical stool or table. On two of these "tables", and possibly on all four originally, there is a small disc of clay, possibly representing a cup or bowl. Facing each pair of seated figures is a standing figure with a jug in his hands. These figures are notably smaller than the seated ones (pl. 15). *Pl. 15*

Levi argues that this model represents the central part of a larger shrine, and that the two standing figures are pouring libations to a chthonic deity or the deified dead. He is convinced that in either case the model is a manifestation of a cult of the dead and he argues that the disturbance of the skeletal remains in the tombs need not preclude the existence of such a cult. However we have seen that it is not merely a question of *disturbance* but of the complete removal of remains, often of their destruction, and frequently of the looting of the personal belongings buried with them. These are unlikely to be the actions of a society who hold to the concept of a physical after-life. If we are to follow Levi at all, then it seems we must either accept his alternative interpretation of the seated figures—as chthonic deities who were perhaps responsible for the dead—or else identify the seated figures as convenient visual symbols of the spirits of the dead.

Neither interpretation is entirely satisfactory since neither provides a convincing explanation for the appearance of two pairs of seated figures. If these represent deities, then we must presumably envisage a funerary religion elaborate enough to involve and require four deities; if they represent the spirits of the dead, then why should the spirits of two couples be represented on this model? The dual nature of the scene which is modelled must surely be significant in some way and it is far easier to think of situations in life which would suit this duality than situations in a funerary ritual or a cult of the dead. A marriage is probably the most obvious suggestion one can make but there are others which may be offered—a contest between the champions of two villages or two clans, a political or religious ceremony involving two communities or clans—which at least give some meaning to the duality of the model. As for the structure in which the scene is set, it has every appearance of a temporary, outdoor building, such as might be erected for ceremonies of the kind just mentioned. The greater size of the seated figures must surely reflect their status, but whether it represents religious, political or social status (i.e. that they are deities, priests, chieftains or elders) we cannot say. There is presumably some significance in the fact that one pair of seated figures is notably larger than the other. It is impossible to be conclusive about this model, but bearing all considerations in mind, I think it is more likely to represent a ceremony performed in life rather than in the rites of a cult of the dead.

One important question which this model raises is the identification of the Minoan deities which were particularly concerned with death and the dead. If the seated figures on Levi's model are deities, they carry no emblems or attributes by which we may identify them. Some of the artifacts found in and around the tombs however can be confidently identified as either images or attributes of a deity. If we are right in assuming that the zoomorphic and anthropomorphic vessels were used for pouring libations, then the form which they take may be representative of the deity to whom the libations were made. In the chapter describing the grave-goods we saw that these vessels normally fall into one of three groups, representing bulls, birds or women respectively (fig. *Fig. 18* 18). All three elements may comfortably be accommodated in the cult of the Household or Snake Goddess as it exists in the period of the new palaces. The woman-vessels from Koumasa certainly seem to represent this deity, and if only for this reason it seems certain that the Snake Goddess was in some way involved in funerary rites in the Mesara tombs. The chthonic nature of the goddess would have an obvious relevance to such rites. On the other hand, we cannot be sure that the bulls and the birds were at this time elements within the cult of the Snake Goddess. I have discussed this problem at some length elsewhere, and have been unable to find any evidence to suggest that these attributes, and the double-axe, were already incorporated within the cult of the Snake Goddess.[38] At present the evidence suggests that the consolidation of the cult of the Snake Goddess took place during Middle Minoan I–II in the peak sanctuaries which were flourishing at this time. The finds in the circular tombs however enable us to take the development of the cult back one stage further, for it is in the tombs that we can first see these various elements brought into contact with one another.

If, however, it was a case of *contact* rather than of a genuine relationship with the Snake Goddess, then it remains for us to identify the cult with which the bird vessels, bull vessels and double-axes were associated. Bird epiphanies were common in classical Greece and their frequency in Homer is such as to suggest that they were a regular feature of Mycenaean religion too. There can be little doubt that the birds perched a-top the double-axes on the Agia Triadha sarcophagus (pl. 16) and those found in some of the Household Shrines are also representative of a deity or deities. Doves figure most prominently in the Household Shrines and it is tempting to identify the Early Bronze Age bird vessels as representations of this bird, but very few of them can confidently be identified as such.[39] The birds on the Agia Triadha sarcophagus, however, are not doves; they are probably ravens or similar birds. These two birds are particularly relevant to our discussion since they appear on a coffin in a scene which apparently shows a funerary or post-funerary ceremony of some kind. Here, the birds and the double-axes are so closely linked as to suggest that the former are the epiphanies, and the latter the symbols, of a deity. Two female figures riding in a chariot painted on one end of the coffin are usually identified as deities and suggest that the Minoans had a goddess other than the Snake Goddess who was particularly involved with death and the dead. The bird-vases and double-axes from the Mesara tombs may, I suggest, be related to libations and votive offerings made to this goddess.

The relevance of the bull to the funerary proceedings might also be suggested on the evidence provided by the Agia Triadha sarcophagus. On the same side of the coffin as the double-axes and birds two young bulls are carried towards the tomb and the deceased (who stands before it), while on the reverse a bull is seen trussed up on a table. He has been stabbed in the neck, and the blood is collected in a pottery vessel which stands on the ground. Clearly the bull played an important part in funerary proceedings, and the collection of blood from the sacrificed animal may suggest that libations were poured in the animal's blood. The bull vessels might therefore be indicative of a ritual rather than representative of a deity.

There remains the question of the "toasting" ritual. The "toast" may have been drunk as a last act of respect to the deceased, but it could have been drunk as an act of respect for the deity or deities of the dead. There is only one piece of evidence which perhaps points to the latter suggestion. In the alcove immediately outside the doorway in Apesokari 1, a teapot and five handleless cups were found. There were no burials here, but an anthropomorphic concretion which had apparently once stood

Pl. 16

on a six-sided stone slab at the rear of the alcove was found here. It has been plausibly argued that this concretion was regarded as the symbol of a deity.[40] In this case we have the situation of the toasting ritual right alongside the symbol of a god or goddess, and the cups used in the "toasting" placed in front of this symbol.

Whatever one's interpretation of this discovery, there seems to be little doubt that the Minoans of the Early Bronze Age had already adopted at least one and probably two deities who were concerned with death and the dead. One of these, the Snake Goddess, was presumably involved because of her chthonic nature. We might suggest that the apparently universal practice of completely removing all of the soil from the tomb floor and either exposing the clean rock or introducing clean gravel from a stream was adopted in deference to the Goddess. She does not seem to have been closely involved in funerary ritual however, and her widespread adoption first in peak sanctuaries and later in household shrines was no doubt more readily achieved because of this. The chief deity of the dead at present remains nameless, but recognised perhaps by her embodiment as a bird and her adoption of the double-axe as her symbol.

At present there is no conclusive evidence to show whether or not the blessings and protection of this deity were sought only at the time of burial or subsequently as well. Whichever was the case, it seems likely that protection and blessing was sought only for the *spirit* of the deceased. Our evidence suggests that the people of the Mesara did not believe in a physical hereafter, though they may have believed that until it had decomposed, the body was inhabited by the spirit and could be mobilised by it if it was offended. Their attitude to the dead was thus a strange and contradictory mixture. They took care to bury their dead in accordance with certain traditions and with fitting ritual, and yet they were completely careless in the disturbance, and even the destruction, of skeletal remains. They were fearful of the corpse and of offended spirits, and yet they frequently removed the personal belongings of the dead. Strangest of all, in spite of their fears they kept their dead close to the living, building their tombs next to their settlements. In some way which we have yet to examine, the cemeteries were important in the life of contemporary society, just as to the modern archaeologist they are important as evidence *for* that society, its origins, its distribution and its development.

Chapter Seven

THE CEMETERY AND SOCIETY

Apart from the information about ancient art, religion, warfare, and technology that we normally expect to derive from the contents of excavated tombs, it is usual for the archaeologist to learn quite a lot about the physical appearance of the people who built and used the tombs. This information is derived from the skeletal remains found in the tombs, and is particularly valuable because it is primary evidence. With most prehistoric peoples, the only evidence for their physical appearance yielded by contemporary settlements is in the form of figurines, and consequently it is difficult to interpret and particularly open to subjective interpretation. From a group of skeletal remains on the other hand, the archaeologist should be able to obtain a good idea as to the height, build and approximate weight of his subjects, and some idea as to their complexion and features. The skull is particularly important in determining these last facts, since it usually provides an indication which peoples the deceased belonged to. In addition to this information, the modern archaeologist will hope to learn the sex, age at death, and possibly the cause of death of his subject. Thus, from the many thousands of burials which were made in the fifty excavated circular tombs of the Mesara, we might expect to gain a very clear picture indeed of the people who inhabited this region in the Early Bronze Age, their physical type, their life expectation, and perhaps something about the diseases and deficiencies from which they suffered.

In fact we know remarkably little about these things, mainly because no complete skeletons have been found, preserved and studied, and even the number of skulls which have been found and studied amounts to little more than a dozen. Of these, only one (from Agia Triadha A) was found to be brachycephalic, the remainder being equally divided between meso- and dolichocephalic indices.[1] Charles, using a more sophisticated approach to the problem of racial type, has recently re-examined some of the skulls from Platanos, Porti, and Agia Eirene, in addition to two from Lebena, and places six of the nine subjects in his "neomediterranean" type.[2] Two more he classes as "Alpinomediterranean" and the remainder, with a remarkably low cranial index, falls within his "Cordé" type. If we knew the dates of each of these skulls we might be able to draw some useful conclusions even from this small sample, but none of the skulls examined can be dated at all closely. All we can say with any certainty is that by Middle Minoan I the population of the Mesara was composed of a mixture of people of the original "Mediterranean" race and those of a modified type, characterised by a mesocephalic cranial index, presumably resulting from the influx of a small number of brachycephalic "Tauric" immigrants. When this immigration took place we cannot say, but it is unlikely to have occurred after the start of the Early Bronze Age, since there is no suggestion of it in the archaeological record.

At this point one would hope that the tombs themselves, and the grave-goods found in them, would provide evidence of such an immigration. The circular tombs of the Mesara certainly represent a new and distinctive feature in the Cretan tradition and appear at the beginning of the Early Bronze Age. The earliest pottery found within them includes the painted Agios Onouphrios and Lebena wares, which mark a new era in the development of Cretan ceramics—the medium, the style, and the shapes of the wares are all new. It seems entirely reasonable to see the tombs and the pottery within them as visible and lasting expressions of an immigration into Crete at the very end of the Neolithic—an immigration which would no doubt have brought the secrets of metallurgy with it. Evans and Xanthoudides were convinced that there was an immigration into southern Crete from the African shore of the Libyan Sea.[3] Circular tombs, often with a rectangular antechamber, are widespread in North Africa, and from Egypt in particular the Mesara could have "borrowed" the techniques of corbelling, the form of the triangular dagger, the shape of the pointed base figurines, and the use of the foot amulet. But as we shall see in our discussion of the origin of the Mesara tombs, the Libyan ones are not such satisfactory parallels as Evans made them appear, nor are the Egyptian figurines, amulets, daggers, and building techniques.[4] There is also the difficulty that an immigration from the North African coast would not have introduced the "Tauric" race to Crete.

The direction from which we would expect such an immigration would be north or north-eastwards, and in recent years Hutchinson has proposed a small-scale immigration into Crete from the Cyclades, and together with Caskey and Schachermeyr has also suggested an influx of people from Anatolia in, or just before, Early Minoan 1.[5] From these northern sources one could derive not only the "Tauric" element in the population but also early Minoan metalwork, slipped and burnished fabrics (Salame and Pyrgos wares), and characteristic shapes of pottery vessels (one handled cups and jugs, chalices) as well as some of the more unusual ones (barrel vessels, "eared" lids). As for the circular tombs, one might see these as enlarged built graves of the Cycladic type, as suggested by Hutchinson. Again, however, we shall see that this is not an entirely satisfactory solution to the problem of the tombs' origins, and the hypothesis of a Cycladic or Anatolian immigration into the Mesara also leaves unexplained the appearance of Agios Onouphrios ware, the triangular dagger, and the adoption of communal burial chambers.

There remains the seemingly improbable but nevertheless attractive proposal of an immigration into southern Crete from the Levant. From the Proto-Urban culture of Palestine one could derive the inspiration for Agios Onouphrios ware, several ceramic shapes (and especially two-handled jars), and the use of communal burial chambers.[6] From the earlier Halaf culture of Syria could be traced the origins of the Cretan circular tombs, the sacred horns, the double-axe, and the sacred birds.[7] Yet here there are problems of both time and space which, if not insurmountable, cast considerable doubt on the feasibility of our hypothesis.

None of the "immigration" theories yet propounded are sufficiently embracing to provide a plausible explanation for the rise of the Early Minoan culture of the Mesara, and strangely perhaps, it still seems more likely that this culture developed without the assistance of immigrant peoples, though undoubtedly under external influences, particularly those of the Cyclades and western Anatolia.[8] That is to say, in our present state of knowledge, the Mesara tombs and the society which used them are best regarded as indigenous to Crete.

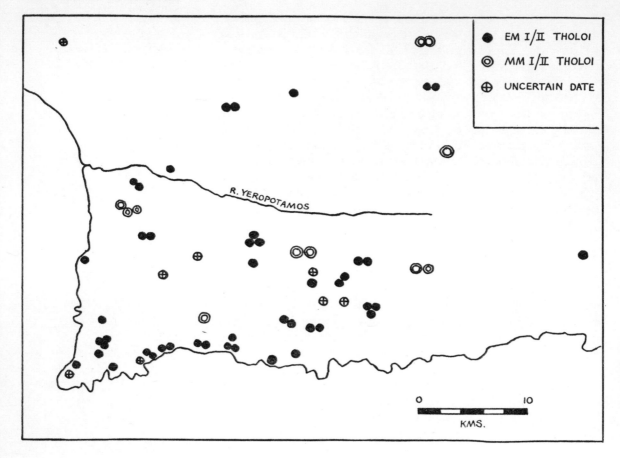

While the tombs provide disappointingly little evidence for the racial make-up and origins of the population, they do give us useful indications of the size, density, and distribution of it. Apart from some of the late tombs, to which we shall return shortly, and the earlier ones at Krasi and probably Gorgolaini, the distribution of the Early Bronze Age circular tombs is confined to the plain of Mesara and the mountains which surround it. The great majority of cemetery sites known in this region, six in every seven, are in fact found south of the Yeropotamos river and mainly in the Asterousia mountains (fig. 26). Alexiou has recently commented on this heavy concentration of early tombs in the Asterousia mountains and suggested that it provides a

Fig. 26 Distribution map of the Early (EM. I–II) and late (MM. I–II) tholos tombs of Mesara type in southern Crete

Fig. 26

powerful argument in support of the Libyan origin of the circular tomb and of the people who favoured it.[9] For reasons discussed in the following chapter, I do not believe that this is necessarily the case, but the distribution pattern of the tombs must certainly have a significance. There is no reason to think that the uneven distribution of tombs north and south of the Yeropotamos results from considerably less archaeological survey work in the northern area. Most of the tombs are in any case discovered by villagers during agricultural work, and farming activities are no less common north of the Yeropotamos than they are south of it. Equally there is no evidence to suggest that the Early Minoan occupants of this part of the region buried their dead in other forms of tomb; the only Early Bronze Age tombs discovered here are typical circular ones. It is reasonable to conclude therefore that the plain and mountains south of the Yeropotamos were much more thickly populated during the Early Bronze Age than was the region to the north of the river. There is no apparent reason why this should have been the case. There is, it is true, a geological difference between the Asterousia mountains to the south (Jurassic) and the foothills to the north (Marine upper Tertiary), but there is no reason to think that this would have made any appreciable difference to agricultural activity and animal husbandry. There are two possible explanations of the uneven distribution which spring to mind however. One is that copper sources appear to be absent north of the Yeropotamos, whereas south of it they are numerous. It may not have taken the early metallurgists long to appreciate this fact. Secondly, the foothills to the north were probably more thickly covered with forest than the Asterousia mountains and may thus have presented greater difficulties to the agriculturalist.

The density of settlement north of the Yeropotamos was, for whatever reason, not at all great. No doubt many sites remain to be found, but it seems clear that the density of sites was never as great as it was south of the river. Here, nearly forty cemetery sites have already been discovered, and the density of their distribution in some areas suggests that many more have yet to be found. At present we can perhaps get some idea of the density of settlement from two areas, one centred on Odiyitria and the other on Salame. In the former region, an area of twenty-five square kilometres contains seven certain or probable cemetery sites. The latter, in the same area, contains six such cemetery sites and three other possible ones. There is no reason to think that such concentrations are exceptional, and indeed a decade ago no tombs at all were known in the vicinity of Odiyitria. Thus there may be no significance in the relatively empty spaces near the western end of the plain, that is, close to the Gulf of Mesara. On the other hand, relatively few tombs are known in any case actually *on* the plain. The distribution of tombs suggests that the Early Bronze Age inhabitants of the Mesara were still essentially hill people who were slow to move away from the foothills and mountains and down into the plain, fertile as it may have been. We should remember that the distribution of the tombs (and the settlements they represent) for the most part reflects the situation from the start of the Early Bronze Age onwards. In other words, the distribution pattern we see on the map (fig. 26) represents the pattern established during Early Minoan I and maintained, very largely, throughout the Early Bronze Age and even into the Late Bronze Age. The expansion of population and the political developments leading to the rise of palatial society added to the pattern, mainly in or on the edge of the plain itself (Kamilari, Apesokari, Drakones and perhaps Vali), but they did not greatly change it.

Fig. 26

The continuity of the population is one of the strongest impressions which emerge from a study of the cemetery sites. It can of course be seen in the material culture, represented by the grave-goods, but the continued use of the cemetery areas throughout the Middle, and often Late, Minoan periods is particularly emphatic evidence of it. Often the continuity is represented by Middle Minoan II–III and Late Minoan burials, in larnakes or pithoi, actually placed within the Early Minoan tomb (pl. 11) as occurs at Vorou, Kamilari and Vali for example.[10] These are late tombs, and were presumably still in good repair, and thus usable, in the Late Bronze Age. Few of the earlier group of tombs can have stood as long as this, though both Porti and Siva S contained burials in pithoi and larnakes.[11] With these tombs therefore, we find continuity marked by later burials around, as opposed to in, them. This is the situation at Platanos, Agia Triadha, and Porti, and Late Minoan remains close to Kephali and Lebena II may indicate similar continuity on these sites.[12] It is important to note that these are all examples where there is not simply continuity of occupation on a settlement site, but where the cemetery site too remains constant.

Pl. 11

A moment ago we mentioned the expansion of population and the political developments giving rise to palatial society, both of which factors operated principally during Early Minoan III and Middle Minoan Ia. These factors cannot, I believe, be totally unrelated to the appearance of the tholos tomb in the north and east of the island, which must also be ascribed to this period. The Early Minoan I tomb at Krasi, and the probable tomb at Gorgolaini, which also seems to belong with the earlier group of tombs, are hardly sufficient to explain the adoption of the tholos in the north and east in Middle Minoan I. This is the very period when the Mesara, for the first time since the Bronze Age began, is not the most advanced region of the island. Both the north, where palatial society is making its first appearance, and the east, where trade with the Levant and Egypt is having a desirable effect, are making headway whilst the Mesara, or rather the village communities characteristic of it, are making little or no progress. In this context, the sudden adoption of the Mesara's characteristic tomb type by the people of the north and east makes little sense. This is all the more so, since even in the Mesara the circular, communal, tomb is going out of favour; individual burials in pithoi or larnakes are rapidly becoming the norm. With these thoughts in mind, it is difficult to explain the appearance of the tholos in the north and east except by postulating small-scale migrations by families or clans from the Mesara to these prospering centres of civilisation. I have written elsewhere of the increased mobility of the population which must have come about with the development of palatial civilisation, and I believe the circular tombs of the north and east are one manifestation of this new mobility.[13] There are eight *possible* Middle Minoan I tombs known outside of the Mesara, one of which lies immediately to the east at Viannos. Of the remainder one is at Knossos (Gypsades) and two others are south of Mallia (Siderokamino and Kalergi). Three more are in Sitia (Myrsini and Pedhino) and the last is south of the gulf of Mirabello (Elleniko).[14] There is no obvious pattern in this distribution, and if we follow the hypothesis of a migration from the Mesara to the north and east, then we must see the process as not only taking place on a small scale but also as being piecemeal and entirely voluntary.

One objection which might immediately be raised against the migration hypothesis is that there is no sign of depopulation, of villages being abandoned, in the Mesara during Middle Minoan I.

This is true, but from what we learn of the structure of society from the tombs, it is clear that we should not expect to see villages abandoned but rather the departure of the odd family or clan from the villages. This would be more difficult to detect archaeologically, but cemetery sites where one tomb goes out of use earlier than the other(s) might perhaps be the result of a family or clan migration. Cemetery sites where this sort of situation may have existed include Platanos (?tomb Γ abandoned earlier than A and B), Apesokari (?tomb I abandoned earlier than II), and Siva (?south tomb in use after north tomb abandoned). One interesting piece of evidence which might indeed point to a family or clan leaving a village to settle elsewhere is the condition of tomb E at Koumasa. Here, all of the bones in the tholos had been swept up against the west side of the tomb, the grave-goods taken, and a layer of white earth spread over the heap of remains. The rest of the tomb was empty—it had been carefully cleared and cleaned, but not reused.

Though the matter has been much debated, and the controversy still rages, I am convinced that the Mesara tombs were built and used by clans rather than by the village community as a whole.[15] Glotz thought the tombs were tribal burial places, but it is probable that in the Early Bronze Age the inhabitants of any single village would have belonged overwhelmingly to a single tribe and it is thus difficult to explain the erection of two, and even three, tombs next to some settlements. We have seen in previous chapters that the villagers were only too anxious to avoid building more tombs than were necessary, being prepared to clear out or sweep to one side earlier remains to make room for new burials. At Lebena, we may recall, the burials were packed into tomb I until it was impossible to enter the chamber at all—but no new tomb was built to replace the full one.[16] Where we have more than one tomb to a cemetery, we find that they are all built at about the same time (and of course we cannot be at all precise about this in terms of years) and are, for most of their period of use, all used together. A glance at our chronological table in Appendix 3 will illustrate this point for several cemeteries, and it is almost certainly true of other ones where the dating evidence is too scarce to allow the cemeteries' appearance in the table. Thus it is difficult to follow Glotz and see the tombs as tribal sepulchres, or to follow the obvious line of thought and see them as village tombs pure and simple.

Equally it is impossible to regard the tombs as the burial places of a few elite families. The number of burials is far too great to allow of this possibility. It has never proved possible to make an actual count of the minimum number of skeletons represented in a tomb, but various excavators have offered opinions and estimates which agree tolerably well. Xanthoudides estimated the burials in Koumasa B and Marathokephalon II to number "many hundreds", whilst at Porti he was convinced that the *lowest estimate* for the burials *inside* the tomb must be "many hundreds".[17] There were also, of course, the mass of skeletal remains cleared from the tomb and placed in the outside chambers. A more specific estimate was made by Halbherr of the number of burials found in Agia Triadha.[18] Bearing in mind that this tomb is considerably larger than Porti and Marathokephalon II, his estimate of two hundred burials in the tomb and fifty more in the antechambers is a lower one than Xanthoudides'. More precise information is offered by Alexiou for the situation in Lebena I. He does not give a figure for the number of burials in the tomb, but he notes that the burials were packed in so that eventually they reached a density of about ten to the square metre.[19] If the density was approximately equal throughout the tomb, then this tomb would have held about six hundred burials! Furthermore, Lebena I is a relatively small tomb, with an internal diameter of about five metres. A figure approaching this total can also, I think, be suggested for the larger tomb at Kamilari. If the evidence noted at Vorou is reliable, and we can assume that two or three clay toasting cups were used at each funerary service, then the one thousand plus cups at Kamilari should represent four to five hundred burials. Some of the Middle Minoan I tombs apparently contained fewer burials, but they are notably small tombs in any case. Thus the total number of burials at Myrsini was a little under a hundred, and Marinatos' description of the burials in Vorou A suggests a similar or slightly lower figure for this tomb.[20]

These figures are at once too small to be suggestive of tribal tombs, and much too large to be indicative of the family vault of a local chieftain or dignitary. They are however the sort of figures we might expect for the tombs of an enlarged family unit such as the clan or *genos*. Furthermore the common appearance of tombs in groups of twos and threes is suited to this interpretation, since the Early Bronze Age village communities were probably about the right size to be comprised of two or three such *gene*. The size of the tombs, and of the stones used in their construction, is entirely consistent with this interpretation, being such as could successfully be tackled by a small group of people.

If we are right in recognising the circular tombs as the tombs of clans, then it follows, I suggest, that the important unit within society was the clan. Over and above the structure within the clan, and the responsibilities to the clan, however, there must have been differences of status and wealth within the larger, village community, and there must have been responsibilities to that community. Of the latter, the tombs provide no evidence, but of the former they perhaps provide a little. Differences of status are notoriously difficult to recognise, but in the Mesara tombs we might regard the gold diadems as symbols of some kind of authority, and the sealstones, which always seem far too few in number to have been worn by everyone buried in the tomb, were probably worn by people of a certain status rather than by a wealthier element who could afford them. On the other hand, gold jewellery at least might simply denote the burial of a wealthy person, as do presumably the scarce imported objects discussed in chapter four. There is no clear evidence at all for the burials of persons with little or no material wealth, or for those with no political or social status. Xanthoudides thought that the burials made in the spaces between the "buttresses" on the south side of Platanos A were those of "poor persons or slaves", but apart from the "poor" finds in this area, there is really little indication as to the nature of these remains.[21] If they were poor both in quality and quantity, that need have no implications for the wealth or status of the bodies with which the finds were originally deposited. The material found here may well all have been cleared from the tomb during its cleaning and fumigation, which as we mentioned in a previous chapter, took place either late in Early Minoan II or early in Early Minoan III. Xanthoudides specifically ascribes to this area only two objects, a sealstone and an amulet-cum-figurine; both of these could be as early as late Early Minoan II.[22] Where complete burials are found outside the tombs, at Porti for example, it is quite certain that they are made after the tomb has all but gone out of use. We know of no Early Bronze Age burials in the Mesara which are not made inside the circular tombs. In death, at least, the Early Bronze Age societies of the Mesara were egalitarian.

With the development of palatial civilisation, and the growth of

towns and overseas commerce, it seems certain that social distinctions must have multiplied and increased. The number of
specialised trades and crafts grew rapidly, in the palaces the rise of
a bureaucracy inevitably gave birth to new social distinctions, and
so too, one imagines, did the proliferation of organised ritual in
the peak sanctuaries. The effects of this process on the village
communities of the Mesara were, I suggest, threefold. The
population became more mobile, it became less egalitarian, and
the solidarity of clan was broken down, probably in favour of the
immediate family unit on the one hand and the community as a
whole on the other. One effect of the increased mobility of the
population has already been suggested to us by the late appearance
of the tholos in the north and east of the island, namely small-
scale migrations within the island. The breakdown of the clan
tradition is, I think, clearly revealed in the gradual abandonment
of the circular tombs during the Middle Minoan period for individual burials in pithoi and larnakes. Initially there were many
examples of compromise between the old and new burial traditions. Larnakes and pithoi were found together in both tombs at
Vorou, in Drakones Δ, Porti, Vali, Myrsini, and Siva S, while
larnax burials alone were also found in Gypsades (pl. 11), *Pl. 11*
Apesokari II, and Viannos.[23] At the same time, the new emphasis
on distinctions of rank, status and wealth may have seen the
burial of some dignitaries or wealthy men of commerce removed
from the tombs and their immediate environs to other situations.
I know of no positive evidence for this, but the absence of gold
jewellery for example from the Middle Minoan I tombs may be
significant in this respect. In the north of the island certainly, we
may compare the paucity of grave-goods in the pithos cemeteries
to the richness of those in the early *tholos* (Middle Minoan II?) at
Arkhanes and in the Chrysollakos ossuary, albeit plundered, at
Mallia.[24]

As the circular tombs themselves were slowly abandoned, there
may have been a lessening of the importance of the cemetery in
communal life. If we were right in recognising the Snake Goddess and several of her attributes or symbols as involved in
funerary ritual, then the rise of the peak sanctuaries in Middle
Minoan I may well have diverted much attention away from the
cemeteries, since I am convinced that these sanctuaries were
dedicated to this deity.[25] Before the peak sanctuaries were erected,
we know of no public sanctuaries, except perhaps for one or two

caves, which could have been the situation of communal or personal ritual dedicated to the Goddess. If only for this reason, it
seems likely that the cemetery sites may have played an important
role in the life of the community other than their funerary one.
There are however other pieces of evidence which point to the
same conclusion.

There is for example the close proximity of the cemeteries to
their respective settlements. More than a dozen cemeteries have
now been linked with their respective settlements and in every
case the tombs have been found within a short distance of the
village. At Salame and Kalathiana for example, only ten metres
separate the cemetery from the settlement, and the tomb at Komo
is a similar distance north of the houses there. There is, however,
no regular situation for the tombs in relation to the settlements; at
Salame and Koumasa the tombs are east of the settlement, at
Trypiti the tomb is south-east of the village, while at Megali
Skinoi and Kalathiana the tombs are to the north. It may be
significant that there are no known examples of a cemetery
placed to the west of the settlement, so that nowhere do the doorways face immediately on to the village. This is interesting since,
if it is true, it perhaps suggests that it was the proximity of the
cemetery as a place of ritual, rather than as the burial ground of
the ancestors, which was desirable.

Some suggestion of rituals which were practised in the immediate vicinity of the tombs but outside both them and their
antechambers is made by the appearance of paved areas and enclosed areas surrounding some of the tombs. The extensive paving
at Koumasa (fig. 27) with an eight metre length of the straight   *Fig. 27*
wall bounding it still preserved, is the greatest area of pavement
yet discovered in a Mesara cemetery, and gives us some idea of
what the original extent of the surviving scraps at Platanos,
Apesokari and Agios Kyrillos may have been.[26] The discovery of
paving outside Apesokari II at once suggests that the whole area
between this tomb and Apesokari I, where traces of a similar
pavement were found, was originally paved. It is possible that
when it was first built in Middle Minoan I, Kamilari I also had a
pavement surrounding it. Certainly it had an enclosure marked
out by an arc of very large, and regular, blocks of stone (fig. 21),   *Fig. 21*
and inside this enclosure Levi found what he termed an altar.[27]
This comprised six flat slabs of stone laid on the ground edge to
edge to form an irregular four-sided area. There were two more

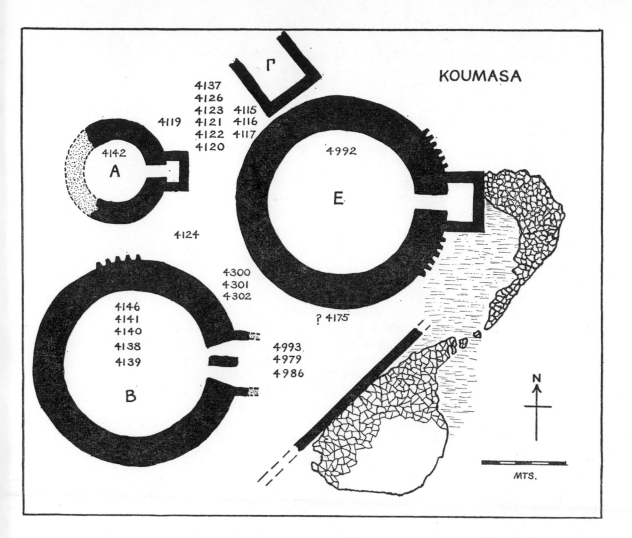

Fig. 27 The distribution of zoomorphic and anthropomorphic vessels in the cemetery at Koumasa

Tholos B:
  4138 Snake-Goddess vessel.
  4146 Vessel in the shape of a tortoise
  4141 Box-like vessel in the shape of a bull
  4140 Box-like vessel in the shape of a bull
  4139 Snake-Goddess vessel
Tholos A:
  4142 Vessel in the form of a bird
Tholos E:
  4992 A jug with two horn-like projections (found in the covering mound, rather than in the tholos itself)
Area A/Γ: (Designated area △ by Xanthoudides)

  4137 Snake-Goddess vessel
  4126 Bull-vessel with acrobats
  4123 Vessel in the form of a ? bird
  4121 Jug in the form of a bird
  4122 Vessel in the form of a bird
  4120 Ring vase, probably representing a bird
  4119 Vessel in the form of a duck
  4115-7 Three jugs with human figures clinging to their necks
Area A/B:
  4124 Vessel in the form of a ? ram
Area B/E:
  4300-2 Three phalli of clay; many other fragmentary examples were found in this area

Outside B Doorway:
  4993 Snake-Goddess vessel
  4986 Vessel in the form of a bull
  4979 Vessel in the form of a woman
Outside E:
  4175 Vessel in the shape of an egg
Uncertain:
  4295 Vessel in the form of a pair of trousers

flat slabs placed on top of each other at one corner of the area
(pl. 13). This may indeed have been an altar, but if so it was a *Pl. 13*
rather irregularly shaped one. There is at least the possibility that
this was the remains of a pavement which originally covered the
surface of the enclosure. Levi noted that at least the west end of
the enclosure had been covered with earth, and had thus gone out
of use, in Middle Minoan II, and one could argue that most of the
pavement had been ripped up at this time.

Whether or not that was so, it can be said without fear of contradiction, that at least five cemetery sites had either pavements or
enclosures, and sometimes both, outside their tombs and antechambers. In one case, other than the dubious example at Kamilari, there was an altar placed on the pavement, this being the
well known example at Apesokari (fig. 28). This suggests that *Fig. 28*
among the rituals practised on the pavements were the pouring of
libations, the making of votive offerings or the offering of sacrifices. Evidence for the first of these practices might be found in the
distribution of anthropomorphic and zoomorphic vessels in the
Koumasa cemetery. Xanthoudides noted the location of most of
the vessels he found and of twenty-seven for which he gives a
location, twenty-one were found not in the tombs at all but in the
enclosed area outside them (fig. 27). Some of these may have been *Fig. 27*
used in funerary rituals, as we suggested in chapter five, since the
tombs at Koumasa did not possess suites of outer chambers, but
some at least of the items found in the enclosure are suggestive of
non-funerary ritual and are not paralleled in the tombs at all.
Notable among these are the six complete, and innumerable
broken, clay phalli, which also turned up in large numbers outside
the tombs at Platanos.[28] These immediately suggest a fertility
ritual of some sort, and if it was not to revive the dead (and the
evidence discussed in the previous chapter suggests it was not)
then it may well have been to bring fertility to the soil or to the
livestock of the community. Also from the enclosure at Platanos
came the two thin, sheet-bronze double-axes mentioned previously. There can be no doubt that these were either votive or
ceremonial axes, since they would have been completely useless
for practical purposes. Furthermore, many similar ones are known
from ritual contexts of later periods.[29] In particular we must again
emphasise the relationship between this discovery at Platanos and
the scene depicted on the Agia Triadha sarcophagus, where we
see two axes of this sort raised on stands and placed in the area *Pl. 16*

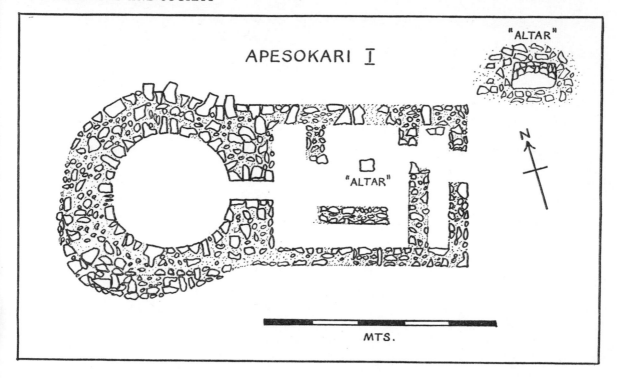

Fig. 28 The Middle Minoan 1
tholos at Apesokari
(Apesokari 1)

before a tomb (pl. 16). The bird which is perched on each of them
is thought to be an epiphany of a goddess. On the evidence of the
sarcophagus however, this goddess, and the bull sacrifice which
accompanies the ritual associated with her, are directly related to
funerary or post-funerary ritual and *may* therefore be irrelevant to
our present discussion.

None of the rituals yet mentioned—libations, deposition of
votives, or making of sacrifices—satisfactorily explain the need for
large areas of pavement outside the tombs. These pavements are
surely to be seen as the precursors of the central and western
courts in the palaces; that is, as the situation of ritual dancing. It
must be said at once that there is no evidence to prove this; nor
could we expect any. There are however one or two indications
that the cemeteries may have been the situation of dancing rituals
and one or two pointers as to the deity or deities for which they
were performed. We have mentioned both in this and previous
chapters the appearance of the Snake Goddess and her symbols

and attributes in the Mesara tombs. The Snake Goddess was not devoted entirely to the affairs of the dead, indeed from Middle Minoan I times onwards she had little or no connection with funerary ritual. Some of the rituals practised at the cemetery sites may therefore have been non-funerary ones associated with this same goddess, and the two Snake Goddess vessels and four bird vases found outside the tombs in the enclosure at Koumasa should perhaps be seen in this context rather than a funerary one. That the rituals of the cult involved dancing is certain since the discovery at Phaistos of a Middle Minoan II plate which shows an image of the Snake Goddess flanked by two women who are clearly dancing (fig. 29). This discovery allows us to interpret *Fig. 29* the scene on a fragmentary plate of the same period, and from the same site, as showing a similar dancing ritual (fig. 29). Some of the rituals performed on the cemetery pavements may, I suggest, have included ceremonial dances related to the cult of the Snake Goddess.

The clay model of four dancers standing in a ring which Levi found in the tomb at Kamilari might well represent such a dance (pl. 14), particularly since the perimeter of the model is decorated *Pl. 14* with sacred horns such as are commonly encountered in shrines of the Snake Goddess. But Hutchinson has warned us that the sacred horns are a feature common to most, if not all, Minoan cults,[30] and the model might therefore portray a dance in honour of some other deity. There are several later parallels to the Kamilari model, including a Late Minoan I group from Palaikastro, a Geometric group from Olympia, a probably Hellenistic model from Corinth, and another of uncertain date and provenance in Vienna.[31] All of these models show three or four persons dancing in a circle. In addition the Palaikastro model shows a lyre player at the centre of the group, the Corinth model a player of pipes, and the Vienna one another pipe player. There is no reason to think that all of these models portray the same dance for the same deity, although the Cretan dance known as the *hyporchema* was famed in classical Greece. These models do however recall Homer's description, in book eighteen of the *Iliad*, of the dance performed for Ariadne at Knossos.[32] There need be no link between the Kamilari model and the dance for Ariadne, but if we follow this train of thought we may find that the possibility is strengthened. As the daughter of Minos, Ariadne might well take the sacred horns and the bull as her symbols. If this was so, then

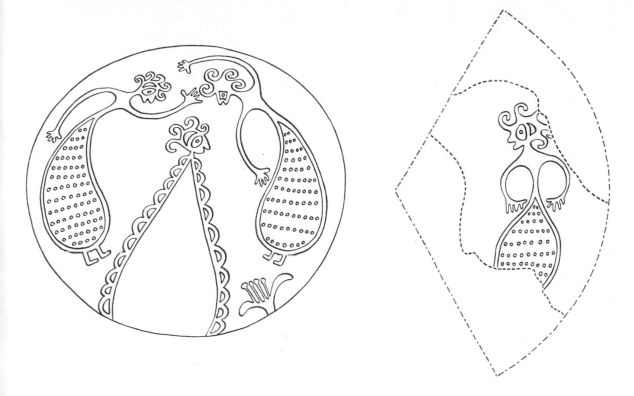

the appearance of bull vessels in the cemeteries and of the horns of consecration on the Kamilari model might be significant. More important however are Nilsson's observations concerning the nature of Ariadne.[33] He has suggested that both the joyous festival in honour of Ariadne the wife of Dionysus, and the festival of mourning celebrated for Ariadne the daughter of Minos, were in fact ceremonies performed in honour of a single deity. Ariadne, he suggests, was a goddess of Spring, honoured for the death and resurrection which she characterised. The rape of Ariadne was the rape of a vegetation goddess, not of a royal princess.

If Nilsson is right, then we can see at once how suitable would be the cemetery as the situation of her rituals, particularly in pre-palatial society when the palaces could not provide an alternative location. Among early farming communities throughout Europe and the Near East, the association of the agricultural and vegetational cycles with the human cycle of life and death was common.

Fig. 29 A Middle Minoan plate, and a fragment from a second, both from Phaistos, depicting dances in honour of the Snake Goddess

It is entirely reasonable to suggest that in Early Bronze Age Crete such an association was contrived, and that the rituals and worship accorded to the vernal goddess in whom the concept was embodied, were practised on the pavements of the cemetery areas. That the deity concerned was Ariadne, or her precursor, cannot be demonstrated but is a plausible hypothesis. In particular we might recall the phalli found in the enclosures at Platanos and Koumasa; dare we suggest that here we are in touch with the origins of the myth of the rape of Ariadne?

That ritual dances to Ariadne were practised on the cemetery pavements is, as we have said, an attractive hypothesis but nothing more. It is however eminently probable that the people of the Mesara had a vernal deity, that he or she was related to the cycle of life and death, and that for this reason the cemeteries were, before the emergence of communal shrines and palatial courts, the situation of ritual and ceremonial performed in honour of this deity. This, the relationship which existed between the Snake Goddess and the cemetery, and the air of social stability and strength which the tombs engendered, together combined to make the cemeteries an important part of the Mesara communities. They were, both geographically and psychologically, an extension of the village; they were the focus of communal life and the symbols of its stability.

Chapter Eight

THE MINOAN THOLOS—ITS
ORIGINS AND HISTORY

The millennium during which the Mesara tombs were built and used, was, as we have seen in chapter two, a most important period in the history of Crete, and of the Aegean as a whole. Although we have no written records for the period and it is thus part of what we call Prehistory, the outline of its historical development can be seen with a reasonable degree of clarity. Surprisingly this is not the case with the tombs themselves. Although we can say something about the history of their construction and usage—when they were built, fumigated or cleared, abandoned, re-used or looted—we can say little about their history as an architectural form. Their origins are much disputed, their architectural development is unclear and seems to be almost non-existent, and their relationship to the Late Bronze Age *tholoi* has yet to be established. We have noted in passing, one or two possible architectural developments in the tombs, and we may add something more on this topic in this chapter. For the most part however, this chapter is concerned with the beginning and the end of the Mesara tombs; it seeks to find an answer to two controversial questions—where did the tholos tombs of the Mesara originate, and were they the prototypes and ancestors of the Mycenaean *tholos* tombs?

There are no built circular tombs of the Neolithic period in Crete, the circular tombs of the Mesara appearing quite suddenly in Early Minoan I. Their sudden appearance and their limited geographical distribution are together suggestive of an immigrant people entering southern Crete in the early third millennium BC

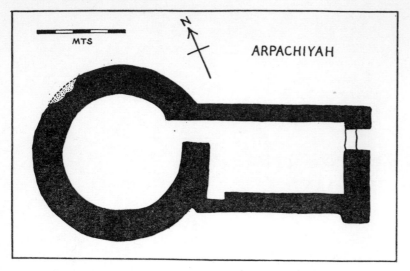

MTS

ARPACHIYAH

Fig. 30   A Halafian "tholos"
at Arpachiyah

to begin the local Bronze Age. The distinctive material culture of
the Mesara both in Early Minoan I and throughout the Early
Bronze Age might also be recognised as the result of an influx of
settlers to the Mesara and its environs at this time. There are
three parts of the eastern Mediterranean from which the circular
built tomb may have been derived, and all three have at some time
been proposed as the home of the Mesara tombs.

The least likely, on chronological and geographical grounds, is
Syria. The Halaf culture which flourished here and in northern
Iraq during the fifth millennium BC provides several interesting
parallels to Minoan cult objects, in addition to its well-known
tholos-like structures best represented at Arpachiyah on the
Tigris. Hutchinson has noted these similarities without comment,
but both Hood and myself have expressed an interest in what we
may call the Levantine hypothesis.[1] The Halafian circular, vaulted
buildings certainly provide the closest parallels outside of Crete to
the Mesara tombs (fig. 30). They are about the same size as the
average tomb, they have walls of a similar thickness and construction, they have an entrance on the east, and a rectangular
antechamber before it. The only structural difference which might
be significant is that the antechamber is far longer than it is wide,
and its overall dimensions are such as to suggest that it is the
equivalent of the suites of outer chambers in tombs like Apeso-

Fig. 30

kari 1 and Agios Kyrillos. Unlike these suites however, the Halafian structures have but a single room. In addition to this structural difference, there is also a notable difference of usage, the Halafian buildings serving as shrines or even workshops rather than tombs.

These differences however are not nearly so great as those of time and distance which separate the Halafian structures from the Cretan ones. The distance from the Syrian coast to the Mesara, something over a thousand kilometres, would not have been an insurmountable obstacle to a migrant group prepared to travel along the southern coast of Turkey, but one would expect some trace of their migration to survive. The chronological difference between the Halafian shrines and the Mesara tombs is of such magnitude, about fifteen hundred years, that if there was a migration it must have been an exceedingly slow one. But in neither the chronological nor the geographical space between Halafian Syria and Early Minoan Crete can we find a trace of the vaulted, circular building tradition. Attractive as the Levantine hypothesis may be, it is therefore entirely unsatisfactory.

The first, and most persistent, hypothesis concerning the origin of the Mesara tombs, directs attention away from the Levant towards North Africa. Evans was the first to suggest a North African origin for the tombs, and he was quickly followed by Xanthoudides. Pendlebury supported the hypothesis in his *Archaeology of Crete*, and most recently Alexiou has committed himself to it.[2] The only voices raised against it have been those of Banti and Hood.[3] Evans was convinced that the Mesara tombs were imitations of circular houses with rectangular antechambers, and for these, and tombs which copied them, he turned to North Africa. Here he found a number of tombs of this type which he immediately proclaimed as ancestral to the Minoan tombs. The Libyan sepulchres had circular stone walls, rectangular ante-chambers (sometimes built inside the perimeter rather than out-side it), trilithon doorways, and communal family burials (fig. 31). *Fig. 31* To these parallels, Xanthoudides added the vaulted tombs of the Early Dynastic period in Egypt, and both Evans and Xanthou-dides repeatedly stressed the many Egyptian parallels for the material culture of the people who used the Mesara tombs. There is too the limited distribution of the tombs, so heavily concen-trated in southern Crete, and more particularly in the Asterousia mountains south of the Mesara proper. This alone is suggestive of

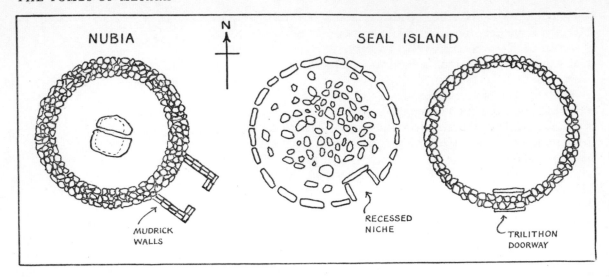

Fig. 31 Three north African circular tombs

a Libyan origin for the tombs. Alexiou has recently developed this argument, emphasising not only the density of the tombs in the Asterousia mountains but also their early date. He believes that they are earlier than the tombs round the edge of the Mesara plain and that the tombs there, and further north, result from subsequent expansion from the original settlements in the mountains facing on to the Libyan Sea.

Taken together this is an impressive array of evidence in support of the Libyan hypothesis; yet Banti long ago cast doubts on the supposed North African origin of certain Early Minoan artifacts and careful analytical study of some of these during the last few years has confirmed her scepticism.[4] Not only are pointed-base figurines, foot amulets, certain sealstone types, and many stone vase types now revealed as considerably later in date than Early Minoan I—and therefore irrelevant to the problem of the tombs—but it has also been argued that they are indigenous types owing nothing to the culture of predynastic and archaic Egypt. These arguments obviously weaken the whole Libyan hypothesis, but they need not invalidate the claim that the Mesara tombs have a Libyan ancestry. However Evans, and those who have followed and supported his hypothesis, have misunderstood the nature of the Libyan tombs which he cites as parallels to the Mesara tombs. They were not *tholoi,* nor even built graves in the normal sense of the word; they were circular, but flat-topped, cairns which were erected above graves already made. Both their method of use and their architecture is thus very different indeed from the tombs of the Mesara, which they resemble only in plan. Furthermore, they are thought to be very much later in date than the third millennium BC. Even the technique of vaulting cannot satisfactorily be derived from archaic Egypt, since the brick vaults of the First and Second Dynasties are not corbelled vaults but barrel vaults.[5] There are thus important differences of both materials and techniques between the Egyptian vaults and those which we believe may have surmounted the tombs of the Mesara.

With the Libyan and Egyptian parallels to the tombs themselves dismissed, the substance of the Libyan hypothesis is gone; yet there remains Alexiou's important point about the distribution and dating of the tombs in southern Crete. The concentration of tombs south of the Yeropotamos was discussed in the previous chapter and one or two possible reasons for it tentatively suggested. The suggestions I made are not particularly convincing but neither is Alexiou's. It might explain why there was an initial concentration in the mountains south of the Yeropotamos, but it does not explain why subsequent expansion did not lead to widespread settlement north of the river. We know of no other Early Bronze Age culture in this region which might have prevented such an expansion. If I am right in supposing that settlement of the northern region did not take place for reasons connected with geological and vegetational conditions there, then presumably these factors could have operated as much in Early Minoan I as later in the Early Bronze Age. The important point which must be resolved is whether or not we have Early Minoan I tombs north of the Yeropotamos, and for that matter, in the foothills looking into the Mesara plain from the south. In the latter area there are the two tombs at Siva (fig. 32) and those at Salame *Fig. 32* and Koutsokera all of which were unquestionably built and used during Early Minoan I. Between the foothills and the river, on the edge of the plain itself, are the Early Minoan I tombs at Agia Triadha, Agia Eirene, and probably Platanos (these last are not certainly of Early Minoan I date). North of the Yeropotamos there are the tombs at Marathokephalon, with undoubted Early Minoan I material, and finally, near the north coast of the island, the small but very early tomb at Krasi. There is at present no way in which we can differentiate between an early and a late

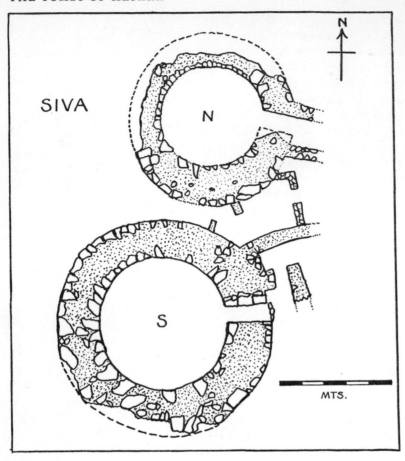

SIVA

N

S

MTS.

Fig. 32   The two tholoi at Siva

phase of Early Minoan I, so that we have no means of distinguishing which of these Early Minoan I tombs are the earliest. It is simply not possible to say that the tombs facing on to the Libyan Sea are earlier than the Early Minoan I tombs looking on to the Yeropotamos or the tombs at Marathokephalon and Krasi. They *may* be earlier, but we do not know and cannot demonstrate that this is so.

The small circular tomb at Krasi is at present the only tomb of this type and of Early Minoan I date to be excavated in the north of the island (fig. 33). It may be an isolated phenomenon, but it seems unlikely and other examples may yet be expected to appear. The tomb at Krasi is certainly a little different from the tombs of

Fig. 33

the Mesara, being built of large, rough blocks, having relatively thin walls, and featuring a built rather than a trilithon doorway. Whether these differences are indicative of a different origin or a different typological stage in the development of the circular tomb is uncertain. Hutchinson seems to have the latter interpretation in mind, when he suggests that the Cycladic built graves might be claimed as an intermediate stage between the circular houses of neolithic Khirokitia (Cyprus) and the tombs of the Mesara.[6] As he observes, the tomb at Krasi resembles the sub-circular, built, Cycladic graves, though in an enlarged form. He takes the line of thought one stage further and suggests that we might "perhaps claim Tholos A at Koumasa, a tomb containing two Cycladic figurines and incised pottery of Early Cycladic I types (. . .), as only an improved and more elaborate form of the Cycladic primitive *tholos*".

The possible Cycladic origin which Hutchinson seems to be suggesting is again an attractive hypothesis. Cycladic built graves of circular or sub-circular shape are now known to go back as far as the Late Neolithic[7] and they are thus of sufficient antiquity to be considered plausible ancestors of the Mesara tombs. They are of course much smaller than the Cretan tombs, rarely exceeding a metre in diameter, and this reflects the mode of burial which was, originally at least, single inhumations. This too is in contrast to the tradition of the Mesara cemeteries. However, a Cycladic origin for the tombs might be linked to other signs of Cycladic influence in the island early in the Bronze Age, and even to some suggestions of Anatolian influence. These influences appear primarily among metalwork and Early Minoan I pottery and chronologically would fit quite comfortably with the appearance of the tombs in Crete in Early Minoan I. Apart from the important differences of scale and usage already mentioned however, there are two other major objections to the Cycladic hypothesis. The first is that no trace of the necessary developments in size and burial customs can be traced in the Cyclades themselves, and in Crete are represented solely by Krasi. The second is that while the tombs are concentrated overwhelmingly in the south, palpable expressions of Cycladic influence are most common in the north and east of the island, as indeed we might expect.[8] Thus the Cycladic hypothesis is in many ways less satisfactory than the Libyan one.

There remains only the theory of an indigenous origin for the

Mesara tombs, but is this really any more satisfactory than the other suggestions which have been made? In the absence of any Neolithic precursors of the circular tombs it seems not. Even if Evans and Xanthoudides were right in suggesting that the tombs were imitations of dwelling huts, we cannot provide any Neolithic prototypes for them. The houses in the Early Neolithic levels at Knossos are rectangular buildings, and so are the Middle and Late Neolithic houses here and at Katsamba and Magasa.[9] All of the excavated Early Minoan houses, including the Early Minoan I examples at Mochlos, Phaistos, and Ellenes, are also rectangular.[10] Our only grounds for thinking that circular huts were used at all during the Early Bronze Age is the shape of the hut-lamp from Lebena, and even this, it could be argued, was made circular for ease of manufacture and convenience of use. Certainly the house walls traced on the surface near cemetery sites like Lebena and Megali Skinoi belong to rectangular rather than circular buildings.[11] This line of enquiry thus leads us no nearer to a solution of our problem.

One possibility remains to be examined. Although rectangular houses had been built from the time when Crete was first inhabited by Neolithic man, there is ample evidence that a large part of the Late Neolithic population at least, lived in caves. In the western part of the island indeed, these are by far the most common type of Neolithic and Early Bronze Age site found. More than a dozen caves with Late and sub-Neolithic material have been found in western Crete.[12] There are three or four similar sites in the east of the island, and in Lasithi the cave excavated by Pendlebury at Trapeza.[13] Not all of these caves can be demonstrated to have been dwelling caves, though this seems reasonably clear at Trapeza, at Lera, and at Melidhoni, to judge from domestic implements such as querns, pounders, rubbers and blades found in the debris. In addition to these caves, there were rock shelters, sometimes roughly walled round at the front, as at Magasa.[14]

Some of the caves in the west of the island seem to have continued in habitation during at least the early part of the Early Bronze Age, but elsewhere caves were now often used as tombs. Trapeza for example became a tomb during the Early Minoan period, and other caves with both Neolithic and Early Bronze Age sherds in them may have seen a similar change of function. There were some caves, however, that had been used for burials during the Neolithic period itself. These are mostly found in western Crete (Koumarospelio, Ellenospelio, Platyvolas) but also occur in the centre and east of the island, particularly at the very end of the Neolithic period and in Early Minoan I (Skaphidia, Kanli Kastelli, Amnisos, Pyrgos, Agios Nikolaos). Since the pottery from the caves in western Crete is thought to be, perhaps, contemporary with Early Minoan I pottery in the centre and east of the island, it may be that all of these cave burials are to be dated to the sub-Neolithic and Early Minoan I periods. In other words the use of caves and rock shelters as tombs may only have developed to any notable extent at all during the transition to the Early Bronze Age. For the most part the caves are used as communal tombs and the practice of communal burial too may only have been widely adopted in Crete at the beginning of the Bronze Age. Its adoption may have coincided with the rapid growth of communal life as represented by the Early Minoan villages.

The appearance of communal burial chambers in the Mesara in Early Minoan I need not therefore surprise us. Their appearance reflects the new social environment of the period, and is part of a widespread change in funerary practice which was taking place throughout the island. The speed at which the change took place varied in different regions, according to the speed at which village communities were established. The Mesara seems to have been in the forefront of this development, while the north and east of the island lagged behind somewhat. As village communities appear in these regions, we see the emergence of distinctive types of built burial chambers. For the most part they date from Early Minoan II, reflecting the retarded development of village life, but like the Mesara cemeteries they provide several separate burial chambers. On some sites, Mochlos and Palaikastro for example, these chambers may actually be separate buildings, but some communities, like that at Arkhanes, may have built a single structure in which several chambers were constructed to allow differentiation of burials.[15] It would be wrong to assume that the social structure of the communities in the north and east was necessarily the same as that in the Mesara, and that multiple chambers imply the strength of the clan tradition, but there is a basic similarity in the situation which deserves to be emphasised. With the onset of communal life in settlements of village size, it became necessary for a community to have two or three burial chambers instead of one. This alone was sufficient reason to abandon cave burials in many areas, for where the density of settlements became great, there would simply not have been enough caves for the purpose. This is particularly true of the Mesara and its environs, where caves are comparatively few. Only two caves used as dwelling sites in the Neolithic period have yet been found there, at Miamou and Agios Kyrillos, and in addition some Early Minoan burials have recently been reported from a cave at Plora.[16] This relative scarcity of caves, together with the early development of village communities in the south, account I believe, for the emergence of built chamber tombs in this region in Early Minoan I.

Could they also account for the shape of these tombs? If the communities of the Mesara each required two or three caves for burial and could not find them in the immediate vicinity, then it may have occurred to them to build artificial caves. The idea of a corbelled structure, whether completely vaulted or not, may have come to them (together with their obsidian) from the Cyclades, but it could have been an independent invention. The real difficulty in accepting the hypothesis of an indigenous origin for the Mesara tombs is the speed with which such a strong tradition must be assumed to have developed. Not only do we find such splendid structures as Megali Skinoi IIIa in Early Minoan I, but a whole group of circular tombs which feature tiny trilithon doors oriented to the east, corbelled construction, antechambers, exposed rock floors, and thick walls. Could such a uniformity have developed so quickly, and without leaving visible evidence for its development? There are two observations which should, I think, be made. Several of the features mentioned were probably predetermined either by the concept of the tombs as caves, or by existing attitudes to death and the dead. Thus the shape and the adoption of a corbelled superstructure were determined by the concept of the tombs as artificial caves. Corbelling was almost certainly the only technique known to them by which they could hope to build anything approaching a complete stone roof. The use of corbelling in turn would have determined the thickness of the walls. The orientation of entrances to the east and the erection of such small doorways may well have been determined by existing beliefs and attitudes. Secondly, we must remember that we cannot distinguish between what is early Early Minoan I and what is late. The Early Minoan I styles of pottery were probably in use, even in the Mesara, for two or three hundred years. Developments could have taken place, and atypical tombs may have been built in this experimental phase, but even if such have been excavated there is no way in which their particularly early date may be established.

Among tombs of Early Minoan I date there are certainly a number of examples which in some way or other are atypical, and which *might* belong to the period of development and experiment. Thus we find Koumasa B has, uniquely, a double entrance, as well as one of the most crudely constructed circuit walls to be found among the Mesara tombs.[17] Its ragged inner face is matched only in the two small tombs at Chrysostomos, to which we will return shortly. A variation of Koumasa B's double door is perhaps represented in the early tomb at Agiopharangos, where there are two separate entrances, one to the east and another to the south.[18] This too is a unique tomb. At least three other Early Minoan I tombs, at Korakies, Marathokephalon and Trypiti, were built with doorways which did not face east but rather towards the south.

The most unusual tombs of all are at Chrysostomos, (fig. 33) Fig. 33 looted but unexcavated, and yielding sherds of Agios Onouphrios I pottery as well as fragments from an Early Minoan III/Middle Minoan Ia stone bowl. Both of these tombs are small and are built of rough boulders put together with little or no clay bonding. Their doorways were in each case of the "built" variety, in contrast to the usual "trilithon" doorways. There were no visible traces of an antechamber to either tomb. These two tombs are, in fact, remarkably close parallels to the tomb at Krasi. While it is difficult to conceive of a small community in the Mesara suddenly, without existing examples to guide them, erecting a tomb like Megali Skinoi IIIa, there is nothing improbable about their erecting tombs like those at Chrysostomos under such conditions. The smaller tomb here, with an internal diameter only a little over two metres, is indeed little more than an enclosed rock shelter, for its builders took advantage of an arc-shaped overhang in the rock outcrop to form a quarter of their circuit wall. Significantly, a very similar tomb, a little larger, was found at Kaloi Limenes (III) only a few kilometres away. Here, surely, we are looking at truly transitional tombs incorporating the structures and the concepts of both the rock shelter and the built tomb. In time I believe more such tombs will come to light in southern Crete, enabling us to demonstrate what at present can only be

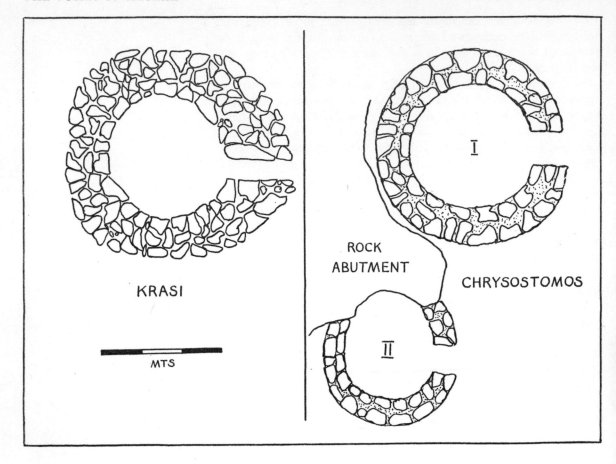

KRASI

MTS

ROCK
ABUTMENT

CHRYSOSTOMOS

I

II

conjectured—that the circular tombs of the Mesara were an indigenous form of sepulchre, created in response to new patterns of settlement and social behaviour, during the first century or so of the Cretan Early Bronze Age.

When we discussed the chronology of the tombs in chapter two, we found that most of those for which a foundation date could be established were built in Early Minoan I or Middle Minoan I. There were a few, like four of the Lebena tombs, which were built during Early Minoan II, and some which *might* have been built during Early Minoan III rather than Middle Minoan I. Even allowing for these tombs of Early Minoan II and perhaps of Early Minoan III, it seemed possible to divide the tombs into

Fig. 33 The small circular tomb at Krasi and the two small tholoi found at Chrysostomos

two groups, an early one and a late one. This division can probably be justified on typological as well as chronological grounds, for although we cannot trace any developments in the tomb architecture among the early group of tombs, we can point to certain features of the late group which seem to represent architectural developments. There are three, perhaps four, developments which can be demonstrated to have taken place by Middle Minoan I.

First, it is true to say that the later tombs are, as a rule, smaller than the early ones. If we take an internal diameter of five metres as our dividing line, we find that while only six out of twenty-eight early tombs are as small as this, eight out of fourteen late tombs fall below five metres. The biggest of the late tombs, Kamilari I, is an impressive structure with an internal diameter of just over seven and a half metres, but there are at least seven Early Minoan I or II tombs which are larger. Secondly, the later tombs feature "built" doorways in contrast to the trilithon doorways of the early group. Myrsini appears to be an exception to this rule, but the remaining seven late tombs for which we have details all feature a "built" door. It looks very much as if taller doorways were also characteristic of the late tombs. Of the four late tombs for which doorway heights are known, three (Drakones Z, Agios Kyrillos, and Gypsades) are *more* than one and a half metres high, only Kamilari (one metre) having a low door comparable to the doors of early tombs. The third development is the erection of a rectangular building containing three or four outer chambers and incorporating the antechamber. Regular suites of this sort occur outside the well dated tombs at Agios Kyrillos, Apesokari I and II, Viannos, and Kamilari I. It is possible that these rooms enclosed inside a large rectangular building were first developed among the early group of tombs, since traces of them survived outside Platanos B and Γ. If this was the case however, it is strange that more of the many early tombs did not have regular suites of this sort. It may be that the suites traced at Platanos were additions to the original tomb structures, made in Middle Minoan I. Finally, there may have been some improvement in the quality of the masonry in the Middle Minoan I tombs. Some of them, like those at Vorou, were as poorly built as many of the early tombs, but the best of the Middle Minoan I tombs are the finest examples of the Mesara tombs that we have. Blocks of reasonably regular shape and size were used to build the tombs at Kamilari II, Vali, Siderokamino (pl. 3), and Agios Kyrillos, allowing the builders to lay coursed masonry. The finest example is the largest of the Kamilari tombs, using large rectangular blocks of stone, faced inside and out and laid in courses, with a superb built doorway closed by a carefully smoothed slab (pl. 5). In quality at least, some of the latest of the Mesara tombs began to approach the Late Bronze Age *tholoi* of the mainland.

Pl. 3

Pl. 5

Nevertheless the gap between the circular tombs of the Mesara and the Mycenaean *tholoi* has always seemed a wide one, and the list of scholars who oppose a generic relationship between the Cretan and the mainland tombs—Persson, Stubbings, Wace, Mylonas, Taylour, Pendlebury, Hutchinson, Schachermeyr—is indeed a formidable one.[19] Formidable too are the arguments with which they press their opposition, and though Xanthoudides and Matz have expressed support for the hypothesis of a Cretan origin, only Hood has attempted to answer these arguments point by point.[20] The case against a Cretan origin is usually argued on any or all of four grounds. These may be summarised as follows. Structural, chronological and geographical differences are too great to be satisfactorily bridged or overlooked, and alternative origins for the *tholoi* are at least as plausible as a Minoan one, if not more so. We must examine these objections in detail.

The structural differences between the Mesara tombs and the *tholoi* are essentially differences of design rather than technique. It is erroneous, for example, to think of the *tholoi* as being constructed of better quality masonry than the tombs of the Mesara. While the "Treasury of Atreus" dwarfs all of the Cretan tombs but Platanos A, and is built of incomparably better masonry, it is also exceptional among the tombs of the mainland. A great many of the Mycenaean *tholoi* are no larger than the average Mesara tomb (*c*. five-six metres internal diameter), and are built of rough-hewn masonry matched and bettered in tombs such as Kamilari and Ayios Kyrillos. There are three features of *tholos* design however which it is difficult to match among the Cretan tombs. First there is the erection of the *tholos* in a hillside cutting, or else the covering of the tomb with a mound of earth. The latter practice seems commonest among the earlier *tholoi,* some of which were built more or less at ground level.[21] In contrast, none of the Mesara tombs have yet revealed any trace of a covering mound, although several were terraced—to varying degrees—into the side of a hill.

The only tomb where the degree of terracing may have approached the deep cuttings made for the mainland *tholoi* is Agios Kyrillos. In the absence of a final report on the tomb, we are dependent on the published photograph, which shows the hillside surrounding, and protecting, the chamber to a depth of about two metres (pl. 9). The small, and almost completely destroyed, third tomb at Kamilari appeared to have been built in a similar situation. These two tombs could perhaps be claimed as examples of a transitional stage between the Minoan and the Mycenaean types. But surely there is no need to search for, or to postulate the existence of, "transitional" tombs of this sort. The concept of a sunken or buried tomb may well have been a Mycenaean contribution to the circular tomb tradition. Hood might be correct in suggesting that the mounds which covered the tombs were intended to dignify them,[22] but there may have been other, religious reasons why the Greeks of the mainland felt it necessary or proper to cover their tombs with earth or bury them into a hillside. In Crete, dug or subterranean graves of any sort are very rare indeed before the Late Bronze Age. Rock shelters, caves, rectangular ossuaries, built circular tombs, and pithos cemeteries all appear to have had the burials placed *on* the ground rather than *in* it. In pre-Mycenaean Greece on the other hand, dug graves are common from the Neolithic period onwards and tumulus burials appear in western Greece not later than the early Middle Helladic period.[23] Indeed, I personally believe that some of the tumulus burials in Epirus, and certainly some of the related round graves of Levkas, date back to the Early Bronze Age. In other words, there seems to have been a long established tradition of subterranean burials on the Greek mainland, and in western Greece this developed into a tumulus tradition, with or without a stimulus from elsewhere.[24] *If* the mainland Greeks adopted the circular built chamber tomb from Crete, they may well have felt it necessary, therefore, to bring it into some sort of compromise with their own traditions and beliefs.

One immediate consequence of placing the tomb in a mound or cutting it into a hillside, was that some sort of entrance passage was needed to enable access to the chamber. Where the passage had to pass through an earth mound, as opposed to the bedrock of a hillside, then the passage would need to be lined with stone walls. Thus the adoption of a subterranean situation for the *tholoi* led, of necessity, to the development of a *dromos* or entrance

Pl. 9

passage—another structural feature which was absent, and not needed, among the Mesara tombs. In contrast to the *dromos* o course, the Cretan tombs had an antechamber and often (particularly amongst the late tombs) a suite of outer rooms. To all intents and purposes these precluded the use of a *dromos* in any case. Thus at Agios Kyrillos, where the tomb *does* appear to have been built right into the hillside, a *dromos* was not needed or built, since access to the tomb through the slope of the hill was gained by means of the outer chambers and antechamber. The Mycenaeans did not, apparently, feel the need for either the antechamber or the other rooms, presumably because the funerary rituals which they practised did not call for them. In the Temple Tomb at Knossos, and the earlier of the Arkhanes *tholoi,* we may see a mixture of the two traditions, since both of these tombs feature a *dromos* and a suite of ritual rooms.[25]

Together with the *dromos,* the Mycenaeans introduced high doorways which were about the same height as a man in most cases, although the "Treasury of Atreus" is again exceptional in having a doorway five metres high! Doorways two metres or more in height are not the norm among the Cretan tombs, where they are more commonly no more than a metre high and are of the trilithon type rather than the "built" doorway. A little earlier in this chapter however, we noted that there was a marked trend towards higher doorways of "built" construction in the tombs erected in Middle Minoan I and II. These two trends brought the Mesara tombs into a closer typological relationship with the Mycenaean *tholoi*.

Whether or not these structural changes were accompanied by a change in the extent and nature of the roof is still uncertain, as we saw in chapter three. Opponents of the Cretan origin of the *tholoi* most persistently quote the difference in the roofing systems of the Mesara tombs and those of the mainland, as the clearest evidence against the hypothesis. Hood has argued that many if not all of the Mesara tombs *were* fully vaulted, though not always in stone, but we saw in chapter three that this was probably not the case. Tombs like Platanos A and B and Koumasa B and E could never have supported a full stone vault and produced no evidence at all for any other sort of vaulting. Many other tombs which *could* conceivably have been fully vaulted in stone, Agia Triadha B for example, could never have stood intact through a millennium of use (and earthquakes) if they had been. On the other hand the size and regularity of the blocks used in tombs like Kamilari 1 and Agios Kyrillos would have allowed the construction of a full stone vault which was probably sound enough and stable enough to have stood for the few centuries in which they were used. One of the architectural trends which we noted in the Middle Minoan 1 tombs, that towards tombs of smaller diameter, could perhaps have been directly related to the development of full stone vaulting, we simply do not know. All we can say is that improvements in the regularity of the masonry and the general trend towards a smaller diameter, would have enabled several of the Middle Minoan 1 tombs to have been *successfully* vaulted in stone. This last and most important structural difference between the Mesara tombs and the mainland *tholoi* might therefore have been eliminated during Middle Minoan 1.

None of the apparent structural differences between the two types of tomb therefore, are too great or too inexplicable to prevent us from accepting a Minoan origin for the *tholos* tomb. More inexplicable certainly is the scarcity of Late Bronze Age *tholoi* in Crete and their abundance on the Greek mainland. We might reasonably expect more in mainland Greece if only for the reasons that the mainland is about fourteen times the size of Crete and had a correspondingly larger population, and the *tholos* tomb was undoubtedly a popular form of sepulchre throughout most of the Mycenaean mainland. Nevertheless, it is strange that if the *tholos* was a development of the Mesara circular tomb, it should never have been particularly popular in Crete itself. Hood partially explains this by pointing to the variety of corbel vaulted tombs in Crete—beehive, keel, and beehive on a rectangular chamber—which cannot be matched on the mainland. He suggests furthermore that in terms of the origin of the corbelled chamber tomb in the Aegean, this variety of tombs in Crete is far more significant than the multiplicity of beehive vaults alone on the mainland.[26] While doubting the validity of this argument, I would certainly agree that the varieties of corbel vaulted tombs in Crete cannot be disregarded and must be taken into account when assessing the popularity of the *tholos* in the island during the Late Bronze Age.

In fact, only seven or eight vaulted tombs with square chambers or keel vaults are at present known in Crete. *Tholoi* with circular chambers are more numerous however. Pendlebury's *Archaeology of Crete,* published in 1939 claimed only a single Late Bronze Age

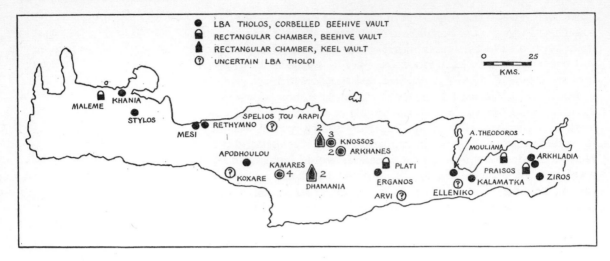

Fig. 34

tholos in the island, though some early reports which he rejected seem likely to have been authentic records of Late Minoan *tholoi*. When Hood published his revised distribution map in 1962 (first published in 1960), he could show about a dozen *tholoi* in Crete, although some of these were uncertain examples.[27] Excavations and fieldwork in the seven or eight years since then have enabled us to add five certain *tholoi,* one probable, and two possible examples to the distribution map (fig. 34).[28] Thus, the *tholos* tomb is not as rare in Crete as we once supposed, although to date it is strangely absent from the Mesara. The reason for this is not clear, but it might reflect the conservatism of the Mesara villages. On the other hand it could be related to the re-use of the existing circular tombs during the Late Bronze Age, such as can be clearly demonstrated at Vali, Kamilari, Drakones and other Early Bronze Age sites.

There remain two major arguments against a Cretan origin for the mainland *tholoi,* namely that the Cretan and mainland tombs are separated by both a geographical and a chronological gap which cannot convincingly be bridged. It must be admitted that the process by which the Cretan tholos may have been transmitted to the Greek mainland cannot easily be identified. Certainly we have no evidence for Cretan immigration into Greece in the late Middle Helladic period. If we look for the earliest examples of *tholoi* yet found in Greece however, we may find a point from

Fig. 34 A map showing the distribution of Late Bronze Age *tholoi* and variant types in Crete

which a plausible line of transmission may be traced. Three mainland *tholoi* have produced pottery which suggests that they were constructed during Middle Helladic III, one of which was found at Karditsa in Thessaly.[29] There is nothing of either this or the preceding period in Thessaly however, to suggest any close contacts with Crete at this time. The two remaining *tholoi* were found in Messenia, at Koryphasion and Moira.[30] This is an altogether more promising area for several reasons, the most obvious of which is its relative nearness to Crete. In terms of the structural development of the circular Mesara tomb towards the mainland *tholos,* Messenia is particularly interesting since it has produced several examples of Middle Helladic tumuli which could provide the prototypes of the covering mounds of the early *tholoi.*[31] One of these early *tholoi,* with a covering mound, was found at Malthi in Messenia.[32] Furthermore, the existence of Middle Helladic tumuli, some of which appear to have contained a low ring wall of stones, suggests that the population of Messenia may have been well disposed towards adopting the circular chamber tomb of Cretan type, since it would not have clashed greatly with their existing funerary tradition. Finally a direct line of contact between Crete and Messenia can be identified on the island of Kythera. The earliest Minoan pottery on the island appears to belong to Early Minoan II, and to this or the succeeding phase we might attribute the well-known stone jug from Kythera. Much larger quantities of Middle Minoan I and II pottery have come to light, mainly in the British excavations at Kastri, and there is little or no doubt that by Middle Minoan II, Kythera was the situation of a Minoan trading station or possibly even a Minoan colony.[33] These early links between Crete and Kythera may well explain the appearance of Minoan types of metalwork in western Greece (toilet scrapers on Levkas and in Epirus, the Malthi double-axe) and also the Minoan influence which has been detected in the Middle Helladic III pottery found in the *tholoi* at Koryphasion.[34] The latter material must surely be significant, coming as it does from one of the earliest mainland *tholoi* yet discovered. Together with the other evidence discussed above, I think it may allow us to formulate a plausible hypothesis—that the circular, built chamber tomb was introduced to the mainland of Greece, via Messenia, in the seventeenth century BC.

Can this hypothesis find chronological compatability with the dating of the Mesara tombs? A great many of the tombs, as we noted in earlier chapters, were still being used for burials in Middle Minoan II (*c.* 1900–1700 BC) which brings them into a close chronological relationship with the earliest of the Messenian *tholoi*. There is still something of a gap however and we must remember too that these were tombs in decline. Not only had they been in use for a millennium, but many communities it seems were slowly abandoning the use of these circular chamber tombs for individual burials in larnakes or pithoi. It seems unlikely that these tombs would have provided the inspiration for the adoption of their type on the mainland. Clearly it is to the latest of the Mesara tombs that we must look for this inspiration. Among these we find at least three which are not built until midway through the period of the old palaces (Middle Minoan Ib/IIa). Although the information gained from the destroyed and looted Kamilari II was insufficient to allow of certainty, we can be sure that both Kamilari I and Gypsades were in regular use throughout Middle Minoan II and III. In other words we know of at least two tombs, both probably built during the nineteenth century BC, which were properly maintained and used as late as the sixteenth century BC. These obviously overlap considerably with the earliest *tholoi* of Middle Helladic III. If Levi is right, then we might add that the small tomb at Kamilari II was *built* less than a century before the *tholoi* at Moira and Koryphasion were erected. There is therefore no chronological incompatability between the latest Mesara type tombs and the earliest mainland *tholoi*; like the other arguments against a Minoan origin for the Late Bronze Age *tholoi,* it is seen, in the light of recent discoveries, to have no substance.

Five years ago, those who believed in a Minoan origin for the *tholos* tomb would have been prepared to leave the argument there. That is to say, they would claim that the mainland Greeks borrowed from Crete the idea of a circular, built chamber tomb, possibly already with a corbelled stone vault, and to this the people of the mainland added the covering mound or sub-terranean situation, and the *dromos*. Today we are able to go further and claim that the *tholos* tomb, as it was known on the mainland, was itself a Minoan creation. The excavations conducted by Dr Sakellarakis at Arkhanes, south of Knossos, have uncovered a *tholos* tomb which was constructed "by the end of Middle Minoan II".[35] It was built therefore, a century or more before the earliest *tholos* tomb yet discovered on the mainland.

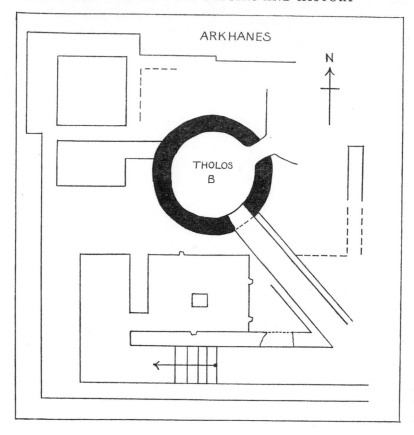

ARKHANES

N

THOLOS
B

Fig. 35 The Middle Minoan II
tholos and associated
funerary complex at Arkhanes

Here we have a chamber about the same diameter as Kamilari 1
(which may have been built only half a century earlier) with a
long *dromos* approaching its entrance on the south-east. To the
north-west of the chamber, and built on to it, were three oblong
rooms, while to the south-west were three more rooms including
a narrow, corridor-like chamber and a large, almost square
"pillar room" (fig. 35). A relationship can surely be established
between this tomb and some of the late tombs of Mesara type.
The orientation of the entrance to the south-east may well have
no significance, though at least two of the Middle Minoan tombs
of Mesara type—Vorou B and Drakones Δ—have entrances
similarly oriented, and Apesokari 1 has a doorway facing east-
south-east. Of much greater interest and significance I feel, are

Fig. 35

the ritual rooms to one side of the *dromos*. They immediately
recall the suites of ritual rooms outside the late tombs at Kamilari
I, Apesokari I and II, Agios Kyrillos and, probably, Viannos. The
earlier tombs Platanos B and Γ also featured suites of outer rooms,
though the date of their construction is uncertain. At least four
of these tombs included in the design of their outer suites a long,
narrow corridor like the one in the suite at Arkhanes. The
oblong room at the end of the corridor is matched in three of the
Mesara suites, while all of the Mesara suites have a large, almost
square chamber as the focus of the ritual ceremonies. These are
presumably to be compared with the similar chamber at Arkhanes
with its central "pillar", so closely resembling the ritual room in
Apesokari I with its central altar (cf. fig. 28).   *Fig. 28*

   At Arkhanes, I believe, we have a truly transitional tomb, just
as the small tombs at Chrysostomos and Kaloi Limenes were
transitional between the cave and rock shelter tombs of the late
and sub-Neolithic and the Mesara tholoi of Early Minoan I. With
the excavations at Arkhanes, we can now follow the Mesara
tombs through a further stage of development until they emerge
as the *tholos* tomb of the Late Bronze Age, devoid of ritual
chambers and set behind a *dromos* and under the earth. In Crete
other developments were to follow—the square chambered
tombs, and those with a keel vault—and the circular, built
chamber tomb was to continue its history through the decline
and destruction of Minoan civilisation and on into the Iron Age.
Here, a full two millennia after the first Mesara tombs were built,
we find small circular tholoi which are not so very different from
their distant ancestors. We may fairly claim that our monuments
of one millennium sired the monuments of a second.

Appendix I

The Structural Details of Forty-Two Tholoi

TOMBS	Int. diameter	Wall thickness	Prvd. height	Int. overhang	Door position	Door height	Door width	Door slab	Built door	Trilithon door	Proj. slabs: rows	Proj. slabs: number	Proj. slabs: orientation	Antechamber: length	Antechamber: width	Other rooms	Pavement/enclosure	Fire traces	Floors: earth/slabs/pebbles
LEBENA II	5.0	1.5		Y	E	0.65	0.9		N									Y	
LEBENA IIa	3.0	0.8			N		0.5												Y
LEBENA III	5.4	2.0	1.0	0.15	E	0.5	0.85	Y	N	Y								N	E
MARATHOKEPHALON II	5.6	2.0	1.2	0.17	S	1.5	1.3					3	?	1.2	1.6	3 or 4			
MEGALI SKINOI IIIa	6.0	2.0	3.4	Y	E			Y	N	Y					Y			Y	N
MEGALI SKINOI IIIb	6.5	2.1	2.0			0.95	0.8		N	Y					Y			Y	
MYRSINI	4.7	1.2		Y	NE				?N	?Y								?Y	
PORTI II	6.65	2.7	1.15	Y	E	0.7	0.7	Y(?)	N	Y	1	6+3	N E / S W	1.75	3.2	2		Y	E
PLATANOS A	13.1	2.45	0.75	Y	E					Y	1			1.5	2.75	9	P/E	Y	E
PLATANOS B	10.23	2.55	1.1	Y	E		?1.8		N	Y	I	24	S	Y	Y	?2	P/E	N	P
PLATANOS Γ	7.3	1.8	0.4		E				N	Y				Y	Y		P/E	Y	P/E
SALAME	5.05	0.85	0.7		E				N	Y									
SIVA N	4.6	1.7	0.9	Y	E		0.9		N		N			?Y	?Y			Y	
SIVA S	5.9	2.0	1.0	Y	E		0.7				N			Y	Y	?Y		N	
TRYPITI	4.9	1.7		Y	SE	1.2	0.75			Y				1.5	3.2				
VALI	4.9																		
VIANNOS																4			
VOROU A	5.5	1.6	1.8	N	N				?Y	?N				?1.0	?1.2	4		Y	P
VOROU B	4.0	2.0		Y	SE				?Y	?N						N			

TOMBS	Int. diameter	Wall thickness	Prvd. height	Int. overhang	Door position	Door height	Door width	Door slab	Built door	Trilithon door	Proj. slabs: rows	Proj. slabs: number	Proj. slabs: orientation	Antechamber: length	Antechamber: width	Other rooms	Pavement/enclosure	Fire traces	Floors: earth/slabs/pebbles
AGIA EIRENE E	8·0	2·0	1·5		E	1·0	1·0	Y	N	Y	1	15	S	2·0	2·2	N			
AGIA EIRENE e	5·45	1·2	0·4	Y	E	1·0	0·81	Y	N	Y								N	
AGIA TRIADHA A	9·0	1·9	1·56	0·40	E	1·0	0·9	Y	N	Y				1·3	1·6	7		Y	
AGIA TRIADHA B	5·6	1·3	2·3	0·15	E	0·81											Y		
AGIOS KYRILLOS			2·0		E	1·75	1·0				3		S			3	?y		P
APESOKARI I	2·4	0·8		Y	ENE		0·45	Y	Y	N	1	4	N	0·7	1·9	4	P	Y	Y
APESOKARI II	5·7		2·0											2·3	3·5	3	P		
CHRISTOS X	6·5	1·5	1·7	Y	E	1·0	0·9	N	N	Y	1		N	Y	Y	N		N	
DRAKONES Δ	5·85	0·8	0·8	Y	SE	0·8	0·75	Y											
DRAKONES Z	7·2	2·1	2·2	Y	E	2·0	1·0		?Y	?N				1·3	2·5			Y	
KALATHIANA K	9·45	2·1	2·7	Y												N		N	P
KALOI LIMENES II	5·5	1·5	2·3	Y	S	0·4+	1·0											N	
KALOI LIMENES III	4·0		0·8	Y	E		0·7							1·9	1·9			Y	
KAMILARI I	7·65	1·7	2·1	Y	ENE	1·0	0·8	Y	N	N	3	(1+3+1)	NE SW	2·0	3·0	4	?P/E	Y	
KAMILARI II	5·0																		
KEPHALI	3·9	1·45	1·9		S	0·8	0·55	Y	Y	Y						Y			S
KNOSSOS (GYP)	4·0				E	1·5+	1·2	Y	N	N			N	N	N	1			E
KOUMASA A	4·1	1·3	1·2	Y	E	0·85	0·85	Y	N	Y			N	0·8	1·45	N	P/E		
KOUMASA B	9·52	2·0	1·6	Y	E	0·93	1·0/0·9	Y	?N	?Y	1	5	N			N	P/E	Y	
KOUMASA E	9·3	2·1	1·5	Y	E	0·7	1·0	Y	?N	?Y	1	12	E	1·75	2·5	N	P/E	Y	
KOUTSOKERA	5·55	1·50	1·30	Y	E	1·0		Y	N	Y									P
LEBENA I	5·1	1·9	1·25	0·25	E	1·0	0·7											Y	E
LEBENA Ib	4·5	1·4	1·4	0·15	SE		0·9	Y										Y	

Appendix 2

THE FINDS MADE IN FORTY-TWO THOLOI

TOMBS	Jugs	Cups	Dishes	Stone Vases	Libation Vessels	Kernoi	"Lids"	Cyc. Figurines	Pointed & round base Figurines	Other Figurines	Double-Axes	Daggers	Tools (Bronze)	Toilet Implements	"Scrapers"	Whetstones	Obsidian (Cores / Blades)	Metal/Clay/Stone Jewellery	Gold Jewellery	Sealstones	Amulets	Imported Scarabs, Daggers, Vessels & Cylinder Seals	Lamps	Palettes	Animal bones & Sea shells	Larnakes	Pithoi	Libation Stones
LEBENA II	Y	Y	Y		Y			Y				Y					Y	Y	Y	Y	Y	IS	Y		SS, AB			
LEBENA II a	Y	Y																		6		IS						
LEBENA III	Y	Y	Y																	IV	Y							
MARATHOKEPHALON II	Y	Y	Y	Y						Y		9		Y	4		c/B	Y	Y	17	IV							
MEGALI SKINOI IIIa	Y	Y	Y					1																				
MYRSINI	Y	Y	Y							Y																	Y	
PORTI Π	Y	Y	Y	Y	Y	Y			2	1		2	Y	Y	2		c/B	Y	Y	13	Y	1D 3S 1C	5	4				Y
PLATANOS A	Y	Y	Y	Y	Y			1 (A/B)	1	2		75+	Y	Y	2		Y	Y	Y	Y	Y							
PLATANOS B	Y	Y	Y	Y	Y		Y		1 (A/B)		2 (A/B)	Y	Y	Y	Y		c/B	Y	Y	Y	Y	1D	1				?1	
PLATANOS Γ	Y	Y	Y	Y	Y		Y										Y	Y	Y	Y	Y							
SALAME	Y	Y										2		2														
SIVA N	Y	Y	Y	Y								2	Y	Y	1		Y	Y	Y	Y	Y				SS		Y	
SIVA S	Y	Y	Y	Y	Y					1		2	Y	Y	1	1	Y	Y	Y	2	Y				SS		Y	
VALI	Y	Y		Y													Y	Y		Y	Y						Y	
VIANNOS	?Y	?Y	?Y																						2			
VOROU A	Y	Y	Y	Y	Y													Y		4	Y	2				Y	1	1
VOROU B	Y	Y	Y	Y	Y													Y			Y					Y	5	1
DEPOSITS																												
AGIOS ANOUPHRIOS	Y	Y	Y	Y				Y				Y		Y			Y	Y	Y	Y	Y	45 / 2V					Y	1
ASPRIPETRA	Y	Y	Y	Y													Y	Y				15					Y	

TOMBS

Tombs	Jugs	Cups	Dishes	Stone Vases	Libation Vessels	Kernoi	"Lids"	Cyc. Figurines	Pointed & round base Figurines	Other Figurines	Double-Axes	Daggers	Tools (Bronze)	Toilet Implements	"Scrapers"	Whetstones	Obsidian (Cores/Blades)	Metal/Clay/Stone Jewellery	Gold Jewellery	Sealstones	Amulets	Imported Scarabs, Daggers, Vessels & Cylinder Seals	Lamps	Palettes	Animal bones & Sea shells	Larnakes	Pithoi	Libation Stones
AGIA EIRENE E	Y	Y	Y									1						Y					1			Y	Y	
AGIA EIRENE e	Y	Y	Y																									
AGIA TRIADHA A	Y	Y	Y	Y	Y		Y	6	6			50			3				Y	108	29	1D / 1C,1S		2	SS, AB		2	
AGIA TRIADHA B	Y	Y	Y	Y	Y							Y																
AGIA KYRIAKI	Y	Y	Y	6						Y		Y					Y											
AGIOS KYRILLOS	Y	Y	Y		Y					1										Y	Y							
APESOKARI I	Y	Y	Y																									
APESOKARI II	Y	Y	Y	12							Y									4					1			
ARKHAIOKHORAPHO	Y																											1
CHRISTOS X	Y	Y	Y	Y											2		Y			Y	Y			1				
DRAKONES Δ	Y	Y	Y	Y		Y								2	3		Y	Y		Y	Y			1	Y		Y	
DRAKONES Z	Y	Y	Y		Y	Y																				Y	Y	
KALATHIANA K	Y	Y	Y							1		7		Y	1	2	Y	Y	Y	6								
KAMILARI I	Y	Y	Y	Y										Y	2	3	Y	Y	Y	20	Y				Y			
KAMILARI II	Y	Y									1		Y					Y										
KEPHALI	Y	Y	Y											Y			Y	Y		3	3							
KNOSSOS (GYP)	Y	Y								Y				Y											1			
KOUMASA A	Y	Y	Y	Y				Y				Y			?Y		Y	Y		Y								
KOUMASA B	Y	Y	Y	Y	Y	Y	Y	2	4	2		24	Y	Y	2	5	Y	Y	Y	20	Y	1D	7	2	Y			
KOUMASA E	Y	Y	Y	Y	Y								Y		?Y		C/B	Y	Y		Y	3D		2				
KOUTSOKERA	Y				?Y																	3D		2				
LEBENA I	Y	Y	Y	Y	Y	Y	Y							Y			Y	Y	Y	30*	Y	1S			AB			
LEBENA Ib	Y	Y	Y	Y				2							1	1	Y	Y	Y						Y		Y	1

Appendix 3

The Chronology of Twenty-Nine Tholoi

Tholos	EM.I	EM.II	EM.III	MM.Ia	MM.II–LM
Agia Eirene E	S ?B	B			LK PH SS
Agia Kyriaki	P O	O2	?SV	SV MW	
Agia Triadha A	O S ?B	B V SV O2	SS ?SV	SV MP SS MW	MM.I– II
Agia Triadha B	S	V		MW SV	B
Agios Kyrillos			?SV	SV MW Z	
Agios Onouphrios	O L	F SS B SV	SS B G	SS Scarabs	
Apesokari I				SV MW MP	
Apesokari II			?SV	SS SV	MW MM.I– BE II

166

Tholos	EM.I	EM.II	EM.III	MM.Ia	MM.II–LM
Aspripetra	O S	O2		Scarab	
Kamilari 1				MW SS SV B	MM.II SS LK LM.II–III
Knossos					MM.II MM.III LM.Ia
Koumasa A	?B	F J FG B	SV	MW	
Koumasa B	S ?B ?BL	O2 Z F FG B SS	G SS SV B	MW SV F B J BE	
Koumasa E	O ?B	B SV	?SV	MW SV	Blossom Bowl
Lebena I		V O2 A SS FG B	G G	MW Scarab	
Lebena Ib		SV F V	?SV	MW SV	
Lebena II	L O S Z F P	B J V	A SV F	MW Scarab	
Lebena IIa		V B		MW Scarab	

Tholos	EM.I	EM.II	EM.III	MM.Ia	MM.II–LM
Lebena III		V FG F	?SV	MW BE SS	MM.Ib
Marathoke- phalon I	O ?B S	SV V B O2 A FG	B G SS SV	B MW SS SV	—
Megali Skinoi IIIa	P O		?SV	MW MP BE	LM (1 Vase)
Platanos A	?B	B J SV	SV B SS	MW SS SV F B	B MM.I/II (3)
Platanos B		SV O2 A	SS SV	MW SV Z SS	MM.I/II- (2) SS B
Platanos Γ		O2	SS SV	MW SS SV	
Porti II	?B	FG J V B	G SV	MW SV MP B Z	MM.I/II
Siva N	L P O ?B S	O2 B	?SV	?SV	
Siva S	L O P	O2 FG B SS	?SS ?SV	SS ?SV	

Tholos	EM.I	EM.II	EM.III	MM.Ia	MM.II–LM
Vali			?SV	SV MW ?SS	LK–LM MM.II
Vorou A			?SV	MW SS SV	

KEY

A	= Amulets	MW	= Middle Minoan I White Painted Wares
B	= Bronzework		
BE	= Barbotine and En-crusted Wares	O	= Agios Onouphrios I Ware
BL	= Burnished "Lids"	O2	= Agios Onouphrios II Ware
F	= Figurines		
FG	= Fine Grey Ware	P	= Pyrgos Ware
G	= Gournia Ware	PH	= Pithoi
J	= Jewellery	S	= Salame Ware
L	= Lebena Ware	SS	= Sealstones
LK	= Larnakes	SV	= Stone Vases
MP	= Middle Minoan I Polychrome Wares	V	= Vasiliki Ware
		Z	= Zoomorphic and analogous vessels

NOTES

1. The omission of artifacts from any column does not necessarily mean that these artifacts were *not* present in the tomb concerned; it means that there is no *record* of such artifacts having been found in the tomb.

2. Where a question mark appears before an abbreviation it implies that the dating of the artifact(s) concerned is uncertain. This applies principally to two groups of objects, some of the triangular daggers (which were used in EM.II but probably first appeared in EM.I) and the majority of the stone vessels (which can only be dated within the brackets EM.III–MM.I).

Appendix 4

Catalogue of Early and Middle Bronze Age built circular chamber tombs of Mesara type

Certain Tholoi (excavated or visible and investigated)

1. 'Agía Eiréne E. Xanthoudides *1924*, 51–53. EM.I–MM.II.
2. 'Agía Eiréne e. Xanthoudides *1924*, 51–53. EM.I–?MM.I.
3. 'Agía Kyriakí. Sakellarakis *1965*, 562–64. EM.I–MM.I.
4. 'Agía Triádha A. Banti *1933*; Stefani *1933*. EM.I–MM.II.
5. 'Agía Triádha B. Parabeni *1905*; Halbherr *1905*. EM.I–MM.II.
6. 'Agiopharángos. Alexiou *1967*, 483. Date unknown.
7. 'Agios Geórgios. Alexiou *1967*, 483. Early Minoan.
8. 'Agios Kýrillos. Sakellarakis *1968*. Middle Minoan I.
9. 'Apesokári I. Matz *1951*. Middle Minoan I.
10. 'Apesokári II. Megaw *1967*, 22; Davaras *1964*, 441. Middle Minoan I.
11. Christós X. Xanthoudides *1924*, 70–72. ?–MM.I.
12. Chrysóstomos I. Branigan *1970*, fig. 38. EM.I–?MM.I.
13. Chrysóstomos II. Branigan *1970*, fig. 38. EM.I–?MM.I.
14. Drakónes Δ. Xanthoudides *1924*, 76–80. ?EM.III–MM.II.
15. Drakónes Z. Xanthoudides *1924*, 76–80. ?EM.III–?MM.I.
16. Kalathianá K. Xanthoudides *1924*, 81–87. ?EM.I–MM.I.
17. Kalói Liménes I. Alexiou *1967*, 483, Davaras *1968*, 405.
18. Kalói Liménes II. Davaras *1968*, 405.
19. Kalói Liménes III. Davaras *1968*, 405.
20. Kamilári I. Levi *1962*. MM.I–III (reused in LM).
21. Kamilári II (Mylona Lakko). Levi *1962*, 107–8. ?MM.II–III.
22. Kamilári III. Unpublished. A tomb of about three–four metres internal diameter, largely destroyed, with a spread of Middle Minoan sherds; situated *c.* 50 metres from Kamilári I. Seen by author, 1966.
23. Kepháli Odiyitrías. Alexiou *1963a*, 312; Alexiou *1963*, 398. EM.I–?MM.I.
24. Knossós (Gypsádes). Hood *1958*, 300–1. MM.II–LM.IA.
25. Korakiés N. Faure *1969*, 181. "Early Minoan–MM.I."
26. Korakiés S. Faure *1969*, 181. "Early Minoan–MM.I."
    A letter from Prof. Faure (dated 9/7/69) informs me that two small tholoi were excavated here, within a few metres of one another.
27. Koumasá A. Xanthoudides *1924*, 32–50. ?EM.I–MM.I.
28. Koumasá B. Xanthoudides *1924*, 4–32. EM.I–MM.I.
29. Koumasá E. Xanthoudides *1924*, 32–50. EM.I–?MM.II.
30. Koutsokéra. Xanthoudides *1924*, 74–5. EM.I–?.
31. Lebéna I (Papoura). Alexiou *1960*; Daux *1959*, 742–4. EM.II–MM.I.
32. Lebéna Ib (Papoura). Daux *1961*, 886–889. EM.II–MM.I.
33. Lebéna II (Yerokambos). Alexiou *1960*; Daux *1959*, 742–4. EM.I–MM.I.

34. Lebéna IIa (Yerokambos). Alexiou *1960*; Daux *1959*, 742–4. EM.II–MM.I.
35. Lebéna III (Zervou). Daux *1961*, 886–889. EM.II–MM.I.
36. Marathoképhalon I. Xanthoudides *1918*. Date unknown, probably EM.I–MM.I.
37. Marathoképhalon II. Xanthoudides *1918*. EM.I–MM.I.
38. Megáli Skinoí IIIa. Alexiou *1967*, 482. EM.I–MM.I.
39. Megáli Skinoí IIIb. Alexiou *1967*, 482. Early Minoan.
40. Megáli Skinoí IIIc. Alexiou *1967*, 482. Date unknown.
41. Myrsíni (Galana Kharakia). Daux *1960*, 821. EM.III/MM.I.
42. Phýlakas. Alexiou *1967*, 484. Date unknown.
43. Plátanos A. Xanthoudides *1924*, 88–125. ?EM.II–MM.II.
44. Plátanos B. Xanthoudides *1924*, 88–125. EM.II–MM.II.
45. Plátanos Γ. Xanthoudides *1924*, 88–125. EM.II–?MM.II.
46. Portí Π. Xanthoudides *1924*, 54–69. ?EM.I–MM.II.
47. Rotási. Platon *1955*, 567. "Early Minoan". "The vases from the EM tholos grave excavated last year . . . in the region of the village of Rotasi, were joined together and are interesting as a group."
48. Saláme. Xanthoudides *1924*, 73–4. EM.I–?.
49. Síva N. Parabeni *1913*, 14–31. EM.I–MM.I.
50. Síva S. Parabeni *1913*, 14–31. EM.I–?MM.I.
51. Trypití (Kalokámbos). Alexiou *1967*, 484. EM.I–?.
52. Valí. Woodward *1927*, 258. ?EM.III–?LM.
53. Viánnos (Galana Kharakia). Hood *1956*, 22. EM.III/MM.I.
54. Voroù A. Marinatos *1931*, 137–170. MM.I.
55. Voroù B. Marinatos *1931*, 137–170. ?MM.I.

Probable Tholoi (excavated but date uncertain or unexcavated but indications good).
56. 'Arkhaiokhorápho. Marinatos *1925*. ?EM–LM. Excavated; foundation date?.
57. Gorgolaíni. Hood *1955*, 30; Platon *1955*, 566. Circular wall, bones, EM sherds.
58. Siderokámino. Faure *1969*, 180. Circular tomb, probably built in MM.I.

Possible Tholoi (surface indications insufficient to indicate the nature and purpose of the structure. Most of the structures are almost certainly tholoi of Mesara type).
59. 'Agios Onoúphrios. Evans *1895* (Supplement). Deposit of material from EM.I–LM, with no known structural associations. Typical tholos assemblage.
60. 'Aspripétra. Marinatos *1918*. Deposit of EM.I–MM.I material with human bones but no recognisable associated structure.
61. Christós. Xanthoudides *1924*, 70. "a section of a circular wall, the last remnant of another tholos possibly never finished".
62 Kalérgi. Pendlebury *1934*, 81; *1939*, 289. "traces of what seems to be a circular tomb", the date is uncertain; Pendlebury thought it of Mesara type.
63. Kato Vatheia. Information from M. S. F. Hood. Traces of a settlement and a large circular? tomb.
64. Kokkiniáno. Pendlebury *1934*, 87. "We found a similar tomb (to Porti). No sherds could be found in it however."
65. Kómo. Evans *1928*, 89, fig. 42. "seemingly a segment of a tomb of the primitive beehive type", on the fringe of an EM.I–MM.I settlement. Pendlebury (*1934*, 89) is dubious of this "tomb", but his remark that it gave the impression of belonging rather to an apsidal building suggests perhaps a tomb with a suite of outer rooms like 'Apesokári I, II, 'Agios Kýrillos etc.
66. Krási. Marinatos *1929*. A circular built chamber tomb of EM.I–MM.I date.

The only problems are its situation (the only known EM.ı tholos outside of the Mesara region) and its unusual construction with large rough boulders. It may be an enlarged built grave of Cycladic type.

67. Megáli Vrýsi ı. Daux *1960*, 833. "Great circular works; probably chamber tombs." Date uncertain.
68. Megáli Vrýsi ıı. Daux *1960*, 833. As above.
69. Merthiés. Pendlebury *1934*, 87. Circular stone building with EM sherds. A stone wall running across its diameter would be unique in a tholos except possibly for 72 below.
70. Pédhino ı. Pendlebury *1934*, 96. "traces of two circular tombs". Sherds on the site were handmade.
71. Pédhino ıı. Pendlebury *1934*, 96. As above.
72. Plakóura. Pendlebury *1934*, 87. Circular stone building with traces of other walls; some EM sherds. Like 68 above, Pendlebury noted traces of a wall running across the diameter.
73. Potamiés. Information from M. S. F. Hood. A small circular ?tomb, near the church of the Archangel Michael, built against an outcrop of rock. Remains of a pithos burial just outside it.
74. Rízikas. Hood *1955*, 30; Platon *1955*, 566. A circular wall, about five metres diameter, built of large stones. No dating evidence given.
75. Tsilástra. Alexiou *1967*, 483. "possibly another tholos" reported here.

Improbable Tholoi (surface indications of built tombs of dubious type or late date).
76. 'Ellenikó (To Vouno). Faure *1967*, 109, pl. XI, 5. Probable remains of a collapsed vaulted tomb of circular shape. No EM remains known nearby but within fifty metres of an LM.ııı site.
77. Paranísi. Pendlebury *1939*, 299. Report of a "small chamber with part of a corbelled roof". Pendlebury clearly did not regard it as an EM tholos for he did not include it in his list of EM sites.

Doubtful (reports which are suggestive of the existence of tholoi but which cannot be confirmed without further information).
78. Kaloí Liménes. Sakellarakis *1965*, 562–4. Description of EM.ıı pottery (pyxides, teapots, two-handled vase) from a "looted grave" near Kaloí Liménes. These could be from any of the other tombs in the vicinity of Kaloí Liménes, subsequently excavated (see No's 17–19).
79. Loúkia. Evans *1928*, map facing page 71. Evans marks an EM tholos at Loúkia but gives no further information.
80. Pómbia. Unpublished. Report to the author, August 1966, by a member of the Greek archaeological service, but see Davaras *1968*, 406.
81. Síva. Platon *1955*, 567; Hood *1955*, 30. "Two narrow gold bands from the region of Síva may also come from a tholos tomb." They might indeed, but such a tomb could be one of those excavated since 1955 at Kamilari, or in the region of Odiyitria.

Rejected Tholoi (tombs identified previously as EM tholoi but rejected by the author).
82. Praesós. Bosanquet *1902*, 240–45. Identified by Xanthoudides (*1924*, 8, fn. 1) as an EM tholos cleared out and re-used in the Geometric period. Neither the architecture nor the finds from the tholos at Praesós provide any suggestion of an EM date.

Bibliography

The following abbreviations are used:

AAA: Athens Annals of Archaeology
AJA: American Journal of Archaeology
Arch. Rep.: Archaeological Reports
ASCC: Acts of the Second Cretological Congress, Khania 1968, 1969.
BCH: Bulletin de Correspondance Hellenique
BPI: Bollettino de Palentologia Italiana
BSA: Annual of the British School at Athens
Deltion: Arkhaiologikon Deltion
Ergon: To Ergon tes Arkhaiologikes Etaireias
IKVF: International Kongress Vor- und Frühgeschichte, 1958.
ILN: Illustrated London News
JHS: Journal of Hellenic Studies
KCh: Kretika Chonika
Mon. Ant.: Monumenti Antichi
MRIL: Memorie del Reale Istituto Lombardo di Scienze e Lettere
Par. Pass.: La Parola del Passato
PPS: Proceedings of the Prehistoric Society
Praktika: Praktika tes en Athenais Arkhaiologikes Etaireias
SMEA: Studi Micenei ed Egeo-Anatolici
TDAUP: Transactions of the Department of Archaeology, University of Pennsylvania
TFMSA: Transactions of the Free Museum of Science and Art, Pennsylvania
World Arch.: World Archaeology

Aberg, N. *1933, Bronzezeitliche und Früheisenzeitliche Chronologie, IV.*
Alexiou, S. *1951,* Protominoikai Taphai para to Kanli Kastelli, Iraklion. *KCh 1951.*
——. *1954,* Anaskaphai en Katsamba. *Praktika 1954.*
——. *1960,* New Light on Minoan Dating; Early Minoan Tombs at Lebena. *ILN Aug. 6th, 1960.*
——. *1963,* Chronika. *KCh 1963.*
——. *1963a,* Arkhaiotetes kai Mneimeia Kretes. *Deltion 18 B' 2.*
——. *1964,* Chronika. *KCh 1964.*
——. *1967,* Arkhaiotetes kai Mneimeia Kentrikes kai Anatol. Kretes. *Deltion 22B' 2.*
Banti, L. *1933,* La Grande Tomba a Tholos di Hagia Triadha. *Annuario 13–14.*
Blegen, C. W. *1954,* An Early Tholos Tomb in West Messenia. *Hesperia 23.*
Bosanquet, R. C. *1902,* Excavations at Praesos I. *BSA 8.*
Branigan, K. *1965,* The Origins of the Hieroglyphic Sign 18. *Kadmos 4.*

——. *1965a*, Four "Miniature Sickles" of Middle Minoan Crete. *KCh 1965*.

——. *1966*, Prehistoric Relations Between Italy and the Aegean. *BPI NS.17*.

——. *1966a*, The Prehistory of Hieroglyphic Signs 12 and 36. *Kadmos 5*.

——. *1966b*, Byblite Daggers in Cyprus and Crete. *AJA 70*.

——. *1967*, The Early Bronze Age Daggers of Crete. *BSA 62*.

——. *1967a*, Further Light on Prehistoric Relations Between Crete and Syria. *AJA 71*.

——. *1968, Copper and Bronzeworking in Early Bronze Age Crete.*

——. *1968a*, Early Minoan Metallurgy—A Re-appraisal. *ASCC. B*.

——. *1968b*, The Mesara Tholoi and Middle Minoan Chronology. *SMEA 5*.

——. *1968c*, Silver and Lead in Prepalatial Crete. *AJA 72*.

——. *1969*, The Earliest Aegean Scripts—The Prepalatial Background. *Kadmos 8*.

——. *1969a*, The Genesis of the Household Goddess. *SMEA 8*.

——. *1969b*, A Transitional Phase in Minoan Metallurgy. *BSA 63*.

——. *1970, The Foundations of Palatial Crete.*

——. *1970a*, Minoan Foot Amulets and their Near Eastern Counterparts. *SMEA 10*.

——. *1971*, Cycladic Figurines and their Derivatives in Crete, *BSA 66*.

Caskey, J. L. *1962*, Excavations in Keos 1960–61. *Hesperia 31*.

——. *1964, Greece, Crete and the Aegean Islands in the Early Bronze Age.*

——. *1964a*, Excavations in Keos 1963. *Hesperia 33*.

Charles, R.-P. *1965, Anthropologie Archéologique de la Crète.*

Daux, G. *1958*, Chroniques des Fouilles en 1957. *BCH 82*.

——. *1959*, Chroniques des Fouilles en 1958. *BCH 83*.

——. *1960*, Chroniques des Fouilles en 1959. *BCH 84*.

——. *1961*, Chroniques des Fouilles en 1960. *BCH 85*.

——. *1964*, Chroniques des Fouilles en 1963. *BCH 88*.

——. *1966*, Chroniques des Fouilles en 1965. *BCH 90*.

Davaras, C. *1964*, Arkhaiotetes kai Mneimeia Kretes. Anaskaphai. *Deltion 19B'3*, 441.

——. *1968*, Perioke Mones Odiyitrias *Deltion 23B' 2*.

Dawkins, R. M. *1904*, Excavations at Palaikastro III. *BSA 10*.

——. *1905*, Excavations at Palaikastro IV. *BSA 11*.

Emery, W. B. *1961, Archaic Egypt.*

Evans, A. J. *1895, Cretan Pictographs and the Mycenaean Script.*

——. *1902*, The Palace at Knossos. *BSA 8*.

——. *1921, The Palace of Minos I.*

——. *1928, The Palace of Minos II.*

——. *1930, The Palace of Minos III.*

——. *1935, The Palace of Minos IV.*

Evans, J. D. *1964*, Excavations in the Neolithic Settlement of Knossos, 1957–60, Part I. *BSA 59*.

Faure, P. *1967*, Aux Frontières de L'État de Lato: 50 Toponymes. *Europa* (ed. W. C. Brice) 94–112.

——. *1969*, Sur Trois Sortes de Sanctuaires Crétois. (suite) *BCH 93*.

Halbherr, F. *1905*, Rapporto . . . Sugli Scavi Eseguiti Dalla Missione Archeologica ad Haghia Triada ed a Festo nell'Anno 1904. *MRIL 21*.

Hall, E. H. *1905*, Early Painted Pottery from Gournia, Crete. *TDAUP I*.

Hammond, N. G. L. *1967*, Tumulus Burial in Albania, the Grave Circles of Mycenae, and the Indo-Europeans. *BSA 62*.

Hazzidakis, J. *1916*, Parartema. Platanos. *Deltion 2.*

Higgins, R. *1957*, The Aegina Treasure Reconsidered. *BICS 4.*

Hogarth, D. G. *1901*, Excavations at Zakro, Crete. *BSA 7.*

Hood, M. S. F. *1955*, Archaeology in Greece 1955. *Arch. Rep. 1955.*

——. *1956*, Archaeology in Greece 1956. *Arch. Rep. 1956.*

——. *1958*, Discoveries During the Latest Knossos Excavations. *ILN Feb. 22, 1958.*

——. *1960*, Tholos Tombs of the Aegean. *Antiquity 34.*

——. *1961*, The Early Bronze Age Chronology of the Aegean Area, with Special Reference to Troy. *IKVF 5.* 398ff.

——. *1962*, The Home of the Heroes, in *The Dawn of Civilisation* (ed. S. Piggott) 195ff.

——. *1963*, Stratigraphic Excavations at Knossos, 1957–61. *KCh 1963.*

——. *1963a*, Archaeology in Greece, 1962. *Arch. Rep. 1963.*

——. *1965*, Minoan Sites in the Far West of Crete. *BSA 60.*

Hood, et al. *1964*, Travels in Crete, 1962, *BSA 59.*

Hutchinson, R. W. *1962, Prehistoric Crete.*

Huxley, G. L. and Coldstream, J. N. *1966*, Kythera, First Minoan Colony. *ILN Aug. 27, 1966.*

Kenyon, K. M. *1960, Archaeology in the Holy Land.*

Levi, D. *1952*, One of the Richest Finds of Minoan Treasures in Crete. *ILN, Jan. 19, 1952.*

——. *1953*, Uncovering One of the Oldest Palaces of Phaistos. *ILN, Dec. 12, 1953.*

——. *1960*, Per Una Nuova Classificazione della Civilta Minoica. *Par. Pass. 15.*

——. *1962*, La Tomba a Tholos di Kamilari Presso a Festòs. *Annuario 39–40.*

——. *1963*, New Discoveries on One of the Greatest of Minoan Sites. *ILN, July 27, 1963.*

——. *1965*, Le Varieta della Primitiva Ceramica Cretese, in *Studi in Onore di Luisa Banti* (Rome 1965).

Long, V. C. R. *1959*, Shrines in Sepulchres. A Re-examination of Three Middle to Late Minoan Tombs. *AJA 63.*

Mallowan, M. E. L. and Rose, J. C. *1933, The Excavations at Arpachiyah.*

Marinatos, S. *1925,* Mesominoiki Oikia en Kato Mesara. *Deltion 9.*

——, *1929*, Protominoikos Tholotos Taphos para to Khorion Krasi Pediadha. *Deltion 12.*

——. *1929a*, Anaskaphai en Krete. To Speos Eileithyies. *Praktika 1929.*

——. *1930*, Anaskaphai en Krete. To Speos Eileithyies. *Praktika 1930.*

——. *1931*, Duo Proimoi Minoikoi Taphoi ek Vorou Mesaras. *Deltion 13.*

——. *1954*, Anaskaphai en Pylo. *Praktika 1954.*

Matz, F. *1951, Forschungen auf Kreta* (Ed.).

——. *1962, Crete and Early Greece.*

Megaw, J. V. S. *1967*, Archaeology in Greece, 1966. *Arch. Rep. 1967.*

Mylonas, G. E. *1951*, The Cult of the Dead in Helladic Times, in *Studies Presented to D. M. Robinson. I.* (Ed. G. E. Mylonas.).

——. *1966, Mycenae and the Mycenaean Age.*

Myres, J. L. *1903,* The Sanctuary Site of Petsofa, *BSA 9.*

Nilsson, M. *1932, The Mycenaean Origins of Greek Mythology.*

Orlandos, A. K. (Ed.) *1960, Ergon 7.*

Parabeni, R. *1905*, Ricerche nel Sepolcreto di Hagia Triada presso Phaestos. *Mon. Ant. 14.*

——. *1913*, Scavi nella Necropoli di Siva. *Ausonia 8.*

Pendlebury, J. D. S. *1934*, Travels in Crete. *BSA 33.*

——. *1939, The Archaeology of Crete.*

Persson, A. W. *1931, The Royal Tombs at Dendra near Midea.*

Platon, N. *1955*, Chronika. *KCh 1955.*

——. *1961*, Chronologie de la Crète et des Cyclades à l'Age du Bronze. *IKVF 5,* 674–5.

——. *1964*, A New Major Minoan Palace Discovered in Crete. *ILN March 7, 1964.*

Proudfoot, E. W. *1963*, Excavation of a Bell Barrow in the parish of Edmonsham, Dorset, England. *PPS 29.*

Renfrew, C. *1967*, Colonialism and Megalithismus. *Antiquity 41.*

——. *1969*, The Development and Chronology of the Early Cycladic Figurines. *AJA 73.*

Renfrew, C. and Springer, J. *1969*, Aegean Marble, A Petrological Study. *BSA 63.*

Sakellarakis, I. *1965*, Arkhaiotetes kai Mneimeia Kretes. Anaskaphai. *Deltion 20, B'3.*

——. *1967*, Minoan Cemeteries at Arkhanes. *Archaeology 20.*

——. *1968*, A Tholos Tomb at Agios Kyrillos in the Mesara. *AAA I.*

Schachermeyr, F. *1964, Die Minoische Kulture des Alten Kreta.*

Seager, R. B. *1907*, Report of Excavations at Vasiliki, Crete, in 1906. *TFMSA II.*

Stefani, E. *1933*, La Grande Tomba a Tholos di Haghia Triada. *Annuario 13–14.*

Stubbings, F. H. *1963, The Rise of Mycenaean Civilisation.*

Taramelli, A. *1897*, The Prehistoric Grotto of Miamu. *AJA I.*

Taylour, Lord W. *1964, The Mycenaeans.*

Tod, M. N. *1903*, Excavations at Palaikastro II. Agios Nikolaos. *BSA 9.*

Ucko, P. J. *1969*, Ethnography and Archaeological Interpretation of Funerary Remains. *World Arch. I, 2.*

Valmin, N. *1938, The Swedish Messenia Expedition.*

Wace, A. J. B. *1949, Mycenae. An Archaeological History and Guide.*

Warren, P. *1965*, The First Minoan Stone Vases and Early Minoan Chronology. *KCh 1965.*

——. *1967*, Minoan Stone Vases as Evidence for Minoan Foreign Connections in the Aegean Late Bronze Age. *PPS 33.*

——. *1968*, A Textile Town—4500 Years Ago. *ILN Feb. 17, 1968.*

——. *1969*, Minoan Village on Crete. *ILN Feb. 8, 1969.*

——. *1970, Minoan Stone Vases.*

Woodward, A. M. *1927*, Archaeology in Greece 1926–27. *JHS 47.*

Xanthoudides, S. *1912*, Cretan Kernoi. *BSA 18.*

——. *1915*, Parartema. Platanos. *Deltion 1.*

——. *1916*, Parartema. Platanos. *Deltion 2.*

——. *1918*, Parartema. Protominoikoi Taphoi Mesaras. *Deltion 4.*

——. *1918a*, Megas Protominoikos Taphos Pyrgos. *Deltion 4.*

——. *1924, The Vaulted Tombs of Mesara.*

Zervos, C. *1956, L'Art de la Crète.*

Zoes, A. *1967*, Eparchei PM.III Epoche. *ASCC I.*

Notes

CHAPTER ONE: THE TOMBS DISCOVERED

1. One is tempted to relate these structures to the arc-shaped ?sanctuary with a bench across its interior, found at Fournou Korifi. *1968*, 25.
2. The reconstruction of the Platanos cemetery area is based on Xanthoudides' plan of a part of it (*1924*, pl. LXII) and his descriptions of it in both the interim and final reports (*1915, 1916, 1924*). It must be emphasised that the reconstruction does not purport to be an accurate plan of the cemetery; Xanthoudides' plan and report are not sufficiently detailed to allow an accurate reconstruction to be made. My intention in drawing this reconstructed plan of the cemetery has been to try to convey the impression of a Mesara cemetery which had been in use for more than a millennium.

CHAPTER TWO: THE MONUMENTS OF A MILLENNIUM

1. Levi *1952, 1953, 1960, 1963, 1965*.
2. Aaberg *1933*.
3. Caskey *1964*, 31, 35; Hutchinson *1962*, 137; Matz *1962*, 239.
4. Warren *1965*, 14–28.
5. Alexiou *1960*.
6. Dawkins *1904*, 198–9.
7. Hall *1905*.
8. Warren *1965*, 16.
9. Warren *1968*, fig. 12.
10. Branigan *1968*, 54–5.
11. Alexiou *1963*, 88ff; Hood *1961*, 389ff; Platon *1961*, 674; Schachermeyr *1964*, 40–156.
12. Zoes *1967*. See also Branigan *1968a*, 34, *1970*, 32.
13. Branigan *1968*, 54–5.
14. Warren *1965*, 36.
15. Warren *1965*, Cat. No's. 5, 13, 32.
16. The terms Early and Middle Bronze Age have not yet been precisely defined for Cretan prehistory and they are used here rather loosely. I include Middle Minoan Ia within the Early Bronze Age, but recognise that this presents a serious problem with regard to Middle Minoan Ib/IIa and IIb, since the Middle Minoan Ia styles of pottery remained in use alongside these later styles and outside of a few palatial centres were probably used exclusively. It would be possible to eliminate the Minoan "Middle Bronze Age" if this line of argument was followed to its conclusion, but this would be an entirely unsatisfactory situation. Until the pottery styles and cultural phases have been given quite separate and distinct labels, this confusion will persist.

17. Branigan *1968b*, 15–24.
18. For a full discussion of Early Minoan Crete, with relevant references, see my previous book, *The Foundations of Palatial Crete*, London *1970*.
19. Both Vasiliki and Fournou Korifi were destroyed by fire in late Early Minoan II, but other Early Minoan II settlement sites have failed to produce evidence of violent destruction at this time. There is no reason to think that these two destroyed sites in Crete should be linked with the widespread destructions in the Argolid at the end of Early Helladic II.

CHAPTER THREE: THE VAULTED TOMBS OF MESARA?

1. Xanthoudides *1924*, 4, 91, 128.
2. Pendlebury *1939*, 64; Hutchinson *1962*, 152; Marinatos *1931*, 168ff.
3. Levi *1962*, 104ff; Alexiou *1960*, 225–6; Daux *1960*, 821.
4. Xanthoudides *1924*, 5.
5. Evans in Xanthoudides *1924*, xi; Seager *1907*, 131.
6. for references, see supra n. 2.
7. for references, see supra n. 3.
8. Hood *1960*.
9. Marinatos *1931*, 140; Xanthoudides *1924*, 77.
10. Xanthoudides *1924*, 70.
11. Xanthoudides *1924*, 91.
12. Xanthoudides *1924*, 70.
13. Xanthoudides *1924*, 70, 90.
14. Parabeni *1905*, 683; Xanthoudides *1924*, 5.
15. Levi *1962*, 12.
16. Pendlebury *1939*, 64; Hutchinson *1962*, 152.
17. Hood *1960*, 171.
18. Warren *1968*, 25; Xanthoudides *1924*, 93.
19. References to, and further discussion of, both contemporary and later vaulted tombs in the Mediterranean area can be found in the concluding chapter of the book.
20. Myrsini may be an exception to this rule, since Platon's brief interim note mentions one preserved "upright"—presumably a slab used as one jamb in a trilithon construction.
21. I am much indebted to Dr Smith (Dept. Civil Engineering, University of Bristol) and Mr R. Maslin, B.Sc. (Mech Engineer) for their lengthy discussions and examinations of the evidence and the problem.

CHAPTER FOUR: GRAVE-GOODS

1. Xanthoudides *1924*, 94 says that no clay vessels were found in tomb A at Platanos, but later (p. 95) ascribes two pottery vessels to tomb A, No's 6892 and 6915. In addition his interim report on the excavation of tomb A includes amongst the list of finds, "cups and simple bowls" of clay.
2. For a discussion of Early Minoan sealstones and of these two "styles", see Branigan *1970*.
3. For a discussion of their meaning see Branigan *1969*.
4. These are discussed in detail in Branigan *1970a*.
5. Branigan *1965*.
6. Branigan *1966*.

7. Renfrew *1969*, 18–20.
8. Renfew and Springer *1969*, 57–58.
9. Branigan *1971*.
10. Warren *1969*, 27.
11. For a full discussion of these see Warren *1970*.
12. Discussed by Warren *1965*, 7–14.
13. Warren *1965*, 9.
14. Xanthoudides *1912*.
15. The woman-vessel from Fournou Korifi (Warren *1969*, fig. 1) is not closely comparable to the Mesara anthropomorphic vessels.
16. Proudfoot *1963*.

CHAPTER FIVE: THE BURIAL OF THE DEAD
1. Stefani *1933*, 150.
2. Stefani *1933*, 151; Evans in Xanthoudides *1924*, xii, fn. 2.
3. Marinatos *1931*, 145, 151–3; Hood *1958*, fig. 8; Daux *1959*, 742–3.
4. Xanthoudides *1924*, 134.
5. Myres *1903*, pls. ix, x. One must, of course, consider the possibility that in burial the normal position was reversed, but this does not seem to be the practice in the Aegean Bronze Age.
6. Branigan *1966*, 98–101; *1967*, 238.
7. Xanthoudides *1924*, 74, 77, 91; Levi *1962*, 107; Hood *1958*, 300; Xanthoudides *1915*, 61.
8. Alexiou *1960*, 227; Xanthoudides *1924*, 89, 34; Marinatos *1931*, 146.
9. Xanthoudides *1918*, fig. 6, lower, second from left; *1924*, pl. XXIVb, 1197; Branigan *1968*, 90, fig. 8, 7.
10. Xanthoudides *1924*, pl. LIV; p. 102, pl. LIV, 1883; pp. 21, 105; *1918*, 19.
11. Xanthoudides *1924*, pls. XXXIXb, 1435, LVI, 1923; *1918*, fig. 6, lower, third from left; Evans *1895*, fig. 139.
12. Banti *1933*, 216; Alexiou *1960*, 226; Daux *1959*, 743.
13. Xanthoudides *1924*, pl. XXXVII, 5074; Marinatos *1931*, 147.
14. Marinatos *1931*, 142, 144; Stefani *1933*, fig. 4, 132; Marinatos *1925*, fig. 12; Xanthoudides *1924*, 91.
15. Ucko *1969*, 269.
16. There was a rectangular building divided into four rooms attached to one side of the tholos at Viannos, but we have no details of the plan.
17. Xanthoudides *1924*, pl. LXII, p. 92.
18. Levi *1962*, 18; *1963*, 134.
19. Davaras *1967*, 441.
20. Sakellarakis *1968*, 51.
21. Marinatos *1931*, 149–50.
22. Stefani *1933*, 151–2.
23. Stefani *1933*, 152; Alexiou *1960*, 227; Daux *1960*, 845; Sakellarakis *1968*, 51; Davaras *1967*, 441.
24. Marinatos *1931*, 149, 153.
25. Marinatos *1931*, 149.
26. Marinatos *1931*, 149; Levi *1962*, fig. 106; Sakellarakis *1968*, fig. 4; Banti *1933*, fig. 4.
27. Davaras *1967*, 441; Sakellarakis *1968*, 51.

28. Alexiou *1960*, figs. 10, 14, 15; Xanthoudides *1924*, pls. XIX, 4138, XX, 4140, 4141, 4146.

29. Xanthoudides *1924*, pls. XIX, 4993, XXX, 4979, 4986.

CHAPTER SIX: DEATH AND THE DEAD

1. Ucko has demonstrated the fallibility of this hypothesis, Ucko *1969*.
2. Evans in Xanthoudides *1924*, xi–xii; Xanthoudides *1924*, 135; Pendlebury *1939*, 63.
3. Alexiou *1960*, fig. 16.
4. For illustrations and discussion of these rectangular ossuaries, see Branigan *1970*.
5. Xanthoudides *1924*, 56, 90, 98.
6. Xanthoudides *1924*, 107, pl. LV, 1934. This dagger is later than the burials in the tomb and chambers, being not earlier than Middle Minoan III.
7. Levi *1962*, figs. 24–27; Xanthoudides *1924*, 34.
8. Levi *1962*, 21–22; Xanthoudides *1924*, 34.
9. Xanthoudides *1924*, 89.
10. Xanthoudides *1924*, 92–3.
11. Xanthoudides *1924*, 92, 7; Stefani *1933*, fig. 5.
12. Xanthoudides *1924*, 6, 132; Hutchinson *1962*, 229–30; Alexiou *1951*.
13. Xanthoudides *1918*, 17–18; *1924*, 71, 82, 51, 92.
14. Xanthoudides *1924*, 89.
15. Alexiou *1960*, 227.
16. Xanthoudides *1924*, 93.
17. Xanthoudides *1924*, 92–3.
18. Xanthoudides *1924*, 52, 6, 56, 76; Alexiou *1967*, 482; Parabeni *1913*, 16.
19. Xanthoudides *1918*, 17; *1924*, 34.
20. Levi *1963*, 134; Xanthoudides *1924*, 34.
21. Ucko (*1969*, 265) suggests it is simply a case of disposal.
22. Marinatos *1931*, 146–7, 150.
23. Marinatos *1931*, 151.
24. Gypsades and Megali Skinoi IIIa.
25. Gypsades, Drakones Z, Agios Kyrillos, and Megali Skinoi IIIa.
26. e.g. Jericho Pre-Pottery B, British neolithic long-barrows, the widespread adoption of trepannation etc.
27. Xanthoudides *1924*, 7, 92; Stefani *1933*, 151; Marinatos *1931*, 151.
28. Stefani *1933*, 150, fig. 5.
29. Marinatos *1931*, 148–9, fig. 21.
30. Marinatos *1931*, 149–50, fig. 24; Xanthoudides *1924*, pl. XXXIII.
31. see Branigan *1969a*, 33–8.
32. Levi *1962*, fig. 158. This is an interesting example, in view of Seager's discovery of two half double-axes at Vasiliki, see Branigan *1966a*.
33. Davaras *1967*, 441; Evans *1902*, 93ff.
34. Xanthoudides *1924*, pl. LVI.
35. Xanthoudides *1924*, pl. XXXVII.
36. Levi *1962*, fig. 96; Branigan *1965a*.
37. Levi *1962*, 122–148, figs. 170a–f, 174a–b, 177a–c.
38. Branigan *1969–a*.
39. Branigan *1969a*, 29–30.
40. Long *1959*, 59.

CHAPTER SEVEN: THE CEMETERY AND SOCIETY

1. Early studies of the Mesara skeletal remains are summarised, together with studies of comparative and contemporary material from elsewhere in Crete, in Xanthoudides *1924*, 126–8. To these studies may be added the brief report on the remains from Vorou, Marinatos *1931*, 165–6.
2. Charles *1965*.
3. Xanthoudides *1924*, xiii, 130.
4. For discussions of foot amulets, triangular daggers, and figurines, see Branigan *1970*, *1967*, 234–6, *1971*.
5. Hutchinson *1962*, 139–40; Caskey *1964*, 32; Schachermeyr *1964*, chapters one and five.
6. Kenyon *1960*, 84–100.
7. These are all illustrated and discussed in Mallowan *1933*.
8. I have discussed this problem at some length in the last chapter of *The Foundations of Palatial Crete*.
9. Alexiou *1967*, 484.
10. Marinatos *1931*, figs. 2, 5, 7; Levi *1962*, figs. 31–42; Woodward *1927*, 258.
11. Xanthoudides *1924*, 56; Parabeni *1931*, 14, 23.
12. Xanthoudides *1924*, 54–5, 93; Parabeni *1905*; Alexiou *1967*, 483.
13. Branigan *1970*, 117.
14. It should be noted that of these eight tombs, there is no certainty that Pedhino and Kalergi are tholoi, nor that they date to Middle Minoan I, and I have expressed doubts in chapter one as to the identification of the remains at Elleniko as a tholos of Mesara type and Early Bronze Age date.
15. Ucko (*1969*, 268–9) cites an interesting, but rarely adopted, alternative practised by the Merina of Madagascar. Here, a community may have several communal tombs, each of which belongs to a "burial association".
16. Daux *1959*, 742–3.
17. Xanthoudides *1924*, 7, 56; *1918*, 17.
18. Halbherr *1905*, 249.
19. Daux *1959*, 743.
20. Marinatos *1931*, 145–7, 152–3; Daux *1960*, 821.
21. Xanthoudides *1924*, 90.
22. Xanthoudides *1924*, 115, pl. XIV, 1047; 121, pl. XV, 229.
23. Marinatos *1931*, 146–7, 152–3; Xanthoudides *1924*, 56, 76; Woodward *1927*, 258; Parabeni *1913*, 14, 23; Hood *1958*, figs. 7, 8; *1956*, 22.
24. Sakellarakis *1967*; Higgins *1957*.
25. Branigan *1969a*.
26. Xanthoudides *1924*, 6, 34, 90, pls. LXI, LXII; Davaras *1967*, 441; Sakellarakis *1968*, 50.
27. Levi *1962*, 80–83, figs. 105–6.
28. Xanthoudides *1924*, 41, 97, pls. XXIXa, LIb.
29. e.g. Arkalochori, Knossos, Gournia, Nirou Khani.
30. Hutchinson *1962*, 224.
31. Zervos *1956*, pl. 794; Levi *1962*, figs. 175–6.
32. Iliad, book 18, 11, 570–8.
33. Nilsson *1932*, 170ff.

CHAPTER EIGHT: THE MINOAN THOLOS—ITS ORIGINS AND HISTORY

1. Hutchinson *1962*, 225; Branigan *1970*, 199; Hood *1960*, 173.
2. Evans *1928*, 34; Xanthoudides *1924*, 128; Pendlebury *1939*, 74; Alexiou *1967*, 484.
3. Banti *1933*, 244–5; Hood *1960*, 173.
4. Warren *1965* (stone vases); Branigan *1968* (metalwork); *1970a* (foot amulets); *1971* (figurines); *1970* (sealstones).
5. Emery *1961*, 185.
6. Hutchinson *1962*, 153.
7. Caskey *1962*, 263ff; *1964a*, 314–17.
8. Branigan *1968c*, 225–6.
9. Evans J. D. *1964*; Alexiou *1954*; Dawkins *1905*, 260–8.
10. Branigan *1970*, 41.
11. Alexiou *1960*, 227; *1967*, 482.
12. Details of most of these can be found in Hood *1965*.
13. Hood et al, *1964*, 84, no. 37; Marinatos *1929a*, *1930*; Faure *1969*, 194ff; Alexiou *1951*.
14. Xanthoudides *1918a*; Hogarth *1901*, 144; Platon *1964*; Tod *1903*, 339–40.
15. Discussed and several illustrated in Branigan *1970*, 155f.
16. Taramelli *1897*; Sakellarakis *1968*, 52; Faure *1969*, 200.
17. Xanthoudides *1924*, 5, pl. XVII.
18. Alexiou *1967*, 483.
19. Persson *1931*, 26; Stubbings *1963*, 17; Wace *1949*, 119; Mylonas *1966*, 132; Taylour *1964*, 79; Pendlebury *1939*, 64; Hutchinson *1962*, 152–3; Schachermeyr *1964*, chapter 23.
20. Xanthoudides *1924*, 135; Matz *1962*, 196; Hood *1960*.
21. Stubbings *1963*, 16.
22. Hood *1960*, 170.
23. Marinatos *1954*, 309ff.
24. see Hammond *1967*.
25. Evans *1935*, 965ff; Sakellarakis *1967*.
26. Hood *1960*, 175.
27. Hood *1962*, 227.
28. At Mesi, Stilos, Arkhanes (2), Ziros (all certain examples); Makriyianni (probable example); Arvi, Koxare (possible examples).
29. Daux *1958*, 758.
30. Blegen *1954*; Orlandos *1960*, 152–8. There are a number of other relatively early *tholoi* in Messenia and Aetolia, discovered during the last decade: Peristeria (Daux *1966*, 806ff) LH.I?; Gouvalari (Daux *1960*, 704, fig. 2); St. Elie (Daux *1964*, 762ff) LH.I?. The finds from Gouvalari were very few but included some hand-made sherds. The tomb itself is interesting since in size and construction techniques it is very similar indeed to many of the Mesara tholoi.
31. Marinatos *1954*.
32. Valmin *1938*, 207.
33. Huxley & Coldstream *1966*; Warren *1967*, pl. IV, L.1. Early Minoan II pottery amongst the finds from Kastri is reported verbally by Huxley and Coldstream.
34. Blegen *1954*.
35. Sakellarakis *1967*, 276–8.

Index